Careers in Protective Services

Careers in Protective Services

SALEM PRESS
A Division of EBSCO Information Services, Inc.
Ipswich, Massachusetts

GREY HOUSE PUBLISHING

Publisher's Cataloging-In-Publication Data
(Prepared by The Donohue Group, Inc.)

Title: Careers in protective services.
Other Titles: Careers in--
Description: [First edition]. | Ipswich, Massachusetts : Salem Press, a division of EBSCO Information Services, Inc. ; Amenia, NY : Grey House Publishing, [2019] | Includes bibliographical references and index.
Identifiers: ISBN 9781642650525 (hardcover)
Subjects: LCSH: Public safety--Vocational guidance--United States. | Human services personnel--Vocational guidance--United States. | Scientists--Vocational guidance--United States.
Classification: LCC HV675 .C37 2019 | DDC 361.023--dc23

First Printing

PRINTED IN THE UNITED STATES OF AMERICA

CONTENTS

PUBLISHER'S NOTE

Careers in Protective Services contains twenty-eight profiles, including emergency medical technicians and paramedics, emergency dispatchers, police officers and detectives, probation officers, epidemiologists, nurses, and correction officers. These career profiles offer details about a particular career path by providing:

Snapshot details including the most current data about
- Median Pay
- Typical Entry-Level Education
- On-the-job Training
- Number of Jobs
- Job Outlook
- Employment Change

Career Overview includes a description of the career in terms of its
- Duties
- Examples of titles for positions in that specific career
- Work environment
- Work schedules

Each profile provides details about **How to become…** that explain how to begin and grow a career within a specific career profile by describing
- Education
- Licenses, certifications, and registrations that may be required
- Advancement opportunities

Profiles also include the most current details about wages compared to other career clusters as well as a look at pay by industry and descriptions of **Similar Occupations** that lists specific jobs that are related in some way to the protective service career being profiled. which includes education requirements and median wage information.

Job Outlook and **Job Prospects** describe current and anticipated rate of growth for a specific career, and compares the rate to other jobs in areas in the same career cluster, as well as to career growth taken as a whole.

Each profile concludes with **Contact information** to offer additional resources such as specific associations or certifying bodies .

Merging scholarship with occupational development, this single comprehensive guidebook provides students passionate about finding a career in protective services with the necessary insight into the wide array of options available in this diverse and dynamic field. The book offers guidance regarding what job seekers can expect in terms of training, advancement, earnings, job prospects, working conditions, relevant associations, and more. *Careers in Protective Services* is specifically designed for a high school and undergraduate audience and is edited to align with secondary or high school curriculum standards.

Scope of Coverage

Understanding the wide scope of jobs open to someone interested in protective services, from first responders to social workers, is important for anyone preparing for a career in protective services, including opportunities working for federal, state, or local governments like police and fire departments or in Homeland Security; for nonprofits and organizations that help care for children, the elderly, or those suffering from mental illness or substance abuse; and even in for-profit, private practices as detectives and investigators.

Careers in Protective Services is enhanced with numerous charts and tables, including projections from the US Bureau of Labor Statistics, and median annual salaries or wages for those occupations profiled. Enhancements, like Fun Facts, Famous Firsts, and dozens of photos, add depth to the discussion. Additional highlights in the book include twenty-four interviews—Conversation With...—conducted with a professional working in a related job that offer insight into specific areas of protective services such as homeland security, information security, social work, emergency management, and more. The respondents share their personal career paths, detail potential for career advancement, offer advice for students, and include a "try this" for those interested in embarking on a career in their profession.

Special Features

Several features continue to distinguish this reference series from other career-oriented reference works. The back matter includes:

Appendix A: Guide to Holland Code. This discusses John Holland's theory that people and work environments can be classified into six different groups: Realistic; Investigative; Artistic; Social; Enterprising; and Conventional. See if the job you want is right for you!

Appendix B: General Bibliography. This is a collection of suggested readings organized into major categories.

Appendix C: Organizations & Web Resources. This is a comprehensive list of organizations, societies, and web addresses to provide further information about membership, training, certification, examinations, and more.

Index: Includes people, concepts, technologies, terms, principles, and all specific occupations discussed in the occupational profile chapters.

Acknowledgments

Thanks are due to Allison Blake, who took the lead in developing the "Conversation With" interviews, with help from Alicia Banks, and Cindy McCormick Hibbert and to the professionals who communicated their work experience through interview questionnaires. Their frank and honest responses provide immeasurable value to *Careers in Protective Services*. The contributions of all are gratefully acknowledged.

INTRODUCTION TO CAREERS IN PROTECTIVE SERVICES

Protective services is a multi-faceted field, from customs and border patrol to elder care and advocacy. Employment in this field is projected to grow 5 percent from 2016 to 2026, about as fast as the average for all occupations, which will result in about 158,200 new jobs.

Adult Protective Services (APS)

These are social services provided to abused, neglected, or exploited older adults and adults with significant disabilities. APS is typically administered by local or state health, aging, or regulatory departments. They often use a multidisciplinary approach to helping older adults, and younger adults with disabilities, who are often victims of abuse or neglect. They begin with initial investigation of mistreatment, to arranging and in some cases providing health and supportive services and legal interventions, and may even include appointment of surrogate decision-makers such as legal guardians.

While some states provide adult protective services to older adults only, as in Ohio where the APS law applies to those 60 and older, most serve adults with disabilities over the age of 18 who meet the state's definition of "vulnerable." Disabilities may be due to aging, developmental disabilities, physical disabilities, mental illness or cognitive impairments.

Forms of abuse include physical, emotional, verbal, and sexual abuse as well as financial exploitation. "Neglect" can be perpetrated by any caregiver who has accepted the responsibility of assisting an older person or an adult with disabilities.

Most states include self-neglect in their definitions of those needing adult protective services. Self-neglect refers to a person who is unable to care for himself or herself due to physical or cognitive impairments.

Child Protective Services (CPS)

Child Protective Services (CPS) is the name of a governmental agency in many states of the United States responsible for providing child protection by responding to reports of child abuse or neglect. Some states use other names, often attempting to reflect more family-centered (as opposed to child-centered) practices, such as "Department of Children & Family Services" (DCFS). CPS is also known by the name of "Department of Social Services" (DSS) or simply "Social Services".

List of Other Names and Acronyms for CPS:

- Department of Children and Families – DCF
- Department of Children and Family Services – DCFS
- Department of Social Services – DSS

- Department of Human Services – DHS
- Department of Child Safety – DCS
- Department of Child Services – DCS
- CPS/DCF is a department under a state's Health and Human Services organization.

Animal Abuse

Cruelty to animals, also called animal abuse, animal neglect or animal cruelty, is the infliction by omission of care (animal neglect) or by commission of actual abuse by humans that cause the suffering or harm of any non-human. More narrowly, it can be the causing of harm or suffering for specific intent—killing animals for food or for their fur, for instance, or in the name of research. Zoosadism is defined as cruelty to animals in which harm or suffering is inflicted as an end in itself.

Laws may govern acceptable methods of killing animals for food, clothing, or other products, or they may concern keeping of animals for entertainment, education, research, or pets. The animal welfare position typically holds that there is nothing inherently wrong with using animals for human purposes, such as food, clothing, entertainment, fun and research, but requires that it be done in a way that minimizes unnecessary pain and suffering. This approach is sometimes referred to as "humane" treatment. Animal rights advocates typically argue that the words "unnecessary" and "humane" avoid the notion that animals have basic rights that can only be upheld when animals are not treated as property or commodities.

Law Enforcement

Law enforcement is any system by which some members of society act in an organized manner to enforce the law by discovering, deterring, rehabilitating, or punishing people who violate the rules and norms governing that society. Although the term may encompass entities such as courts and prisons, it is most frequently applied to those who directly engage in patrols or surveillance to dissuade and discover criminal activity, and those who investigate crimes and apprehend offenders, a task typically carried out by the police. Furthermore, although law enforcement may be most concerned with the prevention and punishment of crimes, organizations exist to discourage a wide variety of non-criminal violations of rules and societal norms.

Correctional officers are responsible for overseeing individuals who have been arrested and are awaiting trial or who have been sentenced to serve time in jail or prison. *Bailiffs* are law enforcement officers who maintain safety and order in courtrooms.

Fire inspectors examine buildings in order to detect fire hazards and ensure that federal, state, and local fire codes are met. Fire investigators, another type of worker in this field, determine the origin and cause of fires and explosions. Forest fire inspectors and prevention specialists assess outdoor fire hazards in public and residential areas.

Firefighters control and put out fires and respond to emergencies where life, property, or the environment is at risk.

Police officers protect lives and property. Detectives and criminal investigators, who are sometimes called agents or special agents, gather facts and collect evidence of possible crimes.

Private detectives and investigators search for information about legal, financial, and personal matters. They offer many services, such as verifying people's backgrounds and statements, finding missing persons, and investigating computer crimes. Security guards and gaming surveillance officers patrol and protect property against theft, vandalism, and other illegal activity.

Social Workers

Social workers help people solve and cope with problems in their everyday lives. Clinical social workers also diagnose and treat mental, behavioral, and emotional issues.

Child and family social workers protect vulnerable children and help families in need of assistance. They help families find housing or services, such as childcare, or apply for benefits, such as food stamps. They intervene when children are in danger of neglect or abuse. Some help arrange adoptions, locate foster families, or work to reunite families.

School social workers work with teachers, parents, and school administrators to develop plans and strategies to improve students' academic performance and social development. Students and their families are often referred to social workers to deal with problems such as aggressive behavior, bullying, or frequent absences from school.

Healthcare social workers help patients understand their diagnosis and make the necessary adjustments to their lifestyle, housing, or healthcare. For example, they may help people make the transition from the hospital back to their homes and communities. In addition, they may provide information on services, such as home healthcare or support groups, to help patients manage their illness or disease. Social workers help doctors and other healthcare professionals understand the effects that diseases and illnesses have on patients' mental and emotional health. Some healthcare social workers specialize in geriatric social work, hospice and palliative care, or medical social work.

Mental health and substance abuse social workers help clients with mental illnesses or addictions. They provide information on services, such as support groups and 12-step programs, to help clients cope with their illness. Many clinical social workers function in these roles as well.

Agricultural and Food Scientists

Snapshot

2017 Median Pay: $62,910 per year, $30.25 per hour
Typical Entry-Level Education: Bachelor's degree
Work Experience in a Related Occupation: None
On-the-job Training: None
Number of Jobs, 2016: 43,000
Job Outlook, 2016-26: 7% (As fast as average)
Employment Change, 2016-26: 3,100

CAREER OVERVIEW

What Agricultural and Food Scientists Do

Agricultural and food scientists research ways to improve the efficiency and safety of agricultural establishments and products.

Duties

Agricultural and food scientists typically do the following:

- Conduct research and experiments to improve the productivity and sustainability of field crops and farm animals
- Create new food products and develop new and better ways to process, package, and deliver them
- Study the composition of soil as it relates to plant growth, and research ways to improve it
- Communicate research findings to the scientific community, food producers, and the public
- Travel between facilities to oversee the implementation of new projects

Agricultural and food scientists play an important role in maintaining and expanding the nation's food supply. Many work in basic or applied research and development. Basic research seeks to understand the biological and chemical processes by which crops and livestock grow. Applied research seeks to discover ways to improve the quality, quantity, and safety of agricultural products.

Many agricultural and food scientists work with little supervision, forming their own hypotheses and developing their research methods. In addition, they often lead teams of technicians or students who help in their research. Agricultural and food scientists who are employed in private industry may need to travel between different worksites.

The following are types of agricultural and food scientists:

Animal scientists typically conduct research on domestic farm animals. With a focus on food production, they explore animal genetics, nutrition, reproduction, diseases, growth, and development. They work to develop efficient ways to produce and process meat, poultry, eggs, and milk. Animal scientists may crossbreed animals to make them more productive or improve other characteristics. They advise farmers on how to upgrade housing for animals, lower animal death rates, increase growth rates, or otherwise increase the quality and efficiency of livestock.

Food scientists and technologists use chemistry, biology, and other sciences to study the basic elements of food. They analyze the nutritional content of food, discover new food sources, and research ways to make processed foods safe and healthy. Food technologists generally work in product development, applying findings from food science research to develop new or better ways of selecting, preserving, processing, packaging, and distributing food. Some food scientists use problem-solving techniques from nanotechnology—the science of manipulating matter on an atomic scale—to develop sensors that can detect contaminants in food. Other food scientists enforce government regulations, inspecting food-processing areas to ensure that they are sanitary and meet waste management standards.

Plant scientists work to improve crop yields and advise food and crop developers about techniques that could enhance production. They may develop ways to control pests and weeds.

Soil scientists examine the composition of soil, how it affects plant or crop growth, and how alternative soil treatments affect crop productivity. They develop methods of conserving and managing soil that farmers and forestry companies can use. Because soil science is closely related to environmental science, people trained in soil science also work to ensure environmental quality and effective land use.

Agricultural and food scientists in private industry commonly work for food production companies, farms, and processing plants. They may improve inspection standards or overall food quality. They spend their time in a laboratory, where they do tests and experiments, or in the field, where they take samples or assess overall conditions. Other agricultural and food scientists work for pharmaceutical companies, where they use biotechnology processes to develop drugs or other medical products. Some look for ways to process agricultural products into fuels, such as ethanol produced from corn.

At universities, agricultural and food scientists do research and investigate new methods of improving animal or soil health, nutrition, and other facets of food quality. They also write grants to organizations, such as the United States Department of Agriculture (USDA) or the National Institutes of Health (NIH), to get funding for their research.

In the federal government, agricultural and food scientists conduct research on animal safety and on methods of improving food and crop production. They spend most of their time conducting clinical trials or developing experiments on animal and plant subjects.

Agricultural and food scientists may eventually present their findings in peer-reviewed journals or other publications.

WORK ENVIRONMENT

Agricultural and food scientists held about 43,000 jobs in 2016. Employment in the detailed occupations that make up agricultural and food scientists was distributed as follows:

Soil and plant scientists	19,900
Food scientists and technologists	17,000
Animal scientists	6,100

The largest employers of agricultural and food scientists were as follows:

Food manufacturing	15%
Colleges, universities, and professional schools; state, local, and private	12
Research and development in the physical, engineering, and life sciences	10
Government	8
Management, scientific, and technical consulting services	8

Agricultural and food scientists work in laboratories, in offices, and in the field. They spend most of their time studying data and reports in a laboratory or an office. Fieldwork includes visits to farms or processing plants.

When visiting a food or animal production facility, agricultural and food scientists must follow biosecurity measures, wear suitable clothing, and tolerate the environment associated with food production processes. This environment may include noise associated with large production machinery, cold temperatures associated with food production or storage, and close proximity to animal byproducts.

Certain positions may require travel, either domestic, international, or both. The amount of travel can vary widely.

Work Schedules

Agricultural and food scientists typically work full time.

HOW TO BECOME AN AGRICULTURAL OR FOOD SCIENTIST

Agricultural and food scientists need at least a bachelor's degree from an accredited postsecondary institution, although many earn advanced degrees. Some animal scientists earn a doctor of veterinary medicine (DVM) degree.

Education

Every state has at least one land-grant college that offers agricultural science degrees. Many other colleges and universities also offer agricultural science degrees or related courses. Degrees in related sciences, such as biology, chemistry, and physics, or in a related engineering specialty also may qualify people for many agricultural science jobs.

Undergraduate coursework for food scientists and technologists and for soil and plant scientists typically includes biology, chemistry, botany, and plant conservation. Students preparing to be food scientists take courses such as food chemistry, food analysis, food microbiology, food engineering, and food-processing operations. Students preparing to be soil and plant scientists take courses in plant pathology, soil chemistry, entomology (the study of insects), plant physiology, and biochemistry.

Undergraduate students in agricultural and food sciences typically gain a strong foundation in their specialty, with an emphasis on teamwork through internships and research opportunities. Students also are encouraged to take humanities courses, which can help them develop good communication skills, and computer courses, which can familiarize them with common programs and databases.

Many people with bachelor's degrees in agricultural sciences find work in related jobs rather than becoming an agricultural or food scientist. For example, a bachelor's degree in agricultural science is a useful background for farming, ranching, agricultural inspection, farm credit institutions, or companies that make or sell feed, fertilizer, seed, or farm equipment. Combined with coursework in business, agricultural and food science could be a good background for managerial jobs in farm-related or ranch-related businesses.

Many students with bachelors' degrees in application-focused food sciences or agricultural sciences earn advanced degrees in applied topics such as toxicology or dietetics. Students who major in a more basic field, such as biology or chemistry, may be better suited for getting their PhD and doing research within the agricultural and food sciences. During graduate school, there is additional emphasis on lab work and original research, in which prospective animal scientists have the opportunity to do experiments and sometimes supervise undergraduates.

Advanced research topics include genetics, animal reproduction, agronomy, and biotechnology, among others. Advanced coursework also emphasizes statistical analysis and experiment design, which are important as PhD candidates begin their research.

Some agricultural and food scientists receive a doctor of veterinary medicine (DVM). Like PhD candidates in animal science, a prospective veterinarian must first have a bachelor's degree before getting into veterinary school.

ADVANCEMENT

Important Qualities

Communication skills. Communication skills are critical for agricultural and food scientists. They must explain their studies: what they were trying to learn, the methods they used, what they found, and what they think the implications of their findings are. They must also communicate well when working with others, including technicians and student assistants.

Critical-thinking skills. Agricultural and food scientists must use their expertise to determine the best way to answer a specific research question.

Data-analysis skills. Agricultural and food scientists, like other researchers, collect data using a variety of methods, including quantitative surveys. They must then apply standard data analysis techniques to understand the data and get the answers to the questions they are studying.

Math skills. Agricultural and food scientists, like many other scientists, must have a sound grasp of mathematical concepts.

Observation skills. Agricultural and food scientists conduct experiments that require precise observation of samples and other data. Any mistake could lead to inconclusive or inaccurate results.

Licenses, Certifications, and Registrations

Some states require soil scientists to be licensed to practice. Licensing requirements vary by state, but generally include holding a bachelor's degree with a certain number of credit hours in soil science, working under a licensed scientist for a certain number of years, and passing an exam.

Otherwise, certifications are generally not required for agriculture and food scientists, but they can be useful in advancing one's career. Agricultural and food scientists can get certifications from organizations such as the American Society of Agronomy, the American Registry of Professional Animal Scientists (ARPAS), the

Institute of Food Technologists (IFT), or the Soil Science Society of America (SSSA), and others. These certifications recognize expertise in agricultural and food science, and enhance the status of those who are certified.

Qualification for certification is generally based on education, previous professional experience, and passing a comprehensive exam. Scientists may need to take continuing education courses to keep their certification, and they must follow the organization's code of ethics.

Other Experience

Internships are highly recommended for prospective food scientists and technologists. Many entry-level jobs in this occupation are related to food manufacturing, and firsthand experience is often valued in that environment.

WAGES

Median annual wages, May 2017

Life scientists: $73,700

Agricultural and food scientists: $62,910

Total, all occupations: $37,690

Note: All Occupations includes all occupations in the U.S. Economy. Source: U.S. Bureau of Labor Statistics, Occupational Employment Statistics

The median annual wage for agricultural and food scientists was $62,910 in May 2017. The lowest 10 percent earned less than $37,890, and the highest 10 percent earned more than $116,520.

Median annual wages for agricultural and food scientists in May 2017 were as follows:

Food scientists and technologists	$63,660
Soil and plant scientists	62,430
Animal scientists	60,760

In May 2017, the median annual wages for agricultural and food scientists in the top industries in which they worked were as follows:

Research and development in the physical, engineering, and life sciences	$75,110
Management, scientific, and technical consulting services	67,950
Government	66,250
Food manufacturing	59,400
Colleges, universities, and professional schools; state, local, and private	52,910

Agricultural and food scientists typically work full time.

JOB OUTLOOK

Percent change in employment, projected 2016-26

Life scientists: 10%

Total, all occupations: 7%

Agricultural and food scientists: 7%

Note: All Occupations includes all occupations in the U.S. Economy. Source: U.S. Bureau of Labor Statistics, Employment Projections program

Overall employment of agricultural and food scientists is projected to grow 7 percent from 2016 to 2026, about as fast as the average for all occupations.

Employment of agricultural and food scientists is projected to grow as research into agricultural production methods and techniques continues. Challenges such as population growth, increased demand for water resources, combating pests and pathogens, changes in climate and weather patterns, and additional demand for agriculture products, such as biofuels, will continue to create demand for research in agricultural efficiency and sustainability.

Animal scientists will be needed to investigate and improve the diets, living conditions, and even genetic makeup of livestock. Food scientists and technologists will work to improve food-processing techniques, ensuring that products are safe, waste is limited, and food is shipped efficiently and safely. Soil and plant scientists will continue to try to understand and map soil composition. They will investigate ways to improve soils, to find uses for byproducts, and selectively breed crops to resist pests and disease, or improve taste.

Job Prospects

Employment projections data for Agricultural and food scientists, 2016-26

Occupational Title	SOC Code	Employment, 2016	Projected Employment, 2026	Change, 2016-26	
				Percent	Numeric
Agricultural and food scientists	19-1010	43,000	46,100	7	3,100
Animal scientists	19-1011	6,100	6,400	6	400
Food scientists and technologists	19-1012	17,000	18,000	6	1,000
Soil and plant scientists	19-1013	19,900	21,700	9	1,800

Source: Bureau of Labor Statistics, Employment Projections program

SIMILAR OCCUPATIONS

This table shows a list of occupations with job duties that are similar to those of agricultural and food scientists.

OCCUPATION	JOB DUTIES	ENTRY-LEVEL EDUCATION	2017 MEDIAN PAY
Agricultural and Food Science Technicians	Agricultural and food science technicians assist agricultural and food scientists by performing duties such as measuring and analyzing the quality of food and agricultural products.	Associate's degree	$39,910
Biochemists and Biophysicists	Biochemists and biophysicists study the chemical and physical principles of living things and of biological processes, such as cell development, growth, heredity, and disease.	Doctoral or professional degree	$91,190
Biological Technicians	Biological technicians help biological and medical scientists conduct laboratory tests and experiments.	Bachelor's degree	$43,800
Chemical Technicians	Chemical technicians use special instruments and techniques to help chemists and chemical engineers research, develop, produce, and test chemical products and processes.	Associate's degree	$47,280

OCCUPATION	JOB DUTIES	ENTRY-LEVEL EDUCATION	2017 MEDIAN PAY
Conservation Scientists and Foresters	Conservation scientists and foresters manage the overall land quality of forests, parks, rangelands, and other natural resources.	Bachelor's degree	$60,970
Environmental Scientists and Specialists	Environmental scientists and specialists use their knowledge of the natural sciences to protect the environment and human health. They may clean up polluted areas, advise policymakers, or work with industry to reduce waste.	Bachelor's degree	$69,400
Farmers, Ranchers, and Other Agricultural Managers	Farmers, ranchers, and other agricultural managers operate establishments that produce crops, livestock, and dairy products.	High school diploma or equivalent	$69,620
Microbiologists	Microbiologists study microorganisms such as bacteria, viruses, algae, fungi, and some types of parasites. They try to understand how these organisms live, grow, and interact with their environments.	Bachelor's degree	$69,960
Veterinarians	Veterinarians care for the health of animals and work to improve public health. They diagnose, treat, and research medical conditions and diseases of pets, livestock, and other animals.	Doctoral or professional degree	$90,420

OCCUPATION	JOB DUTIES	ENTRY-LEVEL EDUCATION	2017 MEDIAN PAY
Zoologists and Wildlife Biologists	Zoologists and wildlife biologists study animals and other wildlife and how they interact with their ecosystems. They study the physical characteristics of animals, animal behaviors, and the impacts humans have on wildlife and natural habitats.	Bachelor's degree	$62,290

Famous First

A 1906 act authorized the Secretary of Agriculture to inspect and condemn any meat product found unfit for human consumption. Unlike previous laws ordering meat inspections, which were enforced to assure European nations from banning pork trade, this law was strongly motivated to protect the American diet. The law was at least partly a response to the publication of Upton Sinclair's The Jungle, an exposé of the Chicago meat packing industry, as well as to other Progressive Era muckraking publications of the day. While Sinclair's account was intended to bring attention to the terrible working conditions in Chicago, public outrage was directed more at the specter or finding themselves endangered by purchasing tainted meat.

Source: https://en.wikipedia.org/wiki/Federal_Meat_Inspection_Act

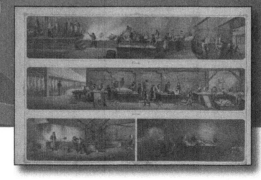

Conversation With . . .
HILLARY MEHL

Assistant Professor, Plant Pathology
Virginia Tech Tidewater Agricultural
Research & Extension Center
Plant Pathologist, 14 years

1. What was your individual career path in terms of education/training, entry-level job, or other significant opportunity?

From a young age, I was fascinated with all aspects of biology; my family would go hiking and camping and collect plants and insects and try to identify them. I majored in botany at Humboldt State University, then went straight into a Ph.D. program at the University of California Davis. I studied plant pathology, which combines my interests in plants, microbiology and fungal biology, and seeks practical ways to manage plant diseases and increase crop yields and quality. As a graduate student, I spent plenty of time in the lab, but I also interacted with growers to identify problems in their crops and conducted field research in grower's fields.

My post-doc was with the U.S. Department of Agriculture in a lab located at the University of Arizona, where I researched biological control of aflatoxin, a toxin produced by a fungus that contaminates food and feed crops. My job here at Virginia Tech is a combination of research and working through the extension service to present the knowledge we gain from research to growers and consultants so they can use it in practice, often through our publications or crop meetings.

I'm working on field crops such as peanuts, cotton, soybeans, small grains and corn, and looking at disease management approaches that combine the use of disease-resistant crops, chemical control, and different cropping practices that can help minimize disease. I'm trying to understand the biology of specific fungal pathogens so we can better understand what they are, what they're doing to plants, and how we can better control them. For example, we're finding strains of frogeye leaf spot of soybean that are resistant to certain fungicides and are trying to find alternative ways to control the disease.

2. What are the most important skills and/or qualities for someone in your profession?

Plant pathology aims to solve real-world problems, so a plant pathologist needs to listen to the needs and concerns of growers and effectively communicate solutions, both verbally and in writing. In addition, analytical skills and curiosity are important to analyze data, make careful observations, and ask good questions. A plant pathologist who does what I do needs to enjoy being outdoors, working in different weather extremes, and traveling to locations with different field conditions.

3. What do you wish you had known going into this profession?

I feel lucky that I got to do what I wanted to do, but there are only so many jobs in academia. It would be beneficial to be aware of other opportunities as an undergraduate so that scientists can train accordingly, rather than go through a doctoral program—where the emphasis is on academic jobs—and find themselves without necessary skills for industry. Knowing this would have given me additional perspective into the field of plant pathology.

4. Are there many job opportunities in your profession? In what specific areas?

A variety of job opportunities are available in academia, industry, and government. In academia, positions include teaching, research, and extension services, and typically require either an M.S. degree (e.g. extension agents, research technicians) or a Ph.D. (researcher, professor, extension specialist). Industry jobs can be in small companies or big corporations, and can range from work as a private consultant who advises growers to a technical representative or researcher working for a chemical or seed company. Federal and state positions may include working for a regulatory agency or conducting research in a government lab.

5. How do you see your profession changing in the next five years? What role will technology play in those changes, and what skills will be required?

As food safety and security become an increasingly global issue, the need for agricultural scientists, including plant pathologists, will increase, but the focus of the work will be more international. Thus, the ability to communicate with and transfer technologies to other countries, especially those in the developing world, will be increasingly important.

6. What do you enjoy most about your job? What do you enjoy least about your job?

I most enjoy solving problems through careful observation, experiments, and analyses, as well as coming up with solutions to growers' problems and helping to improve plant disease management. I least enjoy the times I am unable to come up with solutions—at least not right away—but in the end, these challenges keep the job interesting.

7. Can you suggest a valuable "try this" for students considering a career in your profession?

High school students can look for opportunities at agricultural extension services, which are usually run by states. Undergraduate students at research universities should be able to find ample opportunities to work in a lab or assist with field work. Private industry offers internships. You could also get experience helping out on a farm for the summer.

Fast Fact

Here's what food safety experts will not eat: sliced lemons, raw sprouts, undercooked ground meat, raw oysters, foods from grocery bulk bins, sushi, raw milk, packaged lunch meats and potluck meals. Between the potential for pathogen infection and the mystery of how the food was handled, the experts steer clear.

Source: foodnetwork.com

MORE INFORMATION

For more information about food and animal scientists, including certifications, visit

American Society of Agronomy
https://www.agronomy.org/

American Society of Animal Science
https://www.asas.org/

American Registry of Professional Animal Scientists
https://www.arpas.org/

Future Farmers of America
https://www.ffa.org/

Institute of Food Technologists
https://www.ift.org/

For more information about agricultural and soil scientists, including certifications, visit

Soil Science Society of America
https://www.soils.org/

For information from related governmental agencies, visit

U.S. Food and Drug Administration
https://www.fda.gov/

Smithsonian Institution
https://www.si.edu/

U.S. Department of Agriculture
https://www.usda.gov/

National Institutes of Health
https://www.nih.gov/

Sources

Bureau of Labor Statistics, U.S. Department of Labor, Occupational Outlook Handbook, Agricultural and Food Scientists.

Computer and Information Research Scientists

Snapshot

2017 Median Pay: $114,520 per year, $55.06 per hour

Typical Entry-Level Education: Master's degree

Work Experience in a Related Occupation: None

On-the-job Training: None

Number of Jobs, 2016: 27,900

Job Outlook, 2016-26: 19% (Much faster than average)

Employment Change, 2016-26: 5,400

CAREER OVERVIEW

What Computer and Information Research Scientists Do

Computer and information research scientists study and solve complex problems in computing. Some computer scientists create programs to control robots.

Computer and information research scientists invent and design new approaches

to computing technology and find innovative uses for existing technology. They study and solve complex problems in computing for business, science, medicine, and other fields.

Duties

Computer and information research scientists typically do the following:

- Explore fundamental issues in computing and develop theories and models to address those issues
- Help scientists and engineers solve complex computing problems
- Invent new computing languages, tools, and methods to improve the way in which people work with computers
- Develop and improve the software systems that form the basis of the modern computing experience
- Design experiments to test the operation of these software systems
- Analyze the results of their experiments
- Publish their findings in academic journals and present their findings at conferences

Computer and information research scientists create and improve computer software and hardware.

Creating and improving software involves working with algorithms, which are sets of instructions that tell a computer what to do. Some computing tasks are very difficult and require complex algorithms. Computer and information research scientists try to simplify these algorithms to make computer systems as efficient as possible. The algorithms allow advancements in many types of technology, such as machine learning systems and cloud computing.

Computer and information research scientists design new computer architecture that improves the performance and efficiency of computer hardware. Their work often leads to technological advancements and efficiencies, such as better networking technology, faster computing speeds, and improved information security. In general, computer and information research scientists work at a more theoretical level than do other computer professionals.

Some computer scientists work with electrical engineers, computer hardware engineers, and other specialists on multidisciplinary projects. The following are examples of types of specialties for computer and information research scientists:

Data science. Computer and information research scientists write algorithms that are used to detect and analyze patterns in very large datasets. They improve ways to sort, manage, and display data. Computer scientists build algorithms into software packages that make the data easier for analysts to use. For example, they may create an algorithm to analyze a very large set of medical data in order to find new ways to treat diseases. They may also look for patterns in traffic data to help clear accidents faster.

Robotics. Some computer and information research scientists study how to improve robots. Robotics explores how a machine can interact with the physical world. Computer and information research scientists create the programs that control the robots. They work closely with engineers who focus on the hardware design of robots. Together, these workers test how well the robots do the tasks they were created to do, such as assemble cars or collect data on other planets.

Programming. Computer and information research scientists design new programming languages that are used to write software. The new languages make software writing more efficient by improving an existing language, such as Java, or by making a specific aspect of programming, such as image processing, easier.

WORK ENVIRONMENT

Computer and information research scientists improve ways to sort, manage, and display data. Computer and information research scientists held about 27,900 jobs in 2016. The largest employers of computer and information research scientists were as follows:

Federal government, excluding postal service	28%
Computer systems design and related services	20
Research and development in the physical, engineering, and life sciences	17
Colleges, universities, and professional schools; state, local, and private	8
Software publishers	6

Some computer scientists may work on teams with electrical engineers, computer hardware engineers, and other specialists on multidisciplinary projects:

Work Schedules

Most computer and information research scientists work full time. About 3 in 10 worked more than 40 hours per week in 2016.

HOW TO BECOME A COMPUTER AND INFORMATION RESEARCH SCIENTIST

Most jobs for computer and information research scientists require a master's degree in computer science or a related field. In the federal government, a bachelor's degree may be sufficient for some jobs.

Education

Most computer and information research scientists need a master's degree in computer science or a related field, such as computer engineering. A master's degree usually requires 2 to 3 years of study after earning a bachelor's degree in a computer-related field, such as computer science or information systems.

Computer scientists who work in a specialized field may need knowledge of that field. For example, those working on biomedical applications may need to have taken some biology classes.

ADVANCEMENT

Some computer scientists may become computer and information systems managers

Important Qualities

Analytical skills. Computer and information research scientists must be organized in their thinking and analyze the results of their research to formulate conclusions.

Communication skills. Computer and information research scientists must communicate well with programmers and managers and be able to clearly explain their conclusions to people with no technical background. They often present their research at conferences.

Critical-thinking skills. Computer and information research scientists work on many complex problems.

Detail oriented. Computer and information research scientists must pay close attention to their work, because a small programming error can cause an entire project to fail.

Ingenuity. Computer and information research scientists must continually come up with innovative ways to solve problems, particularly when their ideas do not initially work as intended.

Logical thinking. Computer algorithms rely on logic. Computer and information research scientists must have a talent for reasoning.

Math skills. Computer and information research scientists must have knowledge of advanced math and other technical topics that are critical in computing.

WAGES

Median annual wages, May 2017

Computer and information research scientists: $114,520

Computer occupations: $84,580

Total, all occupations: $37,690

Note: All Occupations includes all occupations in the U.S. Economy. Source: U.S. Bureau of Labor Statistics, Occupational Employment Statistics

The median annual wage for computer and information research scientists was $114,520 in May 2017. The lowest 10 percent earned less than $65,540, and the highest 10 percent earned more than $176,780.

In May 2017, the median annual wages for computer and information research scientists in the top industries in which they worked were as follows:

Software publishers	$132,190
Research and development in the physical, engineering, and life sciences	125,420
Computer systems design and related services	114,790
Federal government, excluding postal service	108,270
Colleges, universities, and professional schools; state, local, and private	77,240

Most computer and information research scientists work full time. About 3 in 10 worked more than 40 hours per week in 2016.

JOB OUTLOOK

Percent change in employment, projected 2016-26

Computer and information research scientists: 19%

Computer occupations: 13%

Total, all occupations: 7%

Note: All Occupations includes all occupations in the U.S. Economy. Source: U.S. Bureau of Labor Statistics, Employment Projections program

Employment of computer and information research scientists is projected to grow 19 percent from 2016 to 2026, much faster than the average for all occupations. However, because it is a small occupation, the fast growth will result in only about 5,400 new jobs over the 10-year period.

The research and development work of computer and information research scientists turns ideas into industry-leading technology. As demand for new and better technology grows, demand for computer scientists will grow as well.

Rapid growth in data collection by businesses will lead to an increased need for data-mining services. Computer scientists will be needed to write algorithms that help businesses make sense of very large amounts of data. With this information, businesses understand their consumers better, making the work of computer and information research scientists increasingly vital.

A growing emphasis on cybersecurity also should lead to new jobs, because computer scientists will be needed to find innovative ways to prevent cyberattacks.

In addition, an increase in demand for software may increase the need for computer scientists who create new programming languages to make software writing more efficient.

Job Prospects

Computer and information research scientists are likely to have excellent job prospects.

For applicants seeking employment in a specialized field, such as finance or biology, knowledge of that field, along with a computer science degree, may be helpful in getting a job.

**Employment projections data for
Computer and information research scientists,**

Occupational Title	SOC Code	Employment, 2016	Projected Employment, 2026	Change, 2016-26	
				Percent	Numeric
Computer and information research scientists	15-1111	27,900	33,200	19	5,400

Source: Bureau of Labor Statistics, Employment Projections program

Fast Fact

Are you surprised to hear 30,000 websites are hacked each day and 6,000 viruses are created each month? On top of that, 80 percent of sent email is spam!

Source: www.gb-advisors.com

SIMILAR OCCUPATIONS

This table shows a list of occupations with job duties that are similar to those of computer and information research scientists.

OCCUPATION	JOB DUTIES	ENTRY-LEVEL EDUCATION	2017 MEDIAN PAY
Computer and Information Systems Managers	Computer and information systems managers, often called information technology (IT) managers or IT project managers, plan, coordinate, and direct computer-related activities in an organization. They help determine the information technology goals of an organization and are responsible for implementing computer systems to meet those goals.	Bachelor's degree	$139,220
Computer Hardware Engineers	Computer hardware engineers research, design, develop, and test computer systems and components such as processors, circuit boards, memory devices, networks, and routers.	Bachelor's degree	$115,120
Computer Programmers	Computer programmers write and test code that allows computer applications and software programs to function properly. They turn the program designs created by software developers and engineers into instructions that a computer can follow.	Bachelor's degree	$82,240
Database Administrators	Database administrators (DBAs) use specialized software to store and organize data, such as financial information and customer shipping records. They make sure that data are available to users and secure from unauthorized access.	Bachelor's degree	$87,020

OCCUPATION	JOB DUTIES	ENTRY-LEVEL EDUCATION	2017 MEDIAN PAY
Software Developers	Software developers are the creative minds behind computer programs. Some develop the applications that allow people to do specific tasks on a computer or another device. Others develop the underlying systems that run the devices or that control networks.	Bachelor's degree	$103,560
Computer Network Architects	Computer network architects design and build data communication networks, including local area networks (LANs), wide area networks (WANs), and Intranets. These networks range from small connections between two offices to next-generation networking capabilities such as a cloud infrastructure that serves multiple customers.	Bachelor's degree	$104,650
Computer Systems Analysts	Computer systems analysts, sometimes called systems architects, study an organization's current computer systems and procedures, and design solutions to help the organization operate more efficiently and effectively. They bring business and information technology (IT) together by understanding the needs and limitations of both.	Bachelor's degree	$88,270
Information Security Analysts	Information security analysts plan and carry out security measures to protect an organization's computer networks and systems. Their responsibilities are continually expanding as the number of cyberattacks increases.	Bachelor's degree	$95,510

OCCUPATION	JOB DUTIES	ENTRY-LEVEL EDUCATION	2017 MEDIAN PAY
Network and Computer Systems Administrators	Computer networks are critical parts of almost every organization. Network and computer systems administrators are responsible for the day-to-day operation of these networks.	Bachelor's degree	$81,100
Web Developers	Web developers design and create websites. They are responsible for the look of the site. They are also responsible for the site's technical aspects, such as its performance and capacity, which are measures of a website's speed and how much traffic the site can handle. In addition, web developers may create content for the site.	Associate's degree	$67,990
Top Executives	Top executives devise strategies and policies to ensure that an organization meets its goals. They plan, direct, and coordinate operational activities of companies and organizations.	Bachelor's degree	$104,700

Conversation With . . .
WILLIAM P. SMYTH

IT Program Analyst, Federal Government
Washington, D.C.
IT Program Analyst, 31 years

1. What was your individual career path in terms of education/training, entry-level job, or other significant opportunity?

I went to Hampton University in Virginia for electrical engineering, but dropped out and joined the U.S. Marine Corps. I ended up doing aviation electronics, which I studied at a community college. I spent six years in the Marines, and played football for the Marine Corps team. NFL teams were scouting me. I went to Atlanta, but wasn't what they were looking for. Then I came to D.C. because the Redskins wanted to see me. However, a motorcycle accident ended my NFL dreams at age 26.

After I healed, I started looking for jobs. At the time, computers were not widespread. I got a downtown D.C. territory repairing electronic typewriters. The law firm Steptoe & Johnson was a client and they had desktop computers. I'd never seen one before, but somebody saw a problem with a cable and asked me to look at it. I traced the cable back, plugged it in, and said, "Try now." That prompted me to get into computers, and I never looked back.

I spent many overnights at law firms setting up networks with little support. It made me really good at my job, even though it could be frustrating. But I'm the kind of person who is persistent and likes to troubleshoot.

Eventually, I moved on to a company called Banctech that built banking machines and computers. I did phone support on networks and was there about five years. The company moved to Texas; I didn't want to go to Texas. So, I found a job as a contractor for a federal agency during Bill Clinton's first term. The agency had no networks or desktop computers, so I was the first one to put in their networks.

After 15 years as a contractor, I was hired eight years ago as a federal employee to support a departmental network and help desk, where I work with a team of 25 people. We handle Freedom of Information requests and run a certification and accreditation program. If someone internally wants to set up a website—for instance, so people can get information from the DOE about solar panels—we review the site and run tests to look for security weaknesses. This is an annual process. In addition, I get pulled in to run projects that are highly technical. For instance, you can't just plug into the internet from our system. Vendors and others who need to do that come to me to find out how.

2. What are the most important skills and/or qualities for someone in your profession?

You really have to understand the theory of computers. If you understand how everything works from the bottom up, you'll be able to troubleshoot. I have to stress that you need a love for this, because things change every six months. If you're not willing to be constantly updated, you'll be far behind pretty quickly.

3. What do you wish you had known going into this profession?

I wish I had known that hacking would become such a big deal. I was on the leading edge when I started, when the internet was DOS-based. I could go onto important websites and there was no protection. Looking back, I could have come up with something to fix vulnerabilities and I wouldn't be working now!

4. Are there many job opportunities in your profession? In what specific areas?

Absolutely. Every day in the news, somebody is getting hacked. However, the security field is intense. You're on the clock 24 hours. Not everybody wants to do that. You can make a lot of money in the security field if you can get those difficult Cisco security certifications. But you can get dismissed real quick, too, if somebody gets into a system you're watching.

5. How do you see your profession changing in the next five years, what role will technology play in those changes, and what skills will be required?

I think it's going to change based on protocols. New protocols—computer languages—are being developed all the time, because every company is trying to stop hackers. And hackers are constantly working on how to get in. You really need to learn programming and protocols.

6. What do you enjoy most about your job? What do you enjoy least about your job?

I most enjoy troubleshooting. When an organization has a problem, I get to figure it out. I least like supporting difficult fellow employees who work in departments other than IT. For instance, I have to approve purchases. If somebody wants a 27-inch monitor, they need to tell me why—and not just assume that they will get it.

7. Can you suggest a valuable "try this" for students considering a career in your profession?

On websites such as http://etherealmind.com or https://learningnetwork.cisco.com/community/learning_center/games, you can play security games, take security tests, or join groups to discuss the topic. You'll find out if you have a real interest in security.

Famous First

During World War II, ballistics computing was done by women, who were hired as "computers." The term computer remained one that referred to mostly women until 1945, after which it took on the modern definition of machinery it presently holds.

Source: https://en.wikipedia.org/wiki/Human_computer

MORE INFORMATION

For more information about computer and information research scientists, visit

Association for Computing Machinery
https://www.acm.org/

IEEE Computer Society
https://www.computer.org/

For information about opportunities for women pursuing information technology careers, visit

National Center for Women & Information Technology
https://www.ncwit.org

To find job openings for computer and information research scientists in the federal government, visit

USAJOBS
https://www.usajobs.gov/

Sources

Bureau of Labor Statistics, U.S. Department of Labor, *Occupational Outlook Handbook*, Computer and Information Research Scientists.

Conservation Scientists and Foresters

Snapshot

2017 Median Pay: $60,970 per year, $29.31 per hour
Typical Entry-Level Education: Bachelor's degree
Work Experience in a Related Occupation: None
On-the-job Training: None
Number of Jobs, 2016: 34,600
Job Outlook, 2016-26: 6% (As fast as average)
Employment Change, 2016-26: 2,000

CAREER OVERVIEW

What Conservation Scientists and Foresters Do

Conservation scientists and foresters study forest and soil quality.

Conservation scientists and foresters manage the overall land quality of forests, parks, rangelands, and other natural resources.

Duties

Conservation scientists typically do the following:

- Oversee forestry and conservation activities to ensure compliance with government regulations and habitat protection
- Negotiate terms and conditions for forest harvesting and for land-use contracts
- Establish plans for managing forest lands and resources
- Monitor forest-cleared lands to ensure that they are suitable for future use
- Work with private landowners, governments, farmers, and others to improve land for forestry purposes, while at the same time protecting the environment
- Foresters typically do the following:
- Supervise activities of forest and conservation workers and technicians
- Choose and prepare sites for new trees, using controlled burning, bulldozers, or herbicides to clear land
- Monitor the regeneration of forests
- Direct and participate in forest fire suppression
- Determine ways to remove timber with minimum environmental damage

Conservation scientists manage, improve, and protect the country's natural resources. They work with private landowners and federal, state, and local governments to find ways to use and improve the land while safeguarding the environment. Conservation scientists advise farmers, ranchers, and other agricultural managers on how they can improve their land for agricultural purposes and to control erosion.

Foresters have a wide range of duties, and their responsibilities vary with their employer. Some primary duties of foresters are drawing up plans to regenerate forested lands, monitoring the progress of those lands, and supervising tree harvests. Another duty of a forester is devising plans to keep forests free from disease, harmful insects, and damaging wildfires. Many foresters supervise forest and conservation workers and technicians, directing their work and evaluating their progress.

Conservation scientists and foresters evaluate data on forest and soil quality, assessing damage to trees and forest lands caused by fires and logging activities. In addition, they lead activities such as suppressing fires and planting seedlings. Fire suppression activities include measuring how quickly fires will spread and how successfully the planned suppression activities turn out.

Conservation scientists and foresters use their skills to determine a fire's impact on a region's environment. Communication with firefighters and other forest workers is an important component of fire suppression and controlled burn activities because the information that conservation scientists and foresters provide can determine how firefighters work.

Conservation scientists and foresters use a number of tools to perform their jobs. They use clinometers to measure the heights of trees, diameter tapes to measure a tree's circumference, and increment borers and bark gauges to measure the growth of trees so that timber volumes can be computed and growth rates estimated.

In addition, conservation scientists and foresters often use remote sensing (aerial photographs and other imagery taken from airplanes and satellites) and Geographic Information System (GIS) data to map large forest or range areas and to detect widespread trends of forest and land use. They make extensive use of hand-held computers and Global Positioning System (GPS) receivers to study these maps.

The following are examples of types of conservation scientists:

Conservation land managers work for land trusts or other conservation organizations to protect the wildlife habitat, biodiversity, scenic value, and other unique attributes of preserves and conservation lands.

Range managers, also called range conservationists, protect rangelands to maximize their use without damaging the environment. Rangelands contain many natural resources and cover hundreds of millions of acres in the United States, mainly in the western states and Alaska.

Range managers may inventory soils, plants, and animals; develop resource management plans; help to restore degraded ecosystems; or help manage a ranch. They also maintain soil stability and vegetation for uses such as wildlife habitats and outdoor recreation.

Like foresters, they work to prevent and reduce wildfires and invasive animal species.

Soil and water conservationists give technical help to people who are concerned with the conservation of soil, water, and related natural resources. For private landowners, they develop programs to make the most productive use of land without damaging it. They also help landowners with issues such as dealing with erosion. They help private landowners and governments by advising on water quality, preserving water supplies, preventing ground-water contamination, and conserving water.

The following are examples of types of foresters:

Procurement foresters buy timber by contacting local forest owners and negotiating a sale. This activity typically involves taking inventory on the type, amount, and location of all standing timber on the property. Procurement foresters then appraise the timber's worth, negotiate its purchase, and draw up a contract. The forester then subcontracts with loggers or pulpwood cutters to remove the trees and to help lay out roads to get to the timber.

Urban foresters live and work in larger cities and manage urban trees. These workers are concerned with quality-of-life issues, including air quality, shade, and storm water runoff.

Conservation education foresters train teachers and students about issues facing forest lands.

Fast Fact

The Camp Fire broke out in Northern California in the fall of 2018. In only two weeks, it destroyed more structures than the state's other seven worst wildfires combined and killed nearly three times more people than those killed by the record-setting Griffith Park Fire 85 years prior.

Source: USA Today.

WORK ENVIRONMENT

Conservation scientists and foresters typically need a bachelor's degree in forestry or a related field.

Conservation scientists held about 22,300 jobs in 2016. The largest employers of conservation scientists were as follows:

Federal government, excluding postal service	32%
State government, excluding education and hospitals	22
Local government, excluding education and hospitals	20
Social advocacy organizations	12
Professional, scientific, and technical services	5

Foresters held about 12,300 jobs in 2016. The largest employers of foresters were as follows:

State government, excluding education and hospitals	25%
Support activities for agriculture and forestry	17
Forestry and logging	13
Federal government, excluding postal service	11
Local government, excluding education and hospitals	11

In the western and southwestern United States, conservation scientists and foresters usually work for the federal government because of the number of national parks in that part of the country. In the eastern United States, they often work for private landowners. Social advocacy organizations employ foresters and conservation scientists in working with lawmakers on behalf of sustainable land use and other issues facing forest land.

Conservation scientists and foresters typically work in offices, in laboratories, and outdoors, sometimes doing fieldwork in remote locations. When visiting or working near logging operations or wood yards, they wear a hardhat and other protective gear.

The work can be physically demanding. Some conservation scientists and foresters work outdoors in all types of weather. They may need to walk long distances through dense woods and underbrush to carry out their work. Insect bites, poisonous plants, and other natural hazards present some risk.

In an isolated location, a forester or conservation scientist may work alone, measuring tree densities and regeneration or performing other outdoor activities. Other foresters work closely with the public, educating them about the forest or the proper use of recreational sites.

Fire suppression activities are an important aspect of the duties of a forester or conservation scientist. Because those activities involve prevention as well as emergency responses, the work of a forester or conservation scientist has occasional risk.

Work Schedules

Most conservation scientists and foresters work full time and have a standard work schedule.

HOW TO BECOME A CONSERVATION SCIENTIST OR FORESTER

Conservation scientists and foresters typically need a bachelor's degree in forestry or a related field.

Education

Conservation scientists and foresters typically need a bachelor's degree in forestry or a related field, such as agricultural science, rangeland management, or environmental science.

Bachelor's degree programs are designed to prepare conservation scientists and foresters for their career or a graduate degree.

Alongside practical skills, theory and education are important parts of these programs.

Bachelor's and advanced degree programs in forestry and related fields typically include courses in ecology, biology, and forest resource measurement. Scientists and foresters also typically have a background in Geographic Information System (GIS) technology, remote sensing, and other forms of computer modeling.

In 2017, more than 50 bachelor's and master's degree programs in forestry, urban forestry, and natural resources and ecosystem management were accredited by the Society of American Foresters.

Licenses, Certifications, and Registrations

Several states have some type of credentialing process for foresters. In some of these states, foresters must be licensed; check with your state for more information. Conservation workers do not need a license.

Although certification is not required, conservation scientists and foresters may choose to earn it because it shows a high level of professional competency.

The Society of American Foresters (SAF) offers certification to foresters. Candidates must have at least a bachelor's degree from an SAF-accredited program or from a forestry program that is substantially equivalent. Candidates also must have qualifying professional experience and pass an exam.

The Society for Range Management offers professional certification in rangeland management or as a range management consultant. To be certified, candidates must hold a bachelor's degree in range management or a related field, have 5 years of full-time related work experience, and pass an exam.

ADVANCEMENT

Important Qualities

Analytical skills. Conservation scientists and foresters must evaluate the results of a variety of field tests and experiments, all of which require precision and accuracy. They use sophisticated computer modeling to prepare their analyses.

Critical-thinking skills. Conservation scientists and foresters reach conclusions through sound reasoning and judgment. They determine how to improve forest conditions, and they must react appropriately to fires.

Decisionmaking skills. Conservation scientists and foresters must use their expertise and experience to determine whether their findings will have an impact on soil, forest lands, and the spread of fires.

Management skills. Conservation scientists and foresters need to work well with the forest and conservation workers and technicians they supervise, so effective communication is critical.

Physical stamina. Conservation scientists and foresters often walk long distances in steep and wooded areas. They work in all kinds of weather, including extreme heat and cold.

Speaking skills. Conservation scientists and foresters must give clear instructions to forest and conservation workers and technicians, who typically do the labor necessary for proper forest maintenance. They also need to communicate clearly with landowners and, in some cases, the general public.

Many conservation scientists and foresters advance to take on managerial duties. They also may conduct research or work on policy issues, often after getting an advanced degree. Foresters in management usually leave fieldwork behind, spending more of their time in an office, working with teams to develop management plans and supervising others.

Soil conservationists usually begin working within one district and may advance to a state, regional, or national level. Soil conservationists also can transfer to occupations such as farm or ranch management advisor or land appraiser.

WAGES

Median annual wages, May 2017

Life scientists: $73,700

Conservation scientists: $61,480

Conservation scientists and foresters: $60,970

Foresters: $60,120

Total, all occupations: $37,690

Note: All Occupations includes all occupations in the U.S. Economy. Source: U.S. Bureau of Labor Statistics, Occupational Employment Statistics

The median annual wage for conservation scientists was $61,480 in May 2017. The lowest 10 percent earned less than $33,740, and the highest 10 percent earned more than $97,490.

The median annual wage for foresters was $60,120 in May 2017. The lowest 10 percent earned less than $40,480, and the highest 10 percent earned more than $84,830.

In May 2017, the median annual wages for conservation scientists in the top industries in which they worked were as follows:

Federal government, excluding postal service	$74,850
Professional, scientific, and technical services	67,470
Social advocacy organizations	60,500
State government, excluding education and hospitals	52,610
Local government, excluding education and hospitals	51,110

In May 2017, the median annual wages for foresters in the top industries in which they worked were as follows:

Federal government, excluding postal service	$64,690
Local government, excluding education and hospitals	58,900
State government, excluding education and hospitals	55,870

Most conservation scientists and foresters work full time and have a standard work schedule.

JOB OUTLOOK

Percent change in employment, projected 2016-26

Life scientists: 10%

Total, all occupations: 7%

Conservation scientists: 6%

Conservation scientists and foresters: 6%

Foresters: 5%

Note: All Occupations includes all occupations in the U.S. Economy. Source: U.S. Bureau of Labor Statistics, Employment Projections program

Employment of conservation scientists and foresters is projected to grow 6 percent from 2016 to 2026, about as fast as the average for all occupations.

Most employment growth is expected to be in state and local government-owned forest lands, particularly in the western United States. In recent years, the prevention and suppression of wildfires has become the primary concern for government agencies managing forests and rangelands. Governments are likely to hire more foresters as the number of forest fires increases and more people live on or near forest lands. Both the development of previously unused lands and changing weather conditions have contributed to increasingly devastating and costly fires.

In addition, continued demand for American timber and wood pellets is expected to drive employment growth for conservation scientists and foresters. Jobs in private forests are expected to grow alongside demand for timber and pellets

Job Prospects

The need to replace retiring workers should create opportunities for conservation scientists and foresters. Job prospects will likely be best for conservation scientists and foresters who have a strong understanding of Geographic Information System (GIS) technology, remote sensing, and other software tools.

Employment projections data for Conservation scientists and foresters, 2016-26

Occupational Title	SOC Code	Employment, 2016	Projected Employment, 2026	Change, 2016-26	
				Percent	Numeric
Conservation scientists and foresters	19-1030	34,600	36,600	6	2,000
Conservation scientists	19-1031	22,300	23,700	6	1,400
Foresters	19-1032	12,300	12,900	5	600

Source: Bureau of Labor Statistics, Employment Projections program

SIMILAR OCCUPATIONS

This table shows a list of occupations with job duties that are similar to those of conservation scientists and foresters.

OCCUPATION	JOB DUTIES	ENTRY-LEVEL EDUCATION	2017 MEDIAN PAY
Agricultural and Food Scientists	Agricultural and food scientists research ways to improve the efficiency and safety of agricultural establishments and products.	Bachelor's degree	$62,910

OCCUPATION	JOB DUTIES	ENTRY-LEVEL EDUCATION	2017 MEDIAN PAY
Environmental Science and Protection Technicians	Environmental science and protection technicians monitor the environment and investigate sources of pollution and contamination, including those affecting public health.	Associate's degree	$45,490
Firefighters	Firefighters control and put out fires and respond to emergencies where life, property, or the environment is at risk.	Postsecondary nondegree award	$49,080
Forest and Conservation Workers	Forest and conservation workers measure and improve the quality of forests. Under the supervision of foresters and forest and conservation technicians, they develop, maintain, and protect forests.	High school diploma or equivalent	$27,650
Zoologists and Wildlife Biologists	Zoologists and wildlife biologists study animals and other wildlife and how they interact with their ecosystems. They study the physical characteristics of animals, animal behaviors, and the impacts humans have on wildlife and natural habitats.	Bachelor's degree	$62,290

Conversation With . . .
TIM KRAEMER

Natural Resources Police
10 years Park Service Ranger, 3 years

1. What was your individual career path in terms of education/training, entry-level job, or other significant opportunity?

I worked summers at Sandy Point State Park starting at age 14 in the food concession. When I was old enough to get a driver's license, I worked at the park's marina renting out motor boats. I did that for seven summers before becoming a seasonal technician doing maintenance projects. Later I became a welder, a plumber, and, for six years, a commercial waterman. In winters, I worked as a seasonal technician for another state park. Finally the park service offered me a full-time job as a ranger recruit. I went on to the police academy for six months, then went to Point Lookout State Park as a full-time ranger. We did law enforcement, conservation enforcement, plus programming, interpretation, and maintenance, which was a large part of the park ranger job.

At the time I became a Natural Resources Police Officer, the job was similar to a park ranger here in Maryland. That has since changed, and many of the assignments we had as rangers are now done by Natural Resources Police Officers, such as law and conservation enforcement. Also, we police officers are on waterways doing commercial seafood inspections and waterways enforcement. I'm on the Potomac River, the Patuxent River and the Chesapeake Bay. Natural Resources Police handle private lands and waterways.

All of those years in the private sector gave me a lot of good experience for the career I have now. For instance, when I check the watermen and the fisheries, I have a better grasp of how those guys work, and I know their gear.

2. What are the most important skills and/or qualities for someone in your profession?

A good work ethic, honesty, integrity, knowledge of fishing laws and hunting laws. You definitely need to be a self-starter. You have to want to be outside, on vessels, and know the mechanical workings of a vessel and fishing gear.

3. What do you wish you had known going into this profession?

I wish I was better with the academic part of it. I'm more of a hands-on learner.

4. Are there many job opportunities in your profession? In what specific areas?

In the last year or two, the state started hiring more Natural Resources Police Officers and they are constantly taking applications in every part of the state.

5. How do you see your profession changing in the next five years? What role will technology play in those changes, and what skills will be required?

We're already starting to see technology play a big role with the Natural Resources Police, with new programs and new report management systems. Officers are issued laptops now that are linked with the new Maritime Law Enforcement Information Network (MLEIN) that we just got trained on. It's a series of cameras and radar stations up and down the Chesapeake Bay that the Natural Resources Police use to track vessels or illegal activities.

In 2007 we had the introduction of new vessels with better outboard/inboard motors and more advanced high tech. The outboards are better, faster, more efficient, more reliable, and more comfortable for officers in harsh environments. They're rigged out for law enforcement use.

I don't ever see us getting away from low-tech completely; there's nothing more reliable than a pad of paper and a pen. Sometimes we're on foot in the middle of a field and you have to travel light and you have to travel fast. A pad of paper doesn't need to be recharged.

6. What do you enjoy most about your job? What do you enjoy least?

It's probably one of the best jobs around. The best part is being in on the water. I like running the boats, as well as the feeling you're making a difference and making sure there's something there tomorrow, such as when you enforce crabbing regulations. Or oysters, which are a big thing. We make sure the kids will have seafood out there to harvest one day. I love being in the state parks, talking to people, doing campground enforcement, and just being there for public information.

Natural resource law changes constantly, and keeping yourself updated on laws and regulations is very challenging. That is probably the hardest part of this job.

7. Can you suggest a valuable "try this" for students considering a career in your profession?

You've really got to want to be outside and talk to people. For people who like to hunt and fish and like fishing and game law, this is a great job. Be a volunteer or, if you're old enough, be a reserve officer.

Famous First

During the late 19th and early 20th centuries, forest preservation programs were established in British India, the United States, and Europe. Sir Dietrich Brandis is considered the father of tropical forestry. The development of plantation forestry was one of the controversial answers to the specific challenges in the tropical colonies. The evolution of forest laws and binding regulations in the 20th century was meant as a way to response to both growing conservation concerns and the increasing technological capacity of logging companies.

Source: https://en.wikipedia.org/wiki/Forestry#Forest_conservation_and_early_globalization

MORE INFORMATION

For more information about conservation scientists and foresters, including schools offering education in forestry, visit

Society of American Foresters
https://www.eforester.org/

For information about careers in forestry, particularly conservation forestry and land management, visit

Forest Stewards Guild
http://www.forestguild.org/

U.S. Forest Service
https://www.fs.fed.us/

Society for Range Management
http://rangelands.org/

Sources

Bureau of Labor Statistics, U.S. Department of Labor, *Occupational Outlook Handbook*, Conservation Scientists and Foresters.

Construction and Building Inspectors

Snapshot

2017 Median Pay: $59,090 per year, $28.41 per hour

Typical Entry-Level Education: High school diploma or equivalent

Work Experience in a Related Occupation: 5 years or more

On-the-job Training: Moderate-term on-the-job training

Number of Jobs, 2016: 105,100

Job Outlook, 2016-26: 10% (Faster than average)

Employment Change, 2016-26: 10,500

CAREER OVERVIEW

What Construction and Building Inspectors Do

Home inspectors inform potential homebuyers of a home's deficiencies.

Construction and building inspectors ensure that construction meets local and national building codes and ordinances, zoning regulations, and contract specifications.

Duties

Construction and building inspectors typically do the following:

- Review plans to ensure they meet building codes, local ordinances, zoning regulations, and contract specifications
- Approve building plans that are satisfactory
- Monitor construction sites periodically to ensure overall compliance
- Use survey instruments, metering devices, and test equipment to perform inspections
- Inspect plumbing, electrical, and other systems to ensure that they meet code
- Verify alignment, level, and elevation of structures to ensure building meets specifications
- Issue violation notices and stop-work orders until building is compliant
- Keep daily logs, including photographs taken during inspections
- Provide written documentation of findings

People want to live and work in safe places, and construction and building inspectors ensure that construction meets codified requirements. Construction and building inspectors examine buildings, highways and streets, sewer and water systems, dams, bridges, and other structures. They also inspect electrical; heating, ventilation, air-conditioning, and refrigeration (HVACR); and plumbing systems. Although no two inspections are alike, inspectors perform an initial check during the first phase of construction and followup inspections throughout the construction project. When the project is finished, they perform a final, comprehensive inspection and provide written and oral feedback related to their findings.

The following are examples of types of construction and building inspectors:

Building inspectors check the structural quality and general safety of buildings. Some specialize further, inspecting only structural steel or reinforced-concrete structures, for example.

Coating inspectors examine the exterior paint and coating on bridges, pipelines, and large holding tanks. Inspectors perform checks at various stages of the painting process to ensure proper coating.

Electrical inspectors examine the installed electrical systems to ensure they function properly and comply with electrical codes and standards. The inspectors visit worksites to inspect new and existing sound and security systems, wiring, lighting, motors, photovoltaic systems, and generating equipment. They also inspect the installed electrical wiring for HVACR systems and appliances.

Elevator inspectors examine lifting and conveying devices, such as elevators, escalators, moving sidewalks, lifts and hoists, inclined railways, ski lifts, and amusement rides. The inspections include both the mechanical and electrical control systems.

Home inspectors typically inspect newly built or previously owned homes, condominiums, townhomes, and other dwellings. Prospective home buyers often hire home inspectors to check and report on a home's structure and overall condition. Sometimes, homeowners hire a home inspector to evaluate their home's condition before placing it on the market.

In addition to examining structural quality, home inspectors examine all home systems and features, including the roof, exterior walls, attached garage or carport, foundation, interior walls, plumbing, electrical, and HVACR systems. They look for violations of building codes, but home inspectors do not have the power to enforce compliance with the codes.

Mechanical inspectors examine the installation of HVACR systems and equipment to ensure that they are installed and function properly. They also may inspect commercial kitchen equipment, gas-fired appliances, and boilers. Mechanical inspectors should not be confused with quality control inspectors, who inspect goods at manufacturing plants.

Plan examiners determine whether the plans for a building or other structure comply with building codes. They also determine whether the structure is suited to the engineering and environmental demands of the building site.

Plumbing inspectors examine the installation of systems that ensure the safety and health of drinking water, the sanitary disposal of waste, and the safety of industrial piping.

Public works inspectors ensure that the construction of federal, state, and local government water and sewer systems, highways, streets, bridges, and dams conforms to detailed contract specifications. Workers inspect excavation and fill operations, the placement of forms for concrete, concrete mixing and pouring, asphalt paving, and grading operations. Public works inspectors may specialize in highways, structural steel, reinforced concrete, or ditches. Others may specialize in dredging operations required for bridges, dams, or harbors.

Specification inspectors ensure that construction work is performed according to design specifications. Specification inspectors represent the owner's interests, not those of the general public. Insurance companies and financial institutions also may use their services.

Some building inspectors are concerned with fire prevention safety. Fire inspectors and investigators ensure that buildings meet fire codes.

WORK ENVIRONMENT

Building inspectors often work outdoors to check the exterior structure of a house.

Construction and building inspectors held about 105,100 jobs in 2016. The largest employers of construction and building inspectors were as follows:

Local government, excluding education and hospitals	39%
Engineering services	16
Self-employed workers	8
Construction	6
State government, excluding education and hospitals	5

Although construction and building inspectors spend most of their time inspecting worksites, they also spend time in a field office reviewing blueprints, writing reports, and scheduling inspections.

Some inspectors may have to climb ladders or crawl in tight spaces to complete their inspections.

Inspectors typically work alone. However, some inspectors may work as part of a team on large, complex projects, particularly because inspectors usually specialize in different areas of construction.

Work Schedules

Most inspectors work full time during regular business hours. However, some may work additional hours during periods of heavy construction activity. Also, if an accident occurs at a construction site, inspectors must respond immediately and may work additional hours to complete their report. Some inspectors—especially those who are self-employed—may have to work evenings and weekends. This is particularly true of home inspectors, who typically inspect homes during the day and write reports in the evening.

HOW TO BECOME A CONSTRUCTION OR BUILDING INSPECTOR

Most employers require construction and building inspectors to have at least a high school diploma and work experience in construction trades. Inspectors also typically learn on the job. Many states and local jurisdictions require some type of license or certification. Inspectors often have a combination of certifications and previous experience in various construction and maintenance trades.

Education

Most employers require inspectors to have at least a high school diploma, even for workers who have considerable related work experience.

Some employers may seek candidates who have studied engineering or architecture or who have a certificate or an associate's degree that includes courses in building inspection, home inspection, construction technology, and drafting. Many community colleges offer programs in building inspection technology. Courses in blueprint reading, vocational subjects, algebra, geometry, and writing are also useful. Courses in business management are helpful for those who plan to run their own inspection business.

Training

Training requirements vary by state, locality, and type of inspector. In general, construction and building inspectors receive much of their training on the job, although they must learn building codes and standards on their own. Working with an experienced inspector, they learn about inspection techniques; codes, ordinances, and regulations; contract specifications; and recordkeeping and reporting duties. Training also may include supervised onsite inspections.

Work Experience in a Related Occupation

Because inspectors must possess the right mix of technical knowledge, work experience, and education, employers prefer applicants who have both training and experience in a construction trade. For example, many inspectors have experience working as carpenters, electricians, or plumbers. Many home inspectors obtain experience in multiple specialties so that they enter the occupation with a combination of certifications and previous experience in various construction trades.

Licenses, Certifications, and Registrations

Most states and local jurisdictions require construction and building inspectors to have a license or certification. Some states have individual licensing programs for construction and building inspectors. Others may require certification by associations such as the International Code Council, the International Association of Plumbing and Mechanical Officials, the International Association of Electrical Inspectors, and the National Fire Protection Association.

Similarly, most states require home inspectors to follow defined trade practices or obtain a state-issued license or certification. Currently, more than a half of states have policies regulating the conduct of home inspectors.

Home inspector license or certification requirements vary by state but may require that inspectors do the following:

- Achieve a specified level of education
- Possess experience with inspections
- Maintain liability insurance
- Pass an exam

Exams are often based on the American Society of Home Inspectors certification exams. Most inspectors must renew their license periodically and take continuing education courses.

Inspectors must have a valid driver's license to travel to inspection sites.

ADVANCEMENT

Important Qualities

Communication skills. Inspectors must explain problems they find in order to help people understand what is needed to fix the problems. In addition, they need to provide a written report of their findings.

Craft experience. Inspectors perform checks and inspections throughout the construction project. Experience in a related construction occupation provides inspectors with the necessary background to become certified.

Detail oriented. Inspectors thoroughly examine many different construction activities. Therefore, they must pay close attention to detail so as to not overlook any items that need to be checked.

Mechanical knowledge. Inspectors use a variety of testing equipment as they check complex systems. In order to perform tests properly, they also must have detailed knowledge of how the systems operate.

Physical stamina. Inspectors are constantly on their feet and often climb and crawl through attics and other tight spaces. As a result, they should be somewhat physically fit.

WAGES

Median annual wages, May 2017

Construction and building inspectors: $59,090

Construction and extraction occupations: $44,730

Total, all occupations: $37,690

Note: All Occupations includes all occupations in the U.S. Economy. Source: U.S. Bureau of Labor Statistics, Occupational Employment Statistics

The median annual wage for construction and building inspectors was $59,090 in May 2017. The lowest 10 percent earned less than $35,220, and the highest 10 percent earned more than $95,340.

In May 2017, the median annual wages for construction and building inspectors in the top industries in which they worked were as follows:

Engineering services	$60,700
Local government, excluding education and hospitals	58,670
Construction	58,300
State government, excluding education and hospitals	55,330

Most inspectors work full time during regular business hours. However, some may work additional hours during periods of heavy construction activity. Also, if an accident occurs at a construction site, inspectors must respond immediately and may work additional hours to complete their report. Some inspectors—especially those who are self-employed—may have to work evenings and weekends. This is particularly true of home inspectors, who typically inspect homes during the day and write reports in the evening.

JOB OUTLOOK

Percent change in employment, projected 2016-26

Construction and extraction occupations: 11%

Construction and building inspectors: 10%

Total, all occupations: 7%

Note: All Occupations includes all occupations in the U.S. Economy. Source: U.S. Bureau of Labor Statistics, Employment Projections program

Employment of construction and building inspectors is projected to grow 10 percent from 2016 to 2026, faster than the average for all occupations.

Public interest in safety and the desire to improve the quality of construction are factors that are expected to continue to create demand for inspectors. Employment growth for inspectors is expected to be strongest in government and in firms specializing in architectural, engineering, and related services.

Job Prospects

Certified construction and building inspectors who can perform a variety of inspections should have the best job opportunities. Inspectors with construction-related work experience or training in engineering, architecture, construction technology, or related fields are also likely to have better job prospects.

Those who are self-employed, such as home inspectors, are more likely to be affected by economic downturns or fluctuations in the real estate market.

Employment projections data for Construction and Building Inspectors, 2016-26

Occupational Title	SOC Code	Employment, 2016	Projected Employment, 2026	Change, 2016-26	
				Percent	Numeric
Construction and building inspectors	47-4011	105,100	115,700	10	10,500

Source: Bureau of Labor Statistics, Employment Projections program

SIMILAR OCCUPATIONS

This table shows a list of occupations with job duties that are similar to those of construction and building inspectors.

OCCUPATION	JOB DUTIES	ENTRY-LEVEL EDUCATION	2017 MEDIAN PAY
Appraisers and Assessors of Real Estate	Appraisers and assessors of real estate provide a value estimate on land and buildings usually before they are sold, mortgaged, taxed, insured, or developed.	Bachelor's degree	$54,010
Architects	Architects plan and design houses, factories, office buildings, and other structures.	Bachelor's degree	$78,470
Carpenters	Carpenters construct, repair, and install building frameworks and structures made from wood and other materials.	High school diploma or equivalent	$45,170
Electricians	Electricians install, maintain, and repair electrical power, communications, lighting, and control systems in homes, businesses, and factories.	High school diploma or equivalent	$54,110

OCCUPATION	JOB DUTIES	ENTRY-LEVEL EDUCATION	2017 MEDIAN PAY
Plumbers, Pipefitters, and Steamfitters	Plumbers, pipefitters, and steamfitters install and repair pipes that carry liquids or gases to, from, and within businesses, homes, and factories.	High school diploma or equivalent	$52,590
Electrical and Electronics Engineering Technicians	Electrical and electronics engineering technicians help engineers design and develop computers, communications equipment, medical monitoring devices, navigational equipment, and other electrical and electronic equipment. They often work in product evaluation and testing, and use measuring and diagnostic devices to adjust, test, and repair equipment. They are also involved in the manufacture and deployment of equipment for automation.	Associate's degree	$63,660
Electrical and Electronics Engineers	Electrical engineers design, develop, test, and supervise the manufacturing of electrical equipment, such as electric motors, radar and navigation systems, communications systems, and power generation equipment. Electronics engineers design and develop electronic equipment, including broadcast and communications systems, such as portable music players and Global Positioning System (GPS) devices.	Bachelor's degree	$97,970
Surveyors	Surveyors make precise measurements to determine property boundaries. They provide data relevant to the shape and contour of the Earth's surface for engineering, mapmaking, and construction projects.	Bachelor's degree	$61,140

OCCUPATION	JOB DUTIES	ENTRY-LEVEL EDUCATION	2017 MEDIAN PAY
Construction Managers	Construction managers plan, coordinate, budget, and supervise construction projects from start to finish.	Bachelor's degree	$91,370
Occupational Health and Safety Specialists and Technicians	Occupational health and safety specialists and technicians collect data on and analyze many types of work environments and work procedures. Specialists inspect workplaces for adherence to regulations on safety, health, and the environment. Technicians work with specialists in conducting tests and measuring hazards to help prevent harm to workers, property, the environment, and the general public.	Bachelor's degree (specialists) High school diploma or equivalent (technicians)	$67,720

Fast Fact

The Camp Fire broke out in Northern California in the fall of 2018. In only two weeks, it destroyed more structures than the state's other seven worst wildfires combined and killed nearly three times more people than those killed by the record-setting Griffith Park Fire 85 years prior.

Source: USA Today.

Conversation With . . .
AUDREY CLINE

Code Official Town of Stratham Building/Codes Department
Stratham, New Hampshire
Building inspector, 10 years

1. What was your individual career path in terms of education/training, entry-level job, or other significant opportunity?

Like many (if not most) building inspectors, code enforcement officers, and code officials, I landed in this field as a mid-career change. I graduated from Boston University with a degree in business administration. A handful of years later, I developed an interest in architecture and attended the architectural engineering program at New Hampshire Technical Institute. After graduation, I worked as a self-employed residential designer. After a decade or so, the work began to feel mundane and I starting casting about for another situation where I could use my skills and training.

I "discovered" the field of building codes when I saw an ad in my local paper for an employment opportunity with the Town of Wolfeboro, N.H. As the town's building official, I managed the building department's processes, which included reviewing plans for compliance with the New Hampshire State Building Code and local zoning ordinances and collaborating with local fire officials for compliance with the New Hampshire State Fire Code. I enjoy the legal aspects of code administration and property rights. My favorite projects are redevelopment or so-called "infill" projects that rejuvenate older buildings and neighborhoods while bringing them up to code to meet structural strength and safety regulations.

2. What are the most important skills and/or qualities for someone in your profession?

It's important to realize that the decisions you make may have a significant effect on personal property rights. It's critical to develop an approach based on the desire to be part of the solution, while fulfilling your responsibility to the public health, safety, and welfare. This is not a career for the faint-of-heart. In the end, credibility is the goal. With credibility, even difficult decisions can be understood as being necessary and fair.

3. What do you wish you had known going into this profession?

There isn't anything I regret about making this career move. What I didn't know, and what was most surprising to me, is that public service is very different from working in the private sector. I had to re-evaluate my basic decisionmaking and judgment processes in order to accommodate the notion of the public good rather than the good of an individual, or indeed, my own preference.

4. Are there many job opportunities in your profession? In what specific areas?

In New Hampshire as well as many other states, the next five to ten years will see a major shortage of people entering this field. In response to the expected shortage, New Hampshire Technical Institute has begun a certificate program designed to attract people to the industry. The program can lead to immediate employment after six courses or can be the foundation for stepping into an associate's or bachelor's degree program in a related field like construction management or architecture/engineering.

While building inspectors and code officials typically work for a city or town, there are home inspection jobs in private industry. When people buy a home, the bank typically requires a home inspection that covers the condition of the home from the foundation to the roof: heating and a/c systems, plumbing and electrical systems, attic/insulation, ceiling, windows and floors. Home inspectors inspect these systems and write up a report for the buyer.

5. How do you see your profession changing in the next five years? What role will technology play in those changes, and what skills will be required?

Just as in fields like medicine and technology, there will be distinct sub-specialties. There will be a need for management personnel who have a thorough grasp of technical codes, as well as the education (such as a degree in public administration) to manage a municipal office. Most building offices are instituting electronic applications, plan review, and inspection protocols.

6. What do you enjoy most about your job? What do you enjoy least about your job?

As the town's building official, I am just as apt to be outside on a job site as in the plan review room or attending a policy committee meeting. I love the variety. Being a resource for builders and potentially saving a project from an expensive or time-consuming retrofit is very satisfying. It can be discouraging to see a project that has derailed because of lack of proper design, planning or implementation. But after ten years, I am still waiting to learn what I least like about my job!

7. **Can you suggest a valuable "try this" for students considering a career in your profession?**

I would urge interested students to contact the association of building officials in their state. If you're in New Hampshire or nearby, contact the New Hampshire Building Officials Association (www.nhboa.net). The association has the ability to set up a shadowing program and will reserve a seat for a curious student at one of our monthly training meetings. I'm sure other state organizations have similar programs.

This conversation was originally published in 2016.

Famous First

The 1960 Valdivia earthquake (Spanish: Terremoto de Valdivia) or the Great Chilean earthquake (Gran terremoto de Chile) of May 22 is the most powerful earthquake ever recorded. Various studies have placed it at 9.4–9.6 on the moment magnitude scale. It occurred in the afternoon (19:11 GMT, 15:11 local time), and lasted approximately 10 minutes. The resulting tsunami affected southern Chile, Hawaii, Japan, the Philippines, eastern New Zealand, southeast Australia and the Aleutian Islands.

Source: https://en.wikipedia.org/wiki/Paramedic#History

MORE INFORMATION

For more information about building codes, certification, and a career as a construction or building inspector, visit

International Code Council
https://www.iccsafe.org/

National Fire Protection Association
https://www.nfpa.org/

For more information about coating inspectors, visit

NACE International
http://www.nace.org/home

For more information about construction inspectors, visit

Association of Construction Inspectors
http://www.aci-assoc.org/

For more information about electrical inspectors, visit

International Association of Electrical Inspectors
https://www.iaei.org//

For more information about elevator inspectors, visit

National Association of Elevator Safety Authorities International
https://www.naesai.org/

For more information about education and training for mechanical and plumbing inspectors, visit

**International Association of
Plumbing and Mechanical
Officials**
http://www.iapmo.org/

For more information about education and training for mechanical and plumbing inspectors, visit

**American Society of Home
Inspectors**
https://www.homeinspector.org/

**International Association of
Certified Home Inspectors
(InterNACHI)**
https://www.homeinspector.org/

Sources

Bureau of Labor Statistics, U.S. Department of Labor, *Occupational Outlook Handbook*, Construction and Building Inspectors.

Correctional Officers and Bailiffs

Snapshot

2017 Median Pay: $43,510 per year, $20.92 per hour
Typical Entry-Level Education: High school diploma or equivalent
Work Experience in a Related Occupation: None
On-the-job Training: Moderate-term on-the-job training
Number of Jobs, 2016: 468,600
Job Outlook, 2016-26: -7% (Decline)
Employment Change, 2016-26: -34,900

CAREER OVERVIEW

What Correctional Officers and Bailiffs Do

Correctional officers must follow procedures to maintain their personal safety as well as the safety of the inmates they oversee.

Correctional officers are responsible for overseeing individuals who have been arrested and are awaiting trial or who have been sentenced to serve time in jail or prison. Bailiffs, also known as *marshals* or *court officers*, are law enforcement officers who maintain safety and order in courtrooms. Their duties, which vary by court, include enforcing courtroom rules, assisting judges, guarding juries, delivering court documents, and providing general security for courthouses.

Duties

Correctional officers typically do the following:
- Enforce rules and keep order within jails or prisons
- Supervise activities of inmates
- Inspect facilities to ensure that they meet security and safety standards
- Search inmates for contraband items
- Report on inmate conduct
- Escort and transport inmates
- Bailiffs typically do the following:
- Ensure the security of the courtroom
- Enforce courtroom rules
- Follow court procedures
- Escort judges, jurors, witnesses, and prisoners
- Handle evidence and court documents

Inside the prison or jail, correctional officers enforce rules and regulations. They maintain security by preventing disturbances, assaults, and escapes, and by inspecting facilities. They check cells and other areas for unsanitary conditions, contraband, signs of a security breach (such as tampering with window bars and doors), and other rule violations. Officers also inspect mail and visitors for prohibited items. They write reports and fill out daily logs detailing inmate behavior and anything else of note that occurred during their shift.

Correctional officers may have to restrain inmates in handcuffs and leg irons to escort them safely to and from cells and to see authorized visitors. Officers also escort prisoners to courtrooms, medical facilities, and other destinations.

Bailiffs' specific duties vary by court, but their primary duty is to maintain order and security in courts of law. They enforce courtroom procedures that protect the integrity of the legal process. For example, they ensure that attorneys and witnesses do not influence juries outside of the courtroom, and they also may isolate juries from the public in some circumstances. As a neutral party, they may handle evidence during court hearings to ensure that only permitted evidence is displayed.

WORK ENVIRONMENT

Because jail and prison security must be provided 24 hours a day, officers work in shifts that cover all hours of the day and night, including weekends and holidays.

Bailiffs held about 18,600 jobs in 2016. The largest employers of bailiffs were as follows:

Local government, excluding education and hospitals	71%
State government, excluding education and hospitals	28

Correctional officers and jailers held about 450,000 jobs in 2016. The largest employers of correctional officers and jailers were as follows.

State government, excluding education and hospitals	54%
Local government, excluding education and hospitals	37
Facilities support services	5
Federal government	4

Correctional officers may work indoors or outdoors, and bailiffs generally work in courtrooms. They both may be required to stand for long periods.

Injuries and Illnesses

Working in a correctional institution can be stressful and dangerous. Correctional officers and jailers may become injured in confrontations with inmates, and they have one of the highest rates of injuries and illnesses of all occupations.

The job demands that officers be alert and ready to react throughout their entire shift.

Work Schedules

Correctional officers usually work full time on rotating shifts. Because jail and prison security must be provided around the clock, officers work all hours of the day and night, including weekends and holidays. Many officers are required to work overtime. Bailiffs' hours are determined by when court is in session.

HOW TO BECOME A CORRECTIONAL OFFICER OR BAILIFF

Correctional officers and bailiffs typically attend a training academy. Although qualifications vary by state and agency, all agencies require a high school diploma. Federal agencies may also require some college education or previous work experience.

Many agencies establish a minimum age for correctional officers, which is typically between 18 and 21 years of age.

Education

Correctional officers and bailiffs must have at least a high school diploma or equivalent.

For employment in federal prisons, the Federal Bureau of Prisons requires entry-level correctional officers to have at least a bachelor's degree or 1 to 3 years of full-time experience in a field providing counseling, assistance, or supervision to individuals.

Training

Correctional officers and bailiffs complete training at an academy. Training typically lasts several months, but this varies by state. The International Association of Directors of Law Enforcement Standards and Training maintains links to states' Peace Officer Standards and Training (POST) programs. Academy trainees receive instruction in a number of subjects, including self-defense, institutional policies, regulations, operations, and security procedures.

ADVANCEMENT

Important Qualities

Decisionmaking skills. Correctional officers and bailiffs must use both their training and common sense to quickly determine the best course of action and to take the necessary steps to achieve a desired outcome.

Detail oriented. Correctional officers and bailiffs follow and enforce strict procedures in correctional facilities and courts to ensure everyone's safety.

Interpersonal skills. Correctional officers and bailiffs must be able to interact and communicate effectively with inmates and others to maintain order in correctional facilities and courtrooms.

Negotiating skills. Correctional officers must be able to assist others in resolving differences in order to avoid conflict.

Physical strength. Correctional officers and bailiffs must have the strength to physically subdue inmates or others.

Self-discipline. Correctional officers must control their emotions when confronted with hostile situations.

WAGES

Median annual wages, May 2017

Law enforcement workers: $54,520

Correctional officers and jailers: $43,540

Correctional officers and bailiffs: $43,510

Bailiffs: $42,960

Total, all occupations: $37,690

Note: All Occupations includes all occupations in the U.S. Economy. Source: U.S. Bureau of Labor Statistics, Occupational Employment Statistics

The median annual wage for bailiffs was $42,960 in May 2017. The lowest 10 percent earned less than $23,950, and the highest 10 percent earned more than $74,060.

The median annual wage for correctional officers and jailers was $43,540 in May 2017. The lowest 10 percent earned less than $29,540, and the highest 10 percent earned more than $74,940.

In May 2017, the median annual wages for bailiffs in the top industries in which they worked were as follows:

State government, excluding education and hospitals	$66,630
Local government, excluding education and hospitals	39,170

Local government, excluding education and hospitals 39,170
In May 2017, the median annual wages for correctional officers and jailers in the top industries in which they worked were as follows:

Federal government	$55,660
Local government, excluding education and hospitals	43,980
State government, excluding education and hospitals	42,510
Facilities support services	36,820

Correctional officers usually work full time on rotating shifts. Because jail and prison security must be provided around the clock, officers work all hours of the day and night, including weekends and holidays. Many officers are required to work overtime. Bailiffs' hours are determined by when court is in session.

Union Membership

Compared with workers in all occupations, correctional officers and bailiffs had a higher percentage of workers who belonged to a union in 2016

JOB OUTLOOK

Percent change in employment, projected 2016-26

Total, all occupations: 7%

Law enforcement workers: 1%

Bailiffs: -2%

Correctional officers and bailiffs: -7%

Correctional officers and jailers: -8%

Note: All Occupations includes all occupations in the U.S. Economy. Source: U.S. Bureau of Labor Statistics, Employment Projections program

Employment of correctional officers and bailiffs is projected to decline 7 percent from 2016 to 2026. State and local budget constraints and prison population levels will determine how many correctional officers are necessary.

Although correctional officers will continue to be needed to watch over the U.S. prison population, changes to criminal laws can have a large effect on how many people are arrested and incarcerated each year.

Faced with high costs for keeping people in prison, many state governments have moved toward laws requiring shorter prison terms and alternatives to prison. While keeping the public safe, community-based programs designed to rehabilitate prisoners and limit their risk of repeated offenses may also reduce prisoner counts.

Bailiffs will continue to be needed to keep order in courtrooms.

Job Prospects

Despite the projected decline in employment, job prospects should still be good due to the need to replace correctional officers who retire, transfer to other occupations, or leave the labor force.

Employment projections data for Correctional officers and bailiffs, 2016-26

Occupational Title	SOC Code	Employment, 2016	Projected Employment, 2026	Change, 2016-26	
				Percent	Numeric
Bailiffs, correctional officers, and jailers	33-3010	468,600	433,700	-7	-34,900
Bailiffs	33-3011	18,600	18,200	-2	-400
Correctional officers and jailers	33-3012	450,000	415,500	-8	-34,500

Source: Bureau of Labor Statistics, Employment Projections program

SIMILAR OCCUPATIONS

This table shows a list of occupations with job duties that are similar to those of correctional officers and bailiffs.

OCCUPATION	JOB DUTIES	ENTRY-LEVEL EDUCATION	2017 MEDIAN PAY
Police and Detectives	Police officers protect lives and property. Detectives and criminal investigators, who are sometimes called agents or special agents, gather facts and collect evidence of possible crimes.	High school diploma or equivalent (police) Bachelor's degree (fish and game wardens) Bachelor's degree (federal agencies)	$62,960
Probation Officers and Correctional Treatment Specialists	Probation officers and correctional treatment specialists provide social services to assist in rehabilitation of law offenders in custody or on probation or parole.	Bachelor's degree	$51,410
Security Guards and Gaming Surveillance Officers	Security guards and gaming surveillance officers patrol and protect property against theft, vandalism, and other illegal activity.	High school diploma or equivalent	$26,960
Firefighters	Firefighters control and put out fires and respond to emergencies where life, property, or the environment is at risk.	Postsecondary nondegree award	$49,080

Conversation With . . .
WILLIAM CROWLEY
Correctional Officer, 9 years

1. **What was your individual career path in terms of education/training, entry-level job, or other significant opportunity?**

   I studied criminal justice in college then became a police officer. I was on the force in Washington, D.C., then Fairfax County in Virginia. Family matters brought me back to Massachusetts. While trying to get on another police department, I worked for an armored car company. I went out on disability. A neighbor worked in corrections, and I decided to try out that career.

2. **What are the most important skills and/or qualities for someone in your profession?**

   You definitely have to be a very patient individual. It also helps if you're a stickler for rules. You have to know how to say 'no.' You also have to be strong-willed in the sense that you need to almost constantly remind yourself that the people you're dealing with are not your friends. If you give in to peer pressure, are offended easily or have a hard time standing up for yourself, then you're going to run into issues.

   Having a good sense of humor also helps.

3. **What do you wish you had known going into this profession?**

   I wish I had known how it would drag on me. They always tell you it's going to wear you down. They tell you you're going to seem to age pretty fast, but they really don't get the point across. A lot of the job is just sitting. You're sitting in the block and you're watching. Physically, it's not a problem. But, you can't go home and talk about the things you've dealt with that day because you don't want to bring that stuff home with you. So it can take a toll, psychologically.

4. What do you wish you had known going into this profession?

There are many job opportunities and they're in all areas. We are like a miniature city. When you first get there, look around, see what all the different jobs are. We have correctional officers (COs) who strictly work in the kitchen. They do all the food buying, prepare all the meals for 900 people every day. You have the grounds officer who brings in inmates from minimum security and supervise them while they do exterior grounds work, like mowing and shoveling snow. If you like electrical work, wood working, etc., you can put in to be an industrial officer. We have COs who are electricians, guys who manufacture steel, cut doors, install locks, armory guys who maintain all the weapons, tool officers who keep track of tools. We have equipment officers. There are COs who work in transportation, bringing inmates to courts around the state. There are training officers who work at the academy and train new correctional officers. There's also a lot of potential to move up the ranks.

5. How do you see your profession changing in the next five years? What role will technology play in those changes, and what skills will be required?

We use computers for everything. I can pull up an inmate's record by his number and access his folder. I can learn whether he has enemy issues and see a list of who his enemies are. I can see a description of each tattoo he has so I can tell if he's added a tattoo while in prison. I can see what medications he takes, whether he has gang affiliation, etc.

I also think in the next five years, you're going to see more help for staff in dealing with stress. I think we'll see the profession getting a little more respect over the next five years because it really is a noble profession.

6. Do you have any general advice or additional professional insights to share with someone in your profession? What is the most fulfilling part of your job, and what is the most frustrating?

Corrections is a great stepping stone to go to other jobs. The only drawback is, it pays so well that when you're making money this good, it's hard to go to a police department where your base pay will be lower.

I think corrections is a harder and more challenging profession than police work. In corrections, if I have an issue with an inmate and he assaults me, I still have to feed him the next day. We still have to work it out. In Massachusetts, we don't have tasers. I don't carry pepper spray. It's just me and my hands and my mind.

7. **Can you suggest a valuable "try this" for students considering a career in your profession?**

   If you know anyone in corrections, ask him about it. Or call the prison facility and ask about tours. You can always watch some shows about prison on television, like Lockup and Hard Time. But most of the time when you're working, you're bored to tears. It's like babysitting, but with grownups.

   This conversation was originally published in 2014.

Famous First

The Eastern State Penitentiary was operational from 1829 until 1971. The penitentiary refined the revolutionary system of separate incarceration first pioneered at the Walnut Street Jail and emphasized reform rather than punishment. Criminals including Al Capone, Willie Sutton James Bruno (Big Joe) and several relatives were incarcerated here. At its completion, the building was the largest and most expensive public structure ever erected in the United States and quickly became a model for more than 300 prisons worldwide.

Source: https://en.wikipedia.org/wiki/Eastern_State_Penitentiary

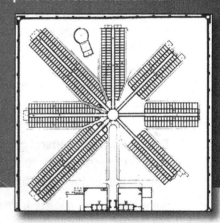

Fast Fact

The U.S. prison population, at more than 2 million, is the highest in the world. Between state, local and federal prisons and jails, incarceration costs $70 billion per year.

Source: www.ranker.com

MORE INFORMATION

For more information about Peace Officer Standards and Training (POST), visit

International Association of Directors of Law Enforcement Standards and Training
https://www.iadlest.org/

For more information about career opportunities for correctional officers at the federal level, visit

Federal Bureau of Prisons
https://www.bop.gov/

For more information about federal government requirements for correctional officers, visit

U.S. Office of Personnel Management
https://www.opm.gov/

Sources

Bureau of Labor Statistics, U.S. Department of Labor, *Occupational Outlook Handbook*, Correctional Officers and Bailiffs.

Emergency Management Directors

Snapshot

2017 Median Pay: $72,760 per year, $34.98 per hour

Typical Entry-Level Education: Bachelor's degree

Work Experience in a Related Occupation: 5 years or more

On-the-job Training: None

Number of Jobs, 2016: 10,100

Job Outlook, 2016-26: 8% (As fast as average)

Employment Change, 2016-26: 800

CAREER OVERVIEW

What Emergency Management Directors Do

Emergency management directors prepare plans and procedures for responding to natural disasters and other emergencies. They also help lead the response during and after emergencies, often in coordination with

public safety officials, elected officials, nonprofit organizations, and government agencies.

Duties

Emergency management directors typically do the following:

- Assess hazards and prepare plans to respond to emergencies and disasters in order to minimize risk to people and property
- Meet with public safety officials, private companies, and the general public to get recommendations regarding emergency response plans
- Organize emergency response training programs and exercises for staff, volunteers, and other responders
- Coordinate the sharing of resources and equipment within the community and across communities to assist in responding to an emergency
- Prepare and analyze damage assessments following disasters or emergencies
- Review emergency plans of individual organizations, such as medical facilities, to ensure their adequacy
- Apply for federal funding for emergency management planning, responses, and recovery, and report on the use of funds allocated
- Review local emergency operations plans and revise them if necessary
- Maintain facilities used during emergency operations

Emergency management directors are responsible for planning and leading the responses to natural disasters and other emergencies. Directors work with government agencies, nonprofits, private companies, and the general public to develop effective plans that minimize damage and disruptions during an emergency.

To develop emergency response plans, directors typically research "best practices" from around the country and from other emergency management agencies. Directors also must prepare plans and procedures that meet local, state, and federal regulations.

Directors must analyze the resources, equipment, and staff available to respond to emergencies. If resources or equipment is lacking, directors must either revise their plans or get the needed resources from another community or state. Many directors coordinate with fire, emergency medical service, police departments, and public works agencies in other communities to locate and share equipment during an emergency. Directors must be in contact with other agencies to collect and share information regarding the scope of the emergency, the potential costs, and the resources or staff needed.

After plans are developed, emergency management directors typically ensure that individuals and groups become familiar with the emergency procedures. Directors often use social media to disseminate plans and warnings to the general public.

Emergency management directors conduct training courses and disaster exercises for staff, volunteers, and local agencies to help ensure an effective and coordinated response to an emergency. Directors also may visit schools, hospitals, or other community groups to update everyone on plans for emergencies.

During an emergency, directors typically maintain a command center at which personnel monitor and manage the emergency operations. Directors help lead the response, making adjustments to or prioritizing certain actions if necessary. These actions may include ordering evacuations, conducting rescue missions, or opening up public shelters for those displaced by the emergency. Emergency management directors also may need to conduct press conferences or other outreach activities to keep the public informed about the emergency.

Following an emergency, directors must assess the damage to their community and must coordinate getting assistance and supplies into the community if necessary. Directors may need to request state or federal assistance to help execute their emergency response plan and provide support to affected citizens, organizations, and communities. Directors may also revise their plans and procedures to prepare for future emergencies or disasters.

Emergency management directors working for hospitals, universities, or private companies may be called *business continuity managers*. Similar to their counterparts in local and state government, business continuity managers prepare plans and procedures to help businesses maintain operations and minimize losses during and after an emergency.

WORK ENVIRONMENT

Most emergency management directors must be on call at all times to assist in emergency response.

Emergency management directors held about 10,100 jobs in 2016. The largest employers of emergency management directors were as follows:

Local government, excluding education and hospitals	52%
State government, excluding education and hospitals	12
Hospitals; state, local, and private	8
Professional, scientific, and technical services	6
Colleges, universities, and professional schools; state, local, and private	5

Although most emergency management directors work in an office, they also typically travel to meet with various government agencies, community groups, and private companies.

During disasters and emergencies, directors often work in stressful situations.

Work Schedules

Most emergency management directors work full time. In addition, most are on call at all times and may need to work overtime to respond to emergencies and to support emergency management operations. Others may work evenings and weekends to meet with various community groups in preparing their emergency response plans.

HOW TO BECOME AN EMERGENCY MANAGEMENT DIRECTOR

Applicants need years of work experience in law enforcement, fire safety, or an emergency management field.

Emergency management directors typically need a bachelor's degree, as well as multiple years of work experience in emergency response, disaster planning, or public administration.

Education

Emergency management directors typically need a bachelor's degree in business or public administration, accounting, finance, emergency management, or public health. Some directors working in the private sector in the area of business continuity management may need to have a degree in computer science, information systems administration, or another information technology (IT) field.

Some smaller municipalities or local governments may hire applicants who have just a high school diploma. However, these applicants usually need extensive work experience in emergency management if they are to be hired.

Work Experience in a Related Occupation

Applicants typically need multiple years of work experience, often with the military, law enforcement, fire safety, or in another emergency management field, before they can be hired as an emergency management director. Previous work experience in these areas enables applicants to make difficult decisions in stressful and time-sensitive situations. Such experience also prepares one to work with various agencies to ensure that proper resources are used to respond to emergencies.

For more information, see the profiles on police and detectives, firefighters, police, fire, and ambulance dispatchers, and EMTs and paramedics.

Licenses, Certifications, and Registrations

Some states require directors obtain certification within a certain timeframe after being hired in the position.

Many agencies and states offer voluntary certificate programs to help emergency management directors obtain additional skills. Some employers may prefer or even require a Certified Emergency Manager (CEM), Certified Business Continuity Professional (CBCP), or equivalent designation. Emergency management directors can attain the CEM designation through the International Association of Emergency Managers (IAEM); the certification must be renewed every 5 years. The CBCP designation is given by the Disaster Recovery Institute International (DRI) and must be renewed every 2 years.

Both associations require applicants to complete a certain number of continuing education courses prior to recertification.

ADVANCEMENT

Important Qualities

Communication skills. Emergency management directors must write out and communicate their emergency preparedness plans to all levels of government, as well as to the public.

Critical-thinking skills. Emergency management directors must anticipate hazards and problems that may arise from an emergency in order to respond effectively.

Decisionmaking skills. Emergency management directors must make timely decisions, often in stressful situations. They must also identify the strengths and weaknesses of all solutions and approaches, as well as the costs and benefits of each action.

Interpersonal skills. Emergency management directors must work with other government agencies, law enforcement and fire officials, and the general public to coordinate emergency responses.

Leadership skills. To ensure effective responses to emergencies, emergency management directors need to organize and train a variety of people.

WAGES

Median annual wages, May 2017

Management occupations: $102,590

Emergency management directors: $72,760

Total, all occupations: $37,690

Note: All Occupations includes all occupations in the U.S. Economy. Source: U.S. Bureau of Labor Statistics, Occupational Employment Statistics

The median annual wage for emergency management directors was $72,760 in May 2017. The lowest 10 percent earned less than $38,270, and the highest 10 percent earned more than $141,620.

In May 2017, the median annual wages for emergency management directors in the top industries in which they worked were as follows:

Professional, scientific, and technical services	$95,890
Colleges, universities, and professional schools; state, local, and private	88,850
Hospitals; state, local, and private	81,790
Local government, excluding education and hospitals	65,910
State government, excluding education and hospitals	60,000

Most emergency management directors work full time. In addition, most are on call at all times and may need to work overtime to respond to emergencies and to support emergency management operations. Others may work evenings and weekends to meet with various community groups in preparing their emergency response plans.

JOB OUTLOOK

Percent change in employment, projected 2016-26

Management occupations: 8%

Emergency management directors: 8%

Total, all occupations: 7%

Note: All Occupations includes all occupations in the U.S. Economy. Source: U.S. Bureau of Labor Statistics, Employment Projections program

Employment of emergency management directors is projected to grow 8 percent from 2016 to 2026, about as fast as the average for all occupations.

The importance of preparing for and minimizing the risks from emergencies will help sustain demand and employment opportunities for emergency management directors. These workers will be needed to help businesses and organizations continue to provide essential services during and after emergencies.

Some local and state governments rely on federal financial assistance to fund their emergency management agencies. Counties may not hire full-time, stand-alone emergency management directors, choosing instead to shift the job responsibilities to the fire chief, police chief, or other government employees.

Job Prospects

Competition for jobs is expected to be strong. Emergency management directors is a relatively small occupation, and only modest increases in state and local government budgets mean that new job openings are likely to be limited.

However, retirements over the next decade may provide some opportunities for jobseekers interested in entering the occupation. Applicants with extensive work experience in an emergency management role will have the best job prospects

**Employment projections data for
Emergency management directors, 2016-26**

Occupational Title	SOC Code	Employment, 2016	Projected Employment, 2026	Change, 2016-26	
				Percent	Numeric
Emergency management directors	11-9161	10,100	10,900	8	800

Source: Bureau of Labor Statistics, Employment Projections program

Famous First

Clara Barton learned of the Red Cross in Geneva, Switzerland and, in 1869, traveled to Europe to become a part of International Red Cross during the Franco-Prussian War. She became President of American National Red Cross, in May 1881. The first chapters opened in upstate New York, where she had connections. John D. Rockefeller and four others donated money to help create a national headquarters near the White House. The famed abolitionist, Frederick Douglass, offered advice and support to Barton,

Source: https://en.wikipedia.org/wiki/American_Red_Cross#History_and_organization

SIMILAR OCCUPATIONS

This table shows a list of occupations with job duties that are similar to those of emergency management directors.

OCCUPATION	JOB DUTIES	ENTRY-LEVEL EDUCATION	2017 MEDIAN PAY
Budget Analysts	Budget analysts help public and private institutions organize their finances. They prepare budget reports and monitor institutional spending.	Bachelor's degree	$75,240
EMTs and Paramedics	Emergency medical technicians (EMTs) and paramedics care for the sick or injured in emergency medical settings. People's lives often depend on the quick reaction and competent care provided by these workers. EMTs and paramedics respond to emergency calls, performing medical services and transporting patients to medical facilities.	Postsecondary nondegree award	$33,380
Firefighters	Firefighters control and put out fires and respond to emergencies where life, property, or the environment is at risk.	Postsecondary nondegree award	$49,080

OCCUPATION	JOB DUTIES	ENTRY-LEVEL EDUCATION	2017 MEDIAN PAY
Management Analysts	Management analysts, often called management consultants, propose ways to improve an organization's efficiency. They advise managers on how to make organizations more profitable through reduced costs and increased revenues.	Bachelor's degree	$82,450
Police and Detectives	Police officers protect lives and property. Detectives and criminal investigators, who are sometimes called agents or special agents, gather facts and collect evidence of possible crimes.	High school diploma or equivalent (police) Bachelor's degree (fish and game wardens) Bachelor's degree (federal agencies)	$62,960
Top Executives	Top executives devise strategies and policies to ensure that an organization meets its goals. They plan, direct, and coordinate operational activities of companies and organizations.	Bachelor's degree	$104,700

Fast Fact

The magnitude 7.0 earthquake that hit Haiti on January 12, 2010, appears to count as one of the world's top ten disasters. The death toll was estimated at 316,000 by the Haitian government in 2011; 160,000 by the journal *Medicine, Conflict and Survival*, and between 46,000-85,000 a draft US Agency for International Development report.

Source: www.ranker.com

MORE INFORMATION

For more information about emergency management directors and their certifications, visit

Recovery Institute International
https://drii.org/

International Association of Emergency Managers
https://www.iaem.org/

National Emergency Management Association
https://www.nemaweb.org/

Sources

Bureau of Labor Statistics, U.S. Department of Labor, *Occupational Outlook Handbook*, Emergency Management Directors.

EMTs and Paramedics

Snapshot

2017 Median Pay: $33,380 per year, $16.05 per hour

Typical Entry-Level Education: Postsecondary nondegree award

Work Experience in a Related Occupation: None

On-the-job Training: None

Number of Jobs, 2016: 248,000

Job Outlook, 2016-26: 15% (Much faster than average)

Employment Change, 2016-26: 37,400

CAREER OVERVIEW

What EMTs and Paramedics Do

EMTs and paramedics assess a patient's condition and administer emergency medical care.

Emergency medical technicians (EMTs) and paramedics care for the sick or injured in emergency medical settings. People's lives often depend on the

quick reaction and competent care provided by these workers. EMTs and paramedics respond to emergency calls, performing medical services and transporting patients to medical facilities.

A 911 operator sends EMTs and paramedics to the scene of an emergency, where they often work with police and firefighters.

Duties

EMTs and paramedics typically do the following:

- Respond to 911 calls for emergency medical assistance, such as cardiopulmonary resuscitation (CPR) or bandaging a wound
- Assess a patient's condition and determine a course of treatment
- Provide first-aid treatment or life support care to sick or injured patients
- Transport patients safely in an ambulance
- Transfer patients to the emergency department of a hospital or other healthcare facility
- Report their observations and treatment to physicians, nurses, or other healthcare facility staff
- Document medical care given to patients
- Inventory, replace, and clean supplies and equipment after use

When transporting a patient in an ambulance, one EMT or paramedic may drive the ambulance while another monitors the patient's vital signs and gives additional care. Some paramedics work as part of a helicopter's or an airplane's flight crew to transport critically ill or injured patients to a hospital.

EMTs and paramedics also transport patients from one medical facility to another. Some patients may need to be transferred to a hospital that specializes in treating their particular injury or illness or to a facility that provides long-term care, such as a nursing home.

If a patient has a contagious disease, EMTs and paramedics decontaminate the interior of the ambulance and may need to report the case to the proper authorities.

The specific responsibilities of EMTs and paramedics depend on their level of certification and the state they work in. The National Registry of Emergency Medical Technicians (NREMT) provides national certification of EMTs and paramedics at four levels: EMR, EMT,

Advanced EMT, and Paramedic. Some states, however, have their own certification programs and use similar titles.

Emergency Medical Responders, or EMRs, are trained to provide basic medical care with minimal equipment. These workers may provide immediate lifesaving interventions while waiting for other emergency medical services (EMS) resources to arrive. Jobs in this category may also go by a variety of titles including Emergency Care Attendants, Certified First Responders, or similar.

An *EMT*, also known as an EMT-Basic, cares for patients at the scene of an incident and while taking patients by ambulance to a hospital. An EMT has the skills to assess a patient's condition and to manage respiratory, cardiac, and trauma emergencies.

An *Advanced EMT*, also known as an EMT-Intermediate, has completed the requirements for the EMT level, as well as instruction in more advanced medical procedures, such as administering intravenous fluids and some medications.

Paramedics provide more extensive prehospital care than do EMTs. In addition to doing the tasks of EMTs, paramedics can give medications orally and intravenously, interpret electrocardiograms (EKGs)—which monitor heart function—and use other monitors and complex equipment.

The specific tasks or procedures EMTs and paramedics are allowed to perform vary by state.

WORK ENVIRONMENT

EMTs and paramedics care for sick or injured patients in a prehospital setting.

EMTs and paramedics held about 248,000 jobs in 2016. The largest employers of EMTs and paramedics were as follows:

Ambulance services	48%
Local government, excluding education and hospitals	28
Hospitals; state, local, and private	18

The above percentages exclude volunteer EMTs and paramedics who do not receive pay.

EMTs and paramedics work both indoors and outdoors, in all types of weather. Their work is physically strenuous and can be stressful, sometimes involving life-or-death situations.

Volunteer EMTs and paramedics share many of the same duties as paid EMTs and paramedics. They volunteer for fire departments, providers of emergency medical services, or hospitals. They may respond to only a few calls per month.

Injuries and Illnesses

EMTs and paramedics have one of the highest rates of injuries and illnesses of all occupations. They are required to do considerable kneeling, bending, and lifting while caring for and moving patients. They may be exposed to contagious diseases and viruses, such as hepatitis B and HIV. Sometimes they can be injured by combative patients. These risks can be reduced by following proper safety procedures, such as waiting for police to clear an area in violent situations or wearing gloves while working with a patient.

Work Schedules

Most paid EMTs and paramedics work full time. About 1 in 3 worked more than 40 hours per week in 2016. Because EMTs and paramedics must be available to work in emergencies, they may work overnight and on weekends. Some EMTs and paramedics work shifts in 12- or 24-hour increments. Volunteer EMTs and paramedics have variable work schedules. For example, they may work only a few days per week.

HOW TO BECOME AN EMT OR PARAMEDIC

EMTs and paramedics need to be physically fit as their job requires bending, lifting, and kneeling.

Emergency medical technicians (EMTs) and paramedics typically complete a postsecondary educational program. All states require EMTs and paramedics to be licensed; requirements vary by state.

Education

Both a high school diploma or equivalent and cardiopulmonary resuscitation (CPR) certification typically are required for entry into postsecondary educational programs in emergency medical technology. Most of these programs are nondegree award programs that can be completed in less than 1 year; others last up to 2 years. Paramedics, however, may need an associate's degree. Programs in emergency medical technology are offered by technical institutes, community colleges, universities, and facilities that specialize in emergency care training. Some states have EMR positions that do not require national certification. These positions typically require state certification.

The Commission on Accreditation of Allied Health Education Programs offers a list of accredited programs for EMTs and paramedics, by state.

Programs at the EMT level include instruction in assessing patients' conditions, dealing with trauma and cardiac emergencies, clearing obstructed airways, using field equipment, and handling emergencies. Formal courses include about 150 hours of specialized instruction, and some instruction may take place in a hospital or ambulance setting.

Programs at the Advanced EMT level typically require about 400 hours of instruction. At this level, candidates learn EMT-level skills as well as more advanced ones, such as using complex airway devices, intravenous fluids, and some medications.

Paramedics have the most advanced level of education. To enter specific paramedical training programs, they must already be EMT certified. Community colleges and universities may offer these programs, which require about 1,200 hours of instruction and may lead to an associate's or bachelor's degree. Paramedics' broader scope of practice may include stitching wounds or administering intravenous medications.

High school students interested in becoming EMTs or paramedics should take courses in anatomy and physiology and consider becoming certified in CPR.

Licenses, Certifications, and Registrations

The National Registry of Emergency Medical Technicians (NREMT) certifies EMTs and paramedics at the national level. All levels of NREMT certification require completing a certified education program and passing the national exam. The national exam has both written and practical parts. Some states have first-level state certifications that do not require national certification.

All states require EMTs and paramedics to be licensed; requirements vary by state. In most states, an individual who has NREMT certification qualifies for licensure; in others, passing an equivalent state exam is required. Usually, an applicant must be over the age of 18. Many states require background checks and may not give a license to an applicant who has a criminal history.

Although some emergency medical services hire separate drivers, most EMTs and paramedics take a course requiring about 8 hours of instruction before they can drive an ambulance.

ADVANCEMENT

Important Qualities

Compassion. EMTs and paramedics must be able to provide emotional support to patients in an emergency, especially patients who are in life-threatening situations or extreme mental distress.

Interpersonal skills. EMTs and paramedics usually work on teams and must be able to coordinate their activities closely with others in stressful situations.

Listening skills. EMTs and paramedics need to listen to patients to determine the extent of their injuries or illnesses.

Physical strength. EMTs and paramedics need to be physically fit. Their job requires a lot of bending, lifting, and kneeling.

Problem-solving skills. EMTs and paramedics must evaluate patients' symptoms and administer appropriate treatments.

Speaking skills. EMTs and paramedics need to clearly explain procedures to patients, give orders, and relay information to others

WAGES

EMTs and paramedics may advance into other related healthcare occupations, such as physician assistants and medical assistants, as well as administrative positions in various healthcare settings, such as ambulatory care companies or hospitals.

Median annual wages, May 2017

Health technologists and technicians: $43,590

Total, all occupations: $37,690

Emergency medical technicians and paramedics: $33,380

Note: All Occupations includes all occupations in the U.S. Economy. Source: U.S. Bureau of Labor Statistics, Occupational Employment Statistics

The median annual wage for EMTs and paramedics was $33,380 in May 2017. The lowest 10 percent earned less than $21,880, and the highest 10 percent earned more than $56,990.

In May 2017, the median annual wages for EMTs and paramedics in the top industries in which they worked were as follows:

Hospitals; state, local, and private	$35,990
Local government, excluding education and hospitals	35,620
Ambulance services	30,800

Most paid EMTs and paramedics work full time. About 1 in 3 worked more than 40 hours per week in 2016. Because EMTs and paramedics must be available to work in emergencies, they may work overnight and on weekends. Some EMTs and paramedics work shifts in 12- or 24-hour increments. Volunteer EMTs and paramedics have variable work schedules. For example, they may work only a few days per week.

JOB OUTLOOK

Percent change in employment, projected 2016-26

Emergency medical technicians and paramedics: 15%

Health technologists and technicians: 14%

Total, all occupations: 7%

Note: All Occupations includes all occupations in the U.S. Economy. Source: U.S. Bureau of Labor Statistics, Employment Projections program

Employment of emergency medical technicians (EMTs) and paramedics is projected to grow 15 percent from 2016 to 2026, much faster than the average for all occupations. Emergencies, such as car crashes, natural disasters, and acts of violence, will continue to require the skills of EMTs and paramedics. The need for volunteer EMTs and paramedics in rural areas and smaller metropolitan areas will also continue.

Growth in the middle-aged and older population will lead to an increase in age-related health emergencies, such as heart attacks and strokes. This increase, in turn, will create greater demand for EMT and paramedic services. An increase in the number of specialized medical facilities will require more EMTs and paramedics to transfer patients with specific conditions to these facilities for treatment.

Job Prospects

Job opportunities should be good because the growing population will require more emergency services generally. There will also be a need to replace workers who leave the occupation due to the high stress nature of the job or to seek job opportunities in other healthcare occupations.

Employment projections data for EMTs and paramedics, 2016-26

Occupational Title	SOC Code	Employment, 2016	Projected Employment, 2026	Change, 2016-26	
				Percent	Numeric
Emergency medical technicians and paramedics	29-2041	248,000	285,400	15	37,400

Source: Bureau of Labor Statistics, Employment Projections program

SIMILAR OCCUPATIONS

This table shows a list of occupations with job duties that are similar to those of EMTs and paramedics.

OCCUPATION	JOB DUTIES	ENTRY-LEVEL EDUCATION	2017 MEDIAN PAY
Emergency Management Directors	Emergency management directors prepare plans and procedures for responding to natural disasters or other emergencies. They also help lead the response during and after emergencies, often in coordination with public safety officials, elected officials, nonprofit organizations, and government agencies.	Bachelor's degree	$72,760
Firefighters	Firefighters control and put out fires and respond to emergencies where life, property, or the environment is at risk.	Postsecondary nondegree award	$49,080
Medical Assistants	Medical assistants complete administrative and clinical tasks in the offices of physicians, hospitals, and other healthcare facilities. Their duties vary with the location, specialty, and size of the practice.	Postsecondary nondegree award	$32,480
Police and Detectives	Police officers protect lives and property. Detectives and criminal investigators, who are sometimes called agents or special agents, gather facts and collect evidence of possible crimes.	High school diploma or equivalent (police) Bachelor's degree (fish and game wardens) Bachelor's degree (federal agencies)	$62,960

OCCUPATION	JOB DUTIES	ENTRY-LEVEL EDUCATION	2017 MEDIAN PAY
Physician Assistants	Physician assistants, also known as PAs, practice medicine on teams with physicians, surgeons, and other healthcare workers. They examine, diagnose, and treat patients.	Master's degree	$104,860
Registered Nurses	Registered nurses (RNs) provide and coordinate patient care, educate patients and the public about various health conditions, and provide advice and emotional support to patients and their family members.	Bachelor's degree	$70,000

Famous First

During the United States' Civil War, Union military physicians Joseph Barnes and Jonathan Letterman developed a prehospital care system for soldiers that relied on new techniques and methods of transport. Every regiment had an ambulance cart with a two-wheeled design that accommodated two or three patients. These ambulances were replaced by the "Rucker" ambulance, a four-wheeled design named for Major General Rucker. Other vehicles pressed into service during the civil war included steamboats, which served as mobile hospitals for the troops and railcars to transport wounded soldiers to treatment facilities.

Source: https://en.wikipedia.org/wiki/History_of_the_ ambulance

Fast Fact

Men comprise 65 to 70 percent of the EMT occupation.
Source: woman.thenest.com

Conversation With . . .
BRIAN LUTTRELL

Emergency Medical Technician/Paramedic
38 years in field

1. What was your individual career path in terms of education/training, entry-level job, or other significant opportunity?

My career path started with a basic emergency medical technician (EMT) course. That got me into an entry level position with a private ambulance company.

2. What are the most important skills and/or qualities for someone in your profession?

Being clear-headed, being able to make an educated decision on a moment's notice and being able to detach yourself from the work are very important. Don't be excitable. Someone told me a long time ago, "Keep one thing in mind: this is the patient's emergency, not yours."

As a driver, you need to have good concentration and the ability to multitask. You'll be operating the vehicle, the radio and a siren while communicating from the driver's seat to your partner at the back of the ambulance -- all at the same time.

3. What do you wish you had known going into this profession?

It's important to realize you'll be working long hours. It's a 24-hour, seven day a week, 365 day a year job and you will work all of them. You will work nights, weekends, you will work Christmas, Hanukkah, Thanksgiving. You will work on someone's birthday. You will not be able to go to your kid's ballgame because you will be working.

4. Are there many job opportunities in your profession? In what specific areas?

There are tons of job opportunities. You can work in the private sector for an ambulance company. You can work for a fire department.

5. How do you see your profession changing in the next five years? What role will technology play in those changes, and what skills will be required?

There is more computer-aided dispatching going on now. More of the vehicles are equipped with technology that reports back information. They'll know back at headquarters if you're driving too fast, braking too hard, cornering too hard. They know when you're backing the vehicle up and whether your partner is guiding you. There are blind spots in an ambulance, so your partner has to be outside the vehicle, directing you when you back up. Your partner has to hold a button in the back of the truck while you're backing up. If your partner isn't there holding the button in, a text memo goes to your supervisor.

The computers in the trucks now are giving you directions, but also giving you information pertinent to your call. If I'm transferring a patient from one hospital to another, I'll be getting information on the computer about his heart rate, the med pumps, the medications the patient is on, etc.

6. What is the most fulfilling part of your job, and what is the most frustrating?

The most frustrating part is seeing people being taken care of poorly, whether it's at home or at a skilled nursing facility. It's very frustrating to answer a call where someone is being abused.

What's fulfilling is helping to deliver a baby or save someone's life. Being part of a team is fulfilling. Helping to save someone's life by getting that patient to the right hospital, that feels good.

7. Can you suggest a valuable "try this" for students considering a career in your profession?

Before diving headfirst into this, take a CPR or first aid course. If you're in college, see if there's an emergency medical services department where you can volunteer.

This conversation was originally published in Careers in Healthcare *(Salem) in 2014.*

MORE INFORMATION

For more information about emergency medical technicians and paramedics, visit

National Association of Emergency Medical Technicians
http://www.naemt.org/

National Association of State EMS Officials
https://nasemso.org/

National Highway Traffic Safety Administration, Office of Emergency Medical Services
https://www.ems.gov/

National Registry of Emergency Medical Technicians
https://www.nremt.org/rwd/public

For information about educational programs, visit

Commission on Accreditation of Allied Health Education Programs
https://www.caahep.org/

Sources

Bureau of Labor Statistics, U.S. Department of Labor, *Occupational Outlook Handbook*, EMTs and Paramedics

Environmental Scientists and Specialists

Snapshot

2017 Median Pay: $69,400 per year, $33.37 per hour

Typical Entry-Level Education: Bachelor's degree

Work Experience in a Related Occupation: None

On-the-job Training: None

Number of Jobs, 2016: 89,500

Job Outlook, 2016-26: 11% (Faster than average)

Employment Change, 2016-26: 9,900

CAREER OVERVIEW

What Environmental Scientists and Specialists Do

Environmental scientists and specialists use their knowledge of the natural sciences to protect the environment and human health. They may clean up polluted areas, advise policymakers, or work with industry to reduce waste.

Duties

Environmental scientists and specialists typically do the following:

- Determine data collection methods for research projects, investigations, and surveys
- Collect and compile environmental data from samples of air, soil, water, food, and other materials for scientific analysis
- Analyze samples, surveys, and other information to identify and assess threats to the environment
- Develop plans to prevent, control, or fix environmental problems, such as land or water pollution
- Provide information and guidance to government officials, businesses, and the general public on possible environmental hazards and health risks
- Prepare technical reports and presentations that explain their research and findings

Environmental scientists and specialists analyze environmental problems and develop solutions to them. For example, many environmental scientists and specialists work to reclaim lands and waters that have been contaminated by pollution. Others assess the risks that new construction projects pose to the environment and make recommendations to governments and businesses on how to minimize the environmental impact of these projects. Environmental scientists and specialists may do research and provide advice on manufacturing practices, such as advising against the use of chemicals that are known to harm the environment.

The federal government and many state and local governments have regulations to ensure that there is clean air to breathe and safe water to drink, and that there are no hazardous materials in the soil. The regulations also place limits on development, particularly near sensitive ecosystems, such as wetlands. Environmental scientists and specialists who work for governments ensure that the regulations are followed. Other environmental scientists and specialists work for consulting firms that help companies comply with regulations and policies.

Some environmental scientists and specialists focus on environmental regulations that are designed to protect people's health, while others focus on regulations designed to minimize society's impact on the ecosystem. The following are examples of types of specialists:

Climate change analysts study effects on ecosystems caused by the changing climate. They may do outreach education activities and grant writing typical of scientists.

Environmental health and safety specialists study how environmental factors affect human health. They investigate potential environmental health risks. For example, they may investigate and address issues arising from soil and water contamination caused by nuclear weapons manufacturing. They also educate the public about health risks that may be present in the environment.

Environmental restoration planners assess polluted sites and determine the cost and activities necessary to clean up the area.

Industrial ecologists work with industry to increase the efficiency of their operations and thereby limit the impacts these activities have on the environment. They analyze costs and benefits of various programs, as well as their impacts on ecosystems.

Other environmental scientists and specialists perform work and receive training similar to that of other physical or life scientists, but they focus on environmental issues. For example, ***environmental chemists*** study the effects that various chemicals have on ecosystems. To illustrate, they may study how acids affect plants, animals, and people. Some areas in which they work include waste management and the remediation of contaminated soils, water, and air.

Many people with backgrounds in environmental science become postsecondary teachers or high school teachers

WORK ENVIRONMENT

Environmental scientists and specialists held about 89,500 jobs in 2016. The largest employers of environmental scientists and specialists were as follows:

Management, scientific, and technical consulting services	23%
State government, excluding education and hospitals	23
Local government, excluding education and hospitals	14
Engineering services	9
Federal government, excluding postal service	6

Environmental scientists and specialists work in offices and laboratories. Some may spend time in the field gathering data and monitoring environmental conditions firsthand, but this work is much more likely to be done by environmental science and protection technicians. Fieldwork can be physically demanding, and environmental scientists and specialists may work in all types of weather. Environmental scientists and specialists may have to travel to meet with clients or present research at conferences.

Work Schedules

Most environmental scientists and specialists work full time. They may have to work more than 40 hours a week when working in the field.

HOW TO BECOME AN ENVIRONMENTAL SCIENTIST OR SPECIALIST

Education and Training

For most entry-level jobs, environmental scientists and specialists must have a bachelor's degree in environmental science or a science-related field, such as biology, chemistry, physics, geosciences, or engineering. However, a master's degree may be needed for advancement. Environmental scientists and specialists who have a doctoral degree make up a small percentage of the occupation, and this level of training typically is needed only for the relatively few postsecondary teaching and basic research positions.

A bachelor's degree in environmental science offers a broad approach to the natural sciences. Students typically take courses in biology, chemistry, geology, and physics. Students often take specialized courses in hydrology or waste management as part of their degree as well. Classes in environmental policy and regulation are also beneficial. Students who want to reach the PhD level may find it advantageous to major in a more specific natural science, such as chemistry, biology, physics, or geology, rather than earn a broader environmental science degree.

Many environmental science programs include an internship, which allows students to gain practical experience. Prospective scientists also may volunteer for or participate in internships after graduation to develop skills needed for the occupation.

Students should look for classes and internships that include work in computer modeling, data analysis, and Geographic Information Systems (GISs). Students with experience in these programs will be the best prepared to enter the job market. The University Corporation for Atmospheric Research (UCAR) offers several programs to help students broaden their understanding of environmental sciences.

Important Qualities

Analytical skills. Environmental scientists and specialists base their conclusions on careful analysis of scientific data. They must consider all possible methods and solutions in their analyses.

Communication skills. Environmental scientists and specialists may need to present and explain their findings to audiences of varying backgrounds and write technical reports.

Interpersonal skills. Environmental scientists and specialists typically work on teams along with scientists, engineers, and technicians. Team members must be able to work together effectively to achieve their goals.

Problem-solving skills. Environmental scientists and specialists try to find the best possible solution to problems that affect the environment and people's health.

Self-discipline. Environmental scientists and specialists may spend a lot of time working alone. They need to stay motivated and get their work done without supervision.

ADVANCEMENT

As environmental scientists and specialists gain experience, they earn more responsibilities and autonomy, and may supervise the work of technicians or other scientists. Eventually, they may be promoted to project leader, program manager, or some other management or research position.

Other environmental scientists and specialists go on to work as researchers or faculty at colleges and universities.

Licenses, Certifications, and Registrations

Environmental scientists and specialists can become Certified Hazardous Materials Managers through the Institute of Hazardous Materials Management. This certification, which must be renewed every 5 years, shows that an environmental scientist or specialist is staying current with developments relevant to the occupation's work. In addition, the Ecological Society of America offers several levels of certification for environmental scientists who wish to demonstrate their proficiency in ecology.

Work Experience in a Related Occupation

Environmental scientists and specialists often begin their careers as field analysts, research assistants, or environmental science and protection technicians in laboratories and offices.

Some environmental scientists and specialists begin their careers as scientists in related occupations, such as hydrology or engineering, and then move into the more interdisciplinary field of environmental science.

WAGES

Median annual wages, May 2017

Physical scientists: $78,790

Environmental scientists and specialists, including health: $69,400

Total, all occupations: $37,690

Note: All Occupations includes all occupations in the U.S. Economy. Source: U.S. Bureau of Labor Statistics, Occupational Employment Statistics

The median annual wage for environmental scientists and specialists was $69,400 in May 2017. The lowest 10 percent earned less than $41,580, and the highest 10 percent earned more than $122,510.

In May 2017, the median annual wages for environmental scientists and specialists in the top industries in which they worked were as follows:

Federal government, excluding postal service	$101,400
Engineering services	69,440
Local government, excluding education and hospitals	69,070
Management, scientific, and technical consulting services	67,960
State government, excluding education and hospitals	63,660

Most environmental scientists and specialists work full time. They may have to work more than 40 hours a week if they work in the field.

JOB OUTLOOK

Percent change in employment, projected 2016-26

Environmental scientists and specialists, including health: 11%

Physical scientists: 10%

Total, all occupations: 7%

Note: All Occupations includes all occupations in the U.S. Economy. Source: U.S. Bureau of Labor Statistics, Employment Projections program

Employment of environmental scientists and specialists is projected to grow 11 percent from 2016 to 2026, faster than the average for all occupations.

Heightened public interest in the hazards facing the environment, as well as increasing demands placed on the environment by population growth, are projected to spur demand for environmental scientists and specialists. Many jobs will remain concentrated in state and local governments, and in industries that provide consulting services. Scientists and specialists will continue to be needed in these industries to analyze environmental problems and develop solutions that ensure communities' health.

Businesses are expected to continue to consult with environmental scientists and specialists to help them minimize the impact their operations have on the environment. For example, environmental consultants help businesses to develop practices that minimize waste, prevent pollution, and conserve resources. Other environmental scientists and specialists are expected to be needed to help planners develop and construct buildings, utilities, and transportation systems that protect natural resources and limit damage to the land.

Job Prospects

Environmental scientists and specialists should have good job opportunities. In addition to growth, many job openings will be created by scientists who retire, advance to management positions, or change careers.

Candidates may improve their employment prospects by gaining hands-on experience through an internship.

Employment projections data for Environmental Scientists and Specialists, 2016-26

Occupational Title	SOC Code	Employment, 2016	Projected Employment, 2026	Change, 2016-26	
				Percent	Numeric
Environmental scientists and specialists, including health	19-2041	89,500	99,400	11	9,900

Source: Bureau of Labor Statistics, Employment Projections program

SIMILAR OCCUPATIONS

This table shows a list of occupations with job duties that are similar to those of environmental scientists and specialists.

OCCUPATION	JOB DUTIES	ENTRY-LEVEL EDUCATION	2017 MEDIAN PAY
Biochemists and Biophysicists	Biochemists and biophysicists study the chemical and physical principles of living things and of biological processes, such as cell development, growth, heredity, and disease.	Doctoral or professional degree	$91,190
Chemists and Materials Scientists	Chemists and materials scientists study substances at the atomic and molecular levels and analyze the ways in which the substances interact with one another. They use their knowledge to develop new and improved products and to test the quality of manufactured goods.	Bachelor's degree	$76,280
Conservation Scientists and Foresters	Conservation scientists and foresters manage the overall land quality of forests, parks, rangelands, and other natural resources.	Bachelor's degree	$60,970
Environmental Engineers	Environmental engineers use the principles of engineering, soil science, biology, and chemistry to develop solutions to environmental problems. They are involved in efforts to improve recycling, waste disposal, public health, and water and air pollution control.	Bachelor's degree	$86,800
Environmental Science and Protection Technicians	Environmental science and protection technicians monitor the environment and investigate sources of pollution and contamination, including those affecting public health.	Associate's degree	$45,490

OCCUPATION	JOB DUTIES	ENTRY-LEVEL EDUCATION	2017 MEDIAN PAY
Geoscientists	Geoscientists study the physical aspects of the Earth, such as its composition, structure, and processes, to learn about its past, present, and future.	Bachelor's degree	$89,850
Hydrologists	Hydrologists study how water moves across and through the Earth's crust. They use their expertise to solve problems in the areas of water quality or availability.	Bachelor's degree	$79,990
Microbiologists	Microbiologists study microorganisms such as bacteria, viruses, algae, fungi, and some types of parasites. They try to understand how these organisms live, grow, and interact with their environments.	Bachelor's degree	$69,960
Occupational Health and Safety Specialists and Technicians	Occupational health and safety specialists and technicians collect data on and analyze many types of work environments and work procedures. Specialists inspect workplaces for adherence to regulations on safety, health, and the environment. Technicians work with specialists in conducting tests and measuring hazards to help prevent harm to workers, property, the environment, and the general public.	Bachelor's degree (specialist) High school diploma or equivalent (technician)	$67,720
Zoologists and Wildlife Biologists	Zoologists and wildlife biologists study animals and other wildlife and how they interact with their ecosystems. They study the physical characteristics of animals, animal behaviors, and the impacts humans have on wildlife and natural habitats.	Bachelor's degree	$62,290

Conversation With . . .
MATT BARNES

Field director, Keystone Conservation
Owner, Shining Horizons Land Management
Rangeland Manager, 12 years

1. **What was your individual career path in terms of education/training, entry-level job, or other significant opportunity?**

   I grew up playing in the woods but didn't know you could have a career allowing you to do that. I dropped out of college twice before going back and realizing I could major in natural resources. Once that happened, I became a straight-A student overnight. I earned a bachelor's degree in wildlife management with a minor in range management, then obtained a master's degree in range science.

   I first worked for the Bureau of Indian Affairs, then the USDA's Natural Resources Conservation Service. At RCS, I worked with ranchers to improve grazing management, which was the focus of my master's thesis. I then managed a ranch for three years on a contract basis, using my theories about grazing management. Now I work with a nonprofit organization to help ranchers in the northern Rockies and Montana manage where and when their livestock graze.

   My interest, most fundamentally, is figuring out how we can have wildness going into the future without having to revert to prehistoric conditions. An ultimate goal is to have a landscape with livestock and people and large carnivores and native species. To me, that means modifying the way humans -- and their livestock -- live on the landscape.

   If you use small pastures and have deep knowledge of what plants are growing where and when, you can rotate livestock so they're always in areas with plentiful forage. That way, they're less likely to spread so far apart that they're an attractive target for predators.

   This was an essentially untested hypothesis when I began. Now case studies by me and others support this belief.

2. **What are the most important skills and/or qualities for someone in your profession?**

   You need a conservation ethic. Obviously, people will disagree about what that means. You need to be observant about what's going on out in the landscape, including both wild and domestic animals and the plant communities. I think a rangelands manager synthesizes all of these different kinds of knowledge and more. You also need to be able to get along with people and to be able to enjoy being by yourself out in the wild for an extended period. You need to know basic outdoor skills.

3. What do you wish you had known going into this profession?

If I had known as a kid that there were careers that involved being in the outdoors besides being a park ranger, I might have discovered this earlier and saved myself four years. But most professions in the world are probably things that an 18-year-old doesn't know exists.

4. Are there many job opportunities in your profession? In what specific areas?

It's a fairly broad field. The government is the primary employer, which is different from most fields. There's competition but less so than for jobs in wildlife biology and conservation. I think it's largely because people don't know what rangeland management is. A typical rangeland manager would work for a government agency managing publicly owned lands, or promote conservation on privately owned rangelands, or manage a ranch. What I'm doing now would not be considered typical.

5. How do you see your profession changing in the next five years, what role will technology play in those changes, and what skills will be required?

It used to be a given that a student graduating in this field grew up on a ranch or handling cattle or hunting and fishing. Those skills are still important but people coming into this field now tend to have much less practical experience than they did in prior decades. They have more of an ecological education.

6. What do you like most about your job? What do you like least about your job?

I get to work in some of the most beautiful places in the world and almost all the people I work with are really fascinating individuals.

On the other hand, there's more office work than you might imagine, especially if you're imagining a park ranger on horseback in the wild. There are days like that and those are the best days. But there are many days spent working on a computer and talking on the phone and that kind of work is just as essential.

7. Can you suggest a valuable "try this" for students considering a career in your profession?

An internship or a summer job related to this field. For a lot of people, this will be where they learn the practical skills they don't get in college.

This conversation was originally published in 2014.

Famous First

During the Industrial Revolution, levels of smoke pollution in the atmosphere increased to an unprecedented level; after 1900 the large volume of industrial chemical discharges added to the growing load of untreated human waste. The first large-scale, modern environmental laws were Britain's Alkali Acts, passed in 1863, to regulate the deleterious air pollution (gaseous hydrochloric acid) given off by the Leblanc process, used to produce soda ash. An Alkali inspector and four sub-inspectors were appointed to curb this pollution. The Alkali Order 1958 placed all major heavy industries that emitted smoke, grit, dust and fumes under their supervision.

Source: https://en.wikipedia.org/wiki/Environmentalism

Fast Fact

Gaia, goddess of the earth, was one of the primordial elemental deities born at the dawn of creation. Her was revived in 1979 by James Lovelock, in Gaia: *A New Look at Life on Earth*

Source: Theoi Greek Mythology, https://www.theoi.com/.

MORE INFORMATION

For more information about environmental scientists and specialists, including training, visit

American Geosciences Institute
https://www.americangeosciences.org/

UCAR (University Corporation for Atmospheric Research)
https://www.ucar.edu/

For more information about certification as a Certified Hazardous Materials Manager, visit

Institute of Hazardous Materials Management
https://www.ihmm.org/certificants/chmm

For more information about certification as an ecologist, visit

Ecological Society of America
https://www.esa.org/esa/

For information about environmental health specialists and related occupations, visit

National Environmental Health Association
https://www.neha.org/

Sources

Bureau of Labor Statistics, U.S. Department of Labor, *Occupational Outlook Handbook*, Environmental Scientists and Specialists.

Epidemiologists

CAREER OVERVIEW

What Epidemiologists Do

Epidemiologists monitor infectious diseases, bioterrorism threats, and other problem areas for public health agencies.

Epidemiologists are public health professionals who investigate patterns and causes of disease and injury in humans. They seek to reduce the risk and occurrence of negative health outcomes through research, community education and health policy.

Duties

Epidemiologists typically do the following:

- Plan and direct studies of public health problems to find ways to prevent and treat them if they arise
- Collect and analyze data—through observations, interviews, and surveys, and by using samples of blood or other bodily fluids—to find the causes of diseases or other health problems
- Communicate their findings to health practitioners, policymakers, and the public
- Manage public health programs by planning programs, monitoring their progress, analyzing data, and seeking ways to improve the programs in order to improve public health outcomes
- Supervise professional, technical, and clerical personnel

Epidemiologists collect and analyze data to investigate health issues. For example, an epidemiologist might collect and analyze demographic data to determine who is at the highest risk for a particular disease. They also may research and investigate the trends in populations of survivors of certain diseases, such as cancer, so that effective treatments can be identified and repeated across the population.

Epidemiologists typically work in applied public health or in research. Applied epidemiologists work for state and local governments, addressing public health problems directly. They often are involved with education outreach and survey efforts in communities. Research epidemiologists typically work for universities or in affiliation with federal agencies, such as the Centers for Disease Control and Prevention (CDC) or the National Institutes of Health (NIH).

Epidemiologists who work in private industry commonly conduct research for health insurance companies or pharmaceutical companies. Those in nonprofit companies often do public health advocacy work. Epidemiologists involved in research are rarely advocates, because scientific research is expected to be unbiased.

Epidemiologists typically specialize in one or more of the following public health areas:

- Infectious diseases
- Chronic diseases
- Maternal and child health

- Public health preparedness and emergency response
- Environmental health
- Injury
- Occupational health
- Oral health
- Substance abuse
- Mental health

WORK ENVIRONMENT

Field work may require interaction with sick patients, yet safety precautions ensure that the likelihood of exposure to disease is minimal.

Epidemiologists held about 6,100 jobs in 2016. The largest employers of epidemiologists were as follows:

State government, excluding education and hospitals	34%
Local government, excluding education and hospitals	19
Hospitals; state, local, and private	15
Colleges, universities, and professional schools; state, local, and private	10
Scientific research and development services	10

Epidemiologists typically work in offices and laboratories at health departments for state and local governments, in hospitals, and at colleges and universities. Epidemiologists are also employed in the federal government by agencies such as the Centers for Disease Control and Prevention (CDC). Work environments can vary widely, however, because of the diverse nature of epidemiological specializations. Epidemiologists also may work in clinical settings or in the field, where they support emergency actions.

Most epidemiologists spend their time studying data and reports in an office setting. Work in laboratories and the field tends to be delegated to specialized scientists and other technical staff. In state and local government public health departments, epidemiologists may be more active in the community and may need to travel to support community education efforts or to administer studies and surveys.

Because modern science has greatly reduced the amount of infectious disease in developed countries, infectious disease epidemiologists are more likely to travel to remote areas and developing nations in order to carry out their studies. Epidemiologists encounter minimal risk when they work in laboratories or in the field, because they have received appropriate training and take extensive precautions before interacting with samples or patients.

Work Schedules

Most epidemiologists work full time and have a standard work schedule. Occasionally, epidemiologists may have to work long or irregular hours in order to complete fieldwork or tend to duties during public health emergencies.

HOW TO BECOME AN EPIDEMIOLOGIST

Epidemiologists need at least a master's degree from an accredited college or university. Most epidemiologists have a master's degree in public health (MPH) or a related field, and some have completed a doctoral degree in epidemiology or medicine.

Education

Epidemiologists typically need at least a master's degree from an accredited college or university. A master's degree in public health with an emphasis in epidemiology is most common, but epidemiologists can earn degrees in a wide range of related fields and specializations. Epidemiologists who direct research projects—

including those who work as postsecondary teachers in colleges and universities—often have a PhD or medical degree in their chosen field.

Coursework in epidemiology includes classes in public health, biological and physical sciences, and math and statistics. Classes emphasize statistical methods, causal analysis, and survey design. Advanced courses emphasize multiple regression, medical informatics, reviews of previous biomedical research, comparisons of healthcare systems, and practical applications of data.

Many master's degree programs in public health, as well as other programs that are specific to epidemiology, require students to complete an internship or practicum that typically ranges in length from a semester to a year.

Some epidemiologists have both a degree in epidemiology and a medical degree. These scientists often work in clinical capacities. In medical school, students spend most of their first 2 years in laboratories and classrooms, taking courses such as anatomy, biochemistry, physiology, pharmacology, psychology, microbiology, and pathology. Medical students also have the option to choose electives such as medical ethics and medical laws. They also learn to take medical histories, examine patients, and diagnose illnesses.

ADVANCEMENT

Important Qualities

Communication skills. Epidemiologists must use their speaking and writing skills to inform the public and community leaders about public health risks. Clear communication is required for an epidemiologist to work effectively with other health professionals.

Critical-thinking skills. Epidemiologists analyze data to determine how best to respond to a public health problem or an urgent health-related emergency.

Detail oriented. Epidemiologists must be precise and accurate in moving from observation and interview to conclusions.

Math and statistical skills. Epidemiologists may need advanced math and statistical skills to design and administer studies and surveys. Skill in using large databases and statistical computer programs may also be important.

Teaching skills. Epidemiologists may be involved in community outreach activities that educate the public about health risks and healthy living.

WAGES

Median annual wages, May 2017

Life scientists: $73,700

Epidemiologists: $69,660

Total, all occupations: $37,690

Note: All Occupations includes all occupations in the U.S. Economy. Source: U.S. Bureau of Labor Statistics, Occupational Employment Statistics

The median annual wage for epidemiologists was $69,660 in May 2017. The lowest 10 percent earned less than $42,810, and the highest 10 percent earned more than $113,560.

In May 2017, the median annual wages for epidemiologists in the top industries in which they worked were as follows:

Scientific research and development services	$103,580
Hospitals; state, local, and private	80,680
Local government, excluding education and hospitals	64,690
State government, excluding education and hospitals	62,370
Colleges, universities, and professional schools; state, local, and private	61,220

Most epidemiologists work full time and have a standard work schedule. Occasionally, epidemiologists may have to work long or irregular hours in order to complete fieldwork or tend to duties during public health emergencies.

JOB OUTLOOK

Percent change in employment, projected 2016-26

Life scientists: 10%

Epidemiologists: 9%

Total, all occupations: 7%

Note: All Occupations includes all occupations in the U.S. Economy. Source: U.S. Bureau of Labor Statistics, Employment Projections program

Employment of epidemiologists is projected to grow 9 percent from 2016 to 2026, about as fast as the average for all occupations. Epidemiological and public health capacity, which is the ability of state and local agencies to provide public health services and respond to emergencies, has increased dramatically over the past decade.

However, there still may be benefits to increasing epidemiological capacity over the projection term. States with large populations tend to have more established programs at this point, but may still expand capacity in certain areas such as mental health and substance abuse. Growth in capacity is expected to be concentrated in states with smaller populations, but large capacity expansions may only require small employment growth.

Epidemiological and public health programs are largely dependent on public funding, and uncertain budgetary conditions are likely to moderate growth.

Epidemiological and infection control capacity is expected to increase in hospitals as more hospitals join programs such as the National Healthcare Safety Network and realize the benefits of strengthened infection control programs.

Job Prospects

Interest in public health and epidemiology has increased over the past decade. The number of master's degree programs in public health specializing in epidemiology, as well as the number of graduates from these programs, has increased. Some entrants are finding strong competition for jobs, but applicants who are willing to work in any of the various specialties found in this occupation, rather than those tied to one specialty, may have less difficulty finding work. Because epidemiology is a diverse field, opportunities can generally be found if one takes a broad view.

Employment projections data for
Epidemiologists, 2016-26

Occupational Title	SOC Code	Employment, 2016	Projected Employment, 2026	Change, 2016-26	
				Percent	Numeric
Epidemiologists	19-1041	6,100	6,600	9	500

Source: Bureau of Labor Statistics, Employment Projections program

SIMILAR OCCUPATIONS

This table shows a list of occupations with job duties that are similar to those of epidemiologists.

OCCUPATION	JOB DUTIES	ENTRY-LEVEL EDUCATION	2017 MEDIAN PAY
Anthropologists and Archeologists	Anthropologists and archeologists study the origin, development, and behavior of humans. They examine the cultures, languages, archeological remains, and physical characteristics of people in various parts of the world.	Master's degree	$62,280
Economists	Economists study the production and distribution of resources, goods, and services by collecting and analyzing data, researching trends, and evaluating economic issues.	Master's degree	$102,490
Environmental Scientists and Specialists	Environmental scientists and specialists use their knowledge of the natural sciences to protect the environment and human health. They may clean up polluted areas, advise policymakers, or work with industry to reduce waste.	Bachelor's degree	$69,400
Geographers	Geographers study the Earth and the distribution of its land, features, and inhabitants. They also examine political or cultural structures and study the physical and human geographic characteristics of regions ranging in scale from local to global.	Bachelor's degree	$76,860

OCCUPATION	JOB DUTIES	ENTRY-LEVEL EDUCATION	2017 MEDIAN PAY
Health Educators and Community Health Workers	Health educators teach people about behaviors that promote wellness. They develop and implement strategies to improve the health of individuals and communities. Community health workers collect data and discuss health concerns with members of specific populations or communities.	Bachelor's degree (health educators) High school diploma or equivalent (community health workers)	$45,360
Medical Scientists	Medical scientists conduct research aimed at improving overall human health. They often use clinical trials and other investigative methods to reach their findings.	Doctoral or professional degree	$82,090
Microbiologists	Microbiologists study microorganisms such as bacteria, viruses, algae, fungi, and some types of parasites. They try to understand how these organisms live, grow, and interact with their environments.	Bachelor's degree	$69,960
Physicians and Surgeons	Physicians and surgeons diagnose and treat injuries or illnesses. Physicians examine patients; take medical histories; prescribe medications; and order, perform, and interpret diagnostic tests. They counsel patients on diet, hygiene, and preventive healthcare. Surgeons operate on patients to treat injuries, such as broken bones; diseases, such as cancerous tumors; and deformities, such as cleft palates.	Doctoral or professional degree	This wage is equal to or greater than $208,000 per year.

OCCUPATION	JOB DUTIES	ENTRY-LEVEL EDUCATION	2017 MEDIAN PAY
Political Scientists	Political scientists study the origin, development, and operation of political systems. They research political ideas and analyze governments, policies, political trends, and related issues.	Master's degree	$115,110
Registered Nurses	Registered nurses (RNs) provide and coordinate patient care, educate patients and the public about various health conditions, and provide advice and emotional support to patients and their family members.	Bachelor's degree	$70,000
Survey Researchers	Survey researchers design and conduct surveys and analyze data. Surveys are used to collect factual data, such as employment and salary information, or to ask questions in order to understand people's opinions, preferences, beliefs, or desires.	Master's degree	$54,270
Mathematicians and Statisticians	Mathematicians and statisticians analyze data and apply mathematical and statistical techniques to help solve real-world problems in business, engineering, healthcare, or other fields.	Master's degree	$84,760

Fast Fact

As of 2016, zika cannot be prevented by medications or vaccines, and it can spread from a pregnant woman to her baby, which can result result in microcephaly, severe brain malformations, and other birth defects.

Source: Centers for Disease Control, www.cdc.gov.

Famous First

John Snow known as the father of epidemiology, investigated the causes of the nineteenth century cholera epidemics. He noticed the significantly higher death rates in two areas, both supplied by Southwark Company. The story of his determination that the Broad Street pump was the cause of the Soho epidemic is considered the classic example of epidemiology. Snow used chlorine in an attempt to clean the water and removed the handle; this ended the outbreak. However, Snow's research and preventive measures to avoid further outbreaks were not fully accepted or put into practice until after his death.

Source: https://en.wikipedia.org/wiki/Epidemiology#History

MORE INFORMATION

For more information about epidemiologists, visit

American College of Epidemiology
https://www.acepidemiology.org/

Council of State and Territorial Epidemiologists
https://www.cste.org/default.aspx

The Society for Healthcare Epidemiology of America
http://www.shea-online.org/

For more information about epidemiology careers in the federal government, visit

Centers for Disease Control and Prevention
https://jobs.cdc.gov/

National Institutes of Health
https://www.nih.gov/

For public health–related information, visit

American Epidemiological Society
https://www.
americanepidemiologicalsociety.
org/

American Public Health Association
https://www.apha.org/

Association of State and Territorial Health Officials
http://www.astho.org/

National Academy for State Health Policy
https://nashp.org/

Public Health Foundation
http://www.phf.org/Pages/default.
aspx

Sources

Bureau of Labor Statistics, U.S. Department of Labor, *Occupational Outlook Handbook*, Epidemiologists.

Fire Inspectors

Snapshot

2017 Median Pay: $56,670 per year, $27.25 per hour

Typical Entry-Level Education: Postsecondary educational program for emergency medical technicians (EMTs), High school diploma or equivalent (forest fire inspectors and prevention specialists)

Work Experience in a Related Occupation: Work experience as a firefighter

On-the-job Training: Moderate-term on-the-job training

Number of Jobs, 2016: 14,100

Job Outlook, 2016-26: 10% (Faster than average)

Employment Change, 2016-26: 1,400

CAREER OVERVIEW

What Fire Inspectors Do

Fire inspectors examine buildings in order to detect fire hazards and ensure that federal, state, and local fire codes are met. Fire investigators, another type of worker in this field, determine the origin and cause of fires and explosions. Forest

fire inspectors and prevention specialists assess outdoor fire hazards in public and residential areas.

Duties

Fire inspectors typically do the following:

- Search for fire hazards
- Ensure that buildings comply with fire codes
- Test fire alarms, sprinklers, and other fire protection equipment
- Inspect fuel storage tanks and air compressors
- Review emergency evacuation plans
- Conduct followup visits to make sure that infractions do not recur
- Review building plans with developers
- Conduct fire and safety education programs
- Maintain fire inspection files
- Administer burn permits and monitor controlled burns
- Fire investigators typically do the following:
- Collect and analyze evidence from scenes of fires and explosions
- Interview witnesses
- Reconstruct the scene of a fire or arson
- Send evidence to laboratories to be tested for fingerprints or accelerants
- Analyze information with chemists, engineers, and attorneys
- Document evidence by taking photographs and creating diagrams
- Determine the origin and cause of a fire
- Keep detailed records and protect evidence for use in a court of law
- Testify in civil and criminal legal proceedings
- Exercise police powers, such as the power of arrest, and carry a weapon

Forest fire inspectors and prevention specialists assess outdoor fire hazards in public and residential areas. They look for fire code infractions and for conditions that pose a wildfire risk. They also recommend ways to reduce fire hazards. During patrols, they enforce fire regulations and report fire conditions to their central command center.

WORK ENVIRONMENT

Fire investigators often work in the field when determining the origin and cause of a fire.

Fire inspectors and investigators held about 12,300 jobs in 2016. The largest employers of fire inspectors and investigators were as follows:

Local government, excluding education and hospitals	78%
State government, excluding education and hospitals	9
Colleges, universities, and professional schools; state, local, and private	2
Investigation and security services	2
Manufacturing	2

Forest fire inspectors and prevention specialists held about 1,700 jobs in 2016. The largest employers of forest fire inspectors and prevention specialists were as follows:

State government, excluding education and hospitals	59%
Local government, excluding education and hospitals	37

Local government, excluding education and hospitals Fire inspectors work both in offices and in the field. In the field, inspectors examine buildings such as apartment complexes and offices. They also may visit and inspect other structures, such as arenas and industrial plants. Fire investigators visit the scene of a fire. They may be exposed to poor ventilation, smoke, fumes, and other hazardous agents.

Forest fire inspectors and prevention specialists spend much of their time outdoors, assessing the risks of fires in places such as forests, fields, and other natural or outdoor environments.

Injuries and Illnesses

Working at the scene of a fire can be dangerous. And injuries can occur when workers are patrolling in remote areas with rugged terrain. As a result, forest fire inspectors and prevention specialists have one of the highest rates of injuries and illnesses of all occupations.

Work Schedules

Fire inspectors and investigators typically work during regular business hours, but investigators may also work evenings, weekends, and holidays because they must be ready to respond when fires occur.

HOW TO BECOME A FIRE INSPECTOR

Many fire inspectors and investigators have a firefighter background.

Fire inspectors and investigators, as well as forest fire inspectors and prevention specialists, typically have previous work experience as a firefighter. These workers need at least a high school diploma or equivalent, and receive on-the-job-training in inspection and investigation.

Fire inspectors and investigators usually must pass a background check, which may include a drug test. Most employers also require inspectors and investigators to have a valid driver's license, and investigators usually need to be U.S. citizens because of their police powers.

Education

Because fire inspectors and investigators typically have previous work experience as a firefighter, many have completed a postsecondary educational program for emergency medical technicians (EMTs). Some employers prefer candidates with a 2- or 4-year degree in fire science, engineering, or chemistry. For those candidates interested in becoming forest fire inspectors and prevention specialists, a high school diploma or equivalent typically is required.

Training

Training requirements vary by state, but programs usually include instruction in a classroom setting in addition to on-the-job training.

Classroom training often takes place at a fire or police academy over the course of several months. A variety of topics are covered, including guidelines for conducting an inspection or investigation, legal codes, courtroom procedures, protocols for handling hazardous and explosive materials, and the proper use of equipment.

In most agencies, after inspectors and investigators have finished their classroom training, they also receive on-the-job training, during which they work with a more experienced officer.

Employers, such as the Bureau of Alcohol, Tobacco, Firearms and Explosives (ATF) and the Federal Bureau of Investigation (FBI), and organizations, such as the National Fire Academy and the International Association of Arson Investigators, offer training programs in fire investigation.

Work Experience in a Related Occupation

Most fire inspectors and investigators are required to have work experience as a firefighter. Forest fire inspectors and prevention specialists typically need firefighting experience before being hired.

Licenses, Certifications, and Registrations

Many states have certification exams that cover standards established by the National Fire Protection Association. Many states require additional training for inspectors and investigators each year in order for them to maintain their certification.

The National Fire Protection Association also offers several certifications, such as Certified Fire Inspector and Certified Fire Protection Specialist, for fire inspectors. Some jobs in the private sector require that job candidates already have these certifications.

In addition, fire investigators may choose to pursue certification from a nationally recognized professional association. Among such certifications and associations are the Certified Fire Investigator (CFI) certification from the International Association of Arson Investigators or the Certified Fire and Explosion Investigator (CFEI) certification from the National Association of Fire Investigators (NAFI). The process of obtaining certification can teach new skills and demonstrate competency.

ADVANCEMENT

Important Qualities

Communication skills. Fire inspectors must clearly explain fire code violations to building and property managers. They must carefully interview witnesses as part of their factfinding mission.

Critical-thinking skills. Fire inspectors must be able to recognize code violations and recommend a way to fix the problem. They must be able to analyze evidence from a fire and come to a reasonable conclusion.

Detail oriented. Fire inspectors must notice details when inspecting a site for code violations or investigating the cause of a fire.

Physical strength. Fire investigators may have to move debris at the site of a fire in order to get a more accurate understanding of the scene.

Famous First

The common law elements of arson vary in different jurisdictions throughout the United States. For example, the element of "dwelling" is no longer required in most states, and arson occurs by the burning of any real property without consent or with unlawful intent. Arson is prosecuted with attention to degree of severity in the alleged offense. First degree arson generally indicates that people were harmed or killed in the course of the fire; second degree arson indicates significant destruction of property occurs. Although it is usually prosecuted as a felony, arson may also be a misdemeanor when it is considered "criminal mischief" or "destruction of property."

Source: https://en.wikipedia.org/wiki/Arson

WAGES

Median annual wages, May 2017

Fire inspectors and investigators: $59,260

Fire inspectors: $56,670

Fire fighting and prevention workers: $49,410

Total, all occupations: $37,690

Forest fire inspectors and prevention specialists: $37,380

Note: All Occupations includes all occupations in the U.S. Economy. Source: U.S. Bureau of Labor Statistics, Occupational Employment Statistics

The median annual wage for fire inspectors and investigators was $59,260 in May 2017. The lowest 10 percent earned less than $34,800, and the highest 10 percent earned more than $95,960.

The median annual wage for forest fire inspectors and prevention specialists was $37,380 in May 2017. The lowest 10 percent earned less than $25,570, and the highest 10 percent earned more than $80,160.

In May 2017, the median annual wages for fire inspectors and investigators in the top industries in which they worked were as follows:

Manufacturing	$72,450
Local government, excluding education and hospitals	60,310
State government, excluding education and hospitals	57,400
Colleges, universities, and professional schools; state, local, and private	51,240
Investigation and security services	51,040

In May 2017, the median annual wages for forest fire inspectors and prevention specialists in the top industries in which they worked were as follows:

| Local government, excluding education and hospitals | $60,370 |
| State government, excluding education and hospitals | 32,360 |

Fire inspectors and investigators typically work during regular business hours, but investigators may also work evenings, weekends, and holidays because they must be ready to respond when fires occur.

Fast Fact

It's believed that humans began to use fire to cook food in a controlled way about one million years ago.

Source: sciencekids.co.nz

JOB OUTLOOK

Percent change in employment, projected 2016-26

Fire inspectors and investigators: $59,260

Fire inspectors: $56,670

Fire fighting and prevention workers: $49,410

Total, all occupations: $37,690

Forest fire inspectors and prevention specialists: $37,380

Note: All Occupations includes all occupations in the U.S. Economy. Source: U.S. Bureau of Labor Statistics, Employment Projections program

Overall employment of fire inspectors is projected to grow 10 percent from 2016 to 2026, faster than the average for all occupations. Employment growth will vary by specialization.

Employment of fire inspectors and investigators is projected to grow 7 percent from 2016 to 2026, about as fast as the average for all occupations. Fire inspectors will be needed to assess potential fire hazards in newly constructed residential, commercial, public, and other buildings in the coming decade. Fire inspectors will also be needed to ensure that existing buildings meet updated and revised federal, state, and local fire codes each year. Although the number of structural fires occurring across the country has been falling for some time, fire investigators will still be needed to determine the cause of fires and explosions.

Employment of forest fire inspectors and prevention specialists is projected to grow 27 percent from 2016 to 2026, much faster than the average for all occupations. However, because it is a small occupation, the fast growth will result in only about 500 new jobs over the 10-year period. Forest fire inspectors and prevention specialists are expected to be needed to help prevent and control the increasingly destructive wildfires that the United States has been experiencing.

Job Prospects

Jobseekers should expect strong competition for the number of available positions.

Those who have completed some fire science education or who have training related to criminal investigation should have the best job prospects.

Employment projections data for Fire inspectors, 2016-26

Occupational Title	SOC Code	Employment, 2016	Projected Employment, 2026	Change, 2016-26	
				Percent	Numeric
Fire inspectors	33-2020	14,100	15,400	10	1,400
Fire inspectors and investigators	33-2021	12,300	13,200	7	900
Forest fire inspectors and prevention specialists	33-2022	1,700	2,200	27	500

Source: Bureau of Labor Statistics, Employment Projections program

SIMILAR OCCUPATIONS

This table shows a list of occupations with job duties that are similar to those of fire inspectors.

OCCUPATION	JOB DUTIES	ENTRY-LEVEL EDUCATION	2017 MEDIAN PAY
Firefighters	Firefighters control and put out fires and respond to emergencies where life, property, or the environment is at risk.	Postsecondary nondegree award	$49,080
Police and Detectives	Police officers protect lives and property. Detectives and criminal investigators, who are sometimes called agents or special agents, gather facts and collect evidence of possible crimes.	High school diploma or equivalent (police) Bachelor's degree (fish and game wardens) Bachelor's degree (federal agencies)	$62,960
Private Detectives and Investigators	Private detectives and investigators search for information about legal, financial, and personal matters. They offer many services, such as verifying people's backgrounds and statements, finding missing persons, and investigating computer crimes.	High school diploma or equivalent	$50,700
Forensic Science Technicians	Forensic science technicians aid criminal investigations by collecting and analyzing evidence. Many technicians specialize in various types of laboratory analysis.	Bachelor's degree	$57,850

Conversation With . . .
TOM FEE

Fire services field, 52 years

Tom Fee is a private fire investigator for Fee Investigations in Pomona, California.

1. What was your individual career path in terms of education/training, entry-level job, or other significant opportunity?

I had a job working for the telephone company right out of high school, but I was looking for a job that paid more money. I applied for police and fire jobs in Pomona, California. I did not have any longtime aspirations to go into those fields, but both were testing at the time and I seized the opportunity. I subsequently got hired into the fire department and fully intended to make a career out of that, and I did. I worked for the city for thirty years.

I came in as a firefighter. I had an injury, so I was doing light duty in fire prevention, then got an opportunity to move into investigation. I took that opportunity and went into a field I felt was very interesting and challenging, which subsequently included bomb investigation. I was later promoted up into administration and was fortunate to be able to retire as fire chief.

I then went into private investigating and have conducted fire, fraud, and explosive investigations. I am the past president of the California Conference of Arson Investigators and the International Association of Arson Investors. I have testified more than 800 times in California and federal courts as an expert in fire and bomb examination. I have participated in hundreds of live burn drills.

The field of fire investigation is like putting a puzzle together. We are fortunate now because the National Fire Protection Association issued Guideline 921 in 1991, which tells you the scientific steps you need to take when conducting investigations. Like any profession, there are certain things you need to learn so you know what you are looking at. Somebody who compares fingerprints knows what each swirl, arch, and loop on a fingerprint means. Fire is very similar. Different fire patterns appear on wood, metal or concrete that show the direction the fire came from and the direction it traveled. You follow these fire movement indicators back to the origin and start looking for what may have caused the fire. Once I have reached the origin, I look for the heat source. I identify each heat source, test that against the facts, and can usually come down to the one thing that most probably caused the fire.

Wildland fire is different from a structure fire. The indicators are different: I look at fenceposts, trees, leaves, smoke deposits and diverse other indicators. Each will display a pattern that tells you which way the fire was moving. By following the fire patterns in reverse, you will arrive at the area of fire origin. Next, you start identifying heat sources. For example, you look for any evidence that somebody had an open campfire, power lines in the area, the presence of incendiary devices, and a variety of other possibilities.

Each fire is different. A normal structure fire may take four to eight hours to determine cause, depending on how large it is, and how much has been destroyed. If it is a large enough facility, you could be there for weeks or months. Wildland fires are the same. I have been on some that took three or four hours, and others, three or four months.

2. What are the most important skills and/or qualities for someone in your profession?

We are moving more and more into the sciences of fire: What can fire do? What can it not do? What is the temperature it burns? The more knowledge you have in that area, the better. Also, you need patience. It takes time to systematically examine debris. You need to make sure that you do not make this a personal challenge. If you follow the science, you will get the answer. If you get new facts, you have to step back and re-evaluate everything from the beginning.

3. What do you wish you had known going into this profession?

I made a lot of mistakes early on and I did not have many mentors who knew the right way of investigating. We are fortunate now because we have standards and guidelines developed by professional people who are very knowledgeable in the field of fire investigation and its sciences.

4. Are there many job opportunities in your profession? In what specific areas?

The most beneficial job is going to work for a fire department. A fire department that serves 50,000 people or more in a metropolitan area will have paid firefighters, which is a good entrance level position for anyone who wants to be a fire investigator. You learn fire behavior and dynamics, and eventually move from being a firefighter into fire investigations. There are also quite a few opportunities in the private field, like working for insurance companies, law firms, public utilities, railroads, and manufacturing firms whose products may have been blamed for causing a fire. We all need to be aware that 70 percent of fire departments across our nation are volunteer; it takes very little effort to get involved with a volunteer fire department.

5. How do you see your profession changing in the next five years? How will technology impact that change, and what skills will be required?

The field of fire service has changed dramatically and it is requiring more and more education if you want to get hired in a paid department. You can still get started in most departments with a high school education and fire academy training, but I think that will change shortly and you will need a two-year or a four-year degree in fire protection engineering or a similar program such as science or engineering.

6. What do you enjoy most about your job? What do you enjoy least about your job?

No two days are the same. Every fire is different from the one you went to yesterday, which keeps your mind sharp and keeps you moving forward in the profession. I least like that every place I go, somebody has suffered a loss whether it is property that has been destroyed or lives lost. I am usually out there because of someone else's tragedy.

7. Can you suggest a valuable "try this" for students considering a career in your profession?

Get ahold of a local fire department with a fire investigation unit and ask to do a ride-a-long as they interview witnesses, collect information, and process a fire scene. Or, look up a private company that does fire investigations for insurance companies and ask them to let you ride-a-long for a day or two. I have done that for dozens of people over the years.

MORE INFORMATION

For more information about federal fire investigator jobs, visit

Bureau of Alcohol, Tobacco,   **Federal Bureau of**
Firearms and Explosives   **Investigation**
https://www.atf.gov/   https://www.fbi.gov/

For more information about fire inspectors' and investigators' training, visit

National Fire Academy
https://www.usfa.fema.gov/
training/nfa/index.html

For information about standards for fire inspectors and investigators, visit

National Fire Protection
Association
https://www.nfpa.org/

For information about certifications, visit

International Association of   **National Association of Fire**
Arson Investigators   **Investigators**
https://www.firearson.com/   https://www.nafi.org/

Sources

Bureau of Labor Statistics, U.S. Department of Labor, *Occupational Outlook Handbook*, Fire Inspectors.

Firefighters

Snapshot

2017 Median Pay: $49,080 per year, $23.60 per hour
Typical Entry-Level Education: Postsecondary nondegree award
Work Experience in a Related Occupation: None
On-the-job Training: Long-term on-the-job training
Number of Jobs, 2016: 327,300
Job Outlook, 2016-26: 7% (As fast as average)
Employment Change, 2016-26: 23,500

CAREER OVERVIEW

What Firefighters Do

Many firefighters are responsible for providing medical attention.

Firefighters control and put out fires and respond to emergencies where life, property, or the environment is at risk.

Duties

Firefighters typically do the following:

- Drive firetrucks and other emergency vehicles
- Put out fires using water hoses, fire extinguishers, and water pumps
- Find and rescue victims in burning buildings or in other emergency situations
- Treat sick or injured people
- Prepare written reports on emergency incidents
- Clean and maintain equipment
- Conduct drills and physical fitness training

When responding to an emergency, firefighters are responsible for connecting hoses to hydrants, operating the pumps that power the hoses, climbing ladders, and using other tools to break through debris. Firefighters also enter burning buildings to extinguish fires and rescue individuals. Many firefighters are responsible for providing medical attention. Two out of three calls to firefighters are for medical emergencies, not fires, according to the National Fire Protection Association.

When firefighters are not responding to an emergency, they are on call at a fire station. During this time, they regularly inspect equipment and perform practice drills. They also eat and sleep and remain on call, as their shifts usually last 24 hours. Some firefighters may provide public education about fire safety, such as presenting about fire safety at a school.

Some firefighters also work in hazardous materials units and are specially trained to control and clean up hazardous materials, such as oil spills and chemical accidents. They work with hazardous materials removal workers in these cases.

Wildland firefighters are specially trained firefighters. They use heavy equipment and water hoses to control forest fires. Wildland firefighters also frequently create fire lines—a swath of cut-down trees and dug-up grass in the path of a fire—to deprive a fire of fuel. They also use prescribed fires to burn potential fire fuel under controlled conditions. Some wildland firefighters, known as smoke jumpers, parachute from airplanes to reach otherwise inaccessible areas.

WORK ENVIRONMENT

Firefighters held about 327,300 jobs in 2016. The largest employers of firefighters were as follows:

Local government, excluding education and hospitals	90%
Administrative and support services	4
Federal government, excluding postal service	3
State government, excluding education and hospitals	2

These employment numbers exclude volunteer firefighters.

Volunteer firefighters share the same duties as paid firefighters and account for the majority of firefighters in many areas. According to the National Fire Protection Association, about two thirds of firefighters were volunteer firefighters in 2015.

When responding to an emergency, these workers often wear protective gear, which can be very heavy and hot. When not on the scene of an emergency, firefighters work at fire stations, where they sleep, eat, work on equipment, and remain on call. Whenever an alarm sounds, firefighters respond, regardless of the weather or time of day.

Injuries and Illnesses

Firefighters have one of the highest rates of injuries and illnesses of all occupations. They often encounter dangerous situations, including collapsing floors and walls, traffic accidents, and overexposure to flames and smoke. As a result, workers must wear protective gear to help lower these risks.

Work Schedules

Firefighters typically work long periods and varied hours. Overtime is common. Most firefighters work 24-hour shifts on duty and are off the following 48 or 72 hours. Some firefighters may work 10/14 shifts, which means 10 hours working and 14 hours off.

When combating forest and wildland fires, firefighters may work for extended periods. For example, wildland firefighters may have to stay for days or weeks when a wildland fire breaks out

HOW TO BECOME A FIREFIGHTER

Firefighters begin their careers by attending fire academy training.

Firefighters typically need a high school diploma and training in emergency medical services. Prospective firefighters must pass written and physical tests, complete a series of interviews, go through training at a fire academy, and hold an emergency medical technician (EMT) certification.

Applicants for firefighter jobs typically must be at least 18 years old and have a valid driver's license. They must also pass a medical exam and drug screening to be hired. After being hired, firefighters may be subject to random drug tests and will also need to complete routine physical fitness assessments.

Education

The entry-level education needed to become a firefighter is a high school diploma or equivalent. However, some classwork beyond high school, such as instruction in assessing patients' conditions, dealing with trauma, and clearing obstructed airways, is usually needed to obtain the emergency medical technician (EMT) certification. EMT requirements vary by city and state.

Training

Entry-level firefighters receive a few months of training at fire academies run by the fire department or by the state. Through classroom instruction and practical training, recruits study firefighting and fire-prevention techniques, local building codes, and emergency medical procedures. They also learn how to fight fires with standard equipment, including axes, chain saws, fire extinguishers, and ladders. After attending a fire academy, firefighters must usually complete a probationary period.

Those wishing to become wildland firefighters may attend apprenticeship programs that last up to 4 years. These programs combine instruction with on-the-job-training under the supervision of experienced firefighters.

In addition to participating in training programs conducted by local or state fire departments and agencies, some firefighters attend federal training sessions sponsored by the National Fire Academy. These training sessions cover topics including anti-arson techniques, disaster preparedness, hazardous materials control, and public fire safety and education.

Licenses, Certifications, and Registrations

Usually, firefighters must be certified as emergency medical technicians. In addition, some fire departments require firefighters to be certified as a paramedic. The National Registry of Emergency Medical Technicians (NREMT). certifies EMTs and paramedics. Both levels of NREMT certification require completing a training or education program and passing the national exam. The national exam has a computer-based test and a practical part. EMTs and paramedics may work with firefighters at the scenes of accidents.

Other Experience

Working as a volunteer firefighter may help in getting a job as a career firefighter.

Fast Fact

Firefighters are expected to get dressed in proper gear in fewer than 2 minutes
Source: lite987.com

ADVANCEMENT

Firefighters can be promoted to engineer, then to lieutenant, captain, battalion chief, assistant chief, deputy chief, and, finally, chief. For promotion to positions beyond battalion chief, many fire departments now require applicants to have a bachelor's degree, preferably in fire science, public administration, or a related field. Some firefighters eventually become fire inspectors or investigators after gaining enough experience.

Important Qualities

Communication skills. Firefighters communicate conditions at an emergency scene to other firefighters and to emergency-response crews.

Compassion. Firefighters, like EMT's and paramedics, need to provide emotional support to those in emergency situations.

Courage. Firefighters' daily job duties involve dangerous situations, such as entering a burning building.

Decisionmaking skills. Firefighters must be able to make quick and difficult decisions in an emergency. The ability to make good decisions under pressure could potentially save someone's life.

Physical stamina. Firefighters may have to stay at disaster scenes for long periods of time to rescue and treat victims. Fighting fires requires prolonged use of strength.

Physical strength. Firefighters must be strong enough to carry heavy equipment and move debris at an emergency site. They also carry victims who are injured or cannot walk.

WAGES

Median annual wages, May 2017

Fire fighting and prevention workers: $49,410

Firefighters: $49,080

Total, all occupations: $37,690

Note: All Occupations includes all occupations in the U.S. Economy. Source: U.S. Bureau of Labor Statistics, Occupational Employment Statistics

The median annual wage for firefighters was $49,080 in May 2017. The lowest 10 percent earned less than $24,490, and the highest 10 percent earned more than $83,570.

In May 2017, the median annual wages for firefighters in the top industries in which they worked were as follows:

Federal government, excluding postal service	$51,060
Local government, excluding education and hospitals	50,000
State government, excluding education and hospitals	48,120
Administrative and support services	29,960

Firefighters typically work long periods and varied hours. Overtime is common. Most firefighters work 24-hour shifts on duty and are off the following 48 or 72 hours. Some firefighters may work 10/14 shifts, which means 10 hours working and 14 hours off.

When combating forest and wildland fires, firefighters may work for extended periods. For example, wildland firefighters may have to stay for days or weeks when a wildland fire breaks out.

Union Membership

Most firefighters belonged to a union in 2016. The largest organizer of firefighters is the International Association of Fire Fighters.

JOB OUTLOOK

Percent change in employment, projected 2016-26

Total, all occupations: 7%

Fire fighting and prevention workers: 7%

Firefighters: 7%

Note: All Occupations includes all occupations in the U.S. Economy. Source: U.S. Bureau of Labor Statistics, Employment Projections program

Employment of firefighters is projected to grow 7 percent from 2016 to 2026, about as fast as the average for all occupations.

Although improved building materials and building codes have resulted in a long-term decrease in fires and fire fatalities, firefighters will still be needed to respond to fires. Fires can spread rapidly, so controlling them quickly is very important. Wildland firefighters will still be needed to combat active fires and manage the environment to reduce the impact of fires. Firefighters will also continue to respond to medical emergencies.

Job Prospects

Job prospects for firefighters will be good despite the number of volunteer firefighters that qualify for career firefighter jobs. There will be positions open from those leaving the occupation.

Physically fit applicants with some postsecondary firefighter education and paramedic training should have the best job prospects.

Employment projections data for Firefighters, 2016-26

Occupational Title	SOC Code	Employment, 2016	Projected Employment, 2026	Change, 2016-26	
				Percent	Numeric
Firefighters	33-2011	327,300	350,900	7	23,500

Source: Bureau of Labor Statistics, Employment Projections program

SIMILAR OCCUPATIONS

This table shows a list of occupations with job duties that are similar to those of firefighters.

OCCUPATION	JOB DUTIES	ENTRY-LEVEL EDUCATION	2017 MEDIAN PAY
EMTs and Paramedics	Emergency medical technicians (EMTs) and paramedics care for the sick or injured in emergency medical settings. People's lives often depend on the quick reaction and competent care provided by these workers. EMTs and paramedics respond to emergency calls, performing medical services and transporting patients to medical facilities.	Postsecondary nondegree award	$33,380

OCCUPATION	JOB DUTIES	ENTRY-LEVEL EDUCATION	2017 MEDIAN PAY
Fire Inspectors	Fire inspectors examine buildings in order to detect fire hazards and ensure that federal, state, and local fire codes are met. Fire investigators, another type of worker in this field, determine the origin and cause of fires and explosions. Forest fire inspectors and prevention specialists assess outdoor fire hazards in public and residential areas.	Postsecondary educational program for emergency medical technicians (EMTs) High school diploma or equivalent (forest fire inspectors and prevention specialists)	$56,670
Forest and Conservation Workers	Forest and conservation workers measure and improve the quality of forests. Under the supervision of foresters and forest and conservation technicians, they develop, maintain, and protect forests.	High school diploma or equivalent	$27,650
Hazardous Materials Removal Workers	Hazardous materials (hazmat) removal workers identify and dispose of asbestos, lead, radioactive waste, and other hazardous materials. They also neutralize and clean up materials that are flammable, corrosive, or toxic.	High school diploma or equivalent	$41,400
Police and Detectives	Police officers protect lives and property. Detectives and criminal investigators, who are sometimes called agents or special agents, gather facts and collect evidence of possible crimes.	High school diploma or equivalent (police) Bachelor's degree (fish and game wardens) Bachelor's degree (federal agencies)	$62,960

Conversation With . . .
CHARLES J. FLANAGAN, Jr

Firefighter, 32 years

Charles Flanagan was a fire captain in Winthrop, Massachusetts, and a safety officer in the Massachusetts Task Force-1 FEMA Urban Search and Rescue.

1. What was your individual career path in terms of education/training, entry-level job, or other significant opportunity?

I joined the Winthrop Fire Department when I was 33 years old, relatively late for a rookie. I was always drawn to firefighting. My grandfather, father, and brother all worked for the Winthrop Fire Department. Between the four of us, the family has 160 years on the job.

My parents encouraged my brothers and me to go to college. I went to Bridgewater State University to become a schoolteacher, but I realized that was not the right career for me and left after two years. I got a job as a shoe salesperson and went to work for a running shoe company, starting as a personal assistant and working my way up to marketing development.

One day when I was in New York City on business, I walked past a fire being battled by fire crews late at night and thought, "I want to do this." I took the state civil service exam that was offered every two years and joined my local department. Then I went to the fire academy and got nationally certified at level 2. Eventually I had enough training and hours to teach courses.

For my first job, I drove the engine to an electrical fire at a nice house on the water. What no one knew is the son had hidden a bunch of fireworks in the basement. For seven to nine minutes, everything was going off. Roman candles, everything.

I am also an Instructor SPEC RESCUE International in Virginia Beach, VA; Certified Fire Instructor, Level III; Emergency Medical Technician; and Structural Collapse Technician.

My career in urban search and rescue began when the Winthrop Fire Department got a special rescue truck to respond to incidents during the construction of a 9.5-mile sewage outfall tunnel under Boston Harbor. I travelled around the country getting trained on my own dime. I learned how to pump out flooded space and use special breathing apparatus underground.

After three years on the rescue truck, I joined the newly created Massachusetts Urban Search and Rescue Team under the Federal Emergency Management Agency. You get deployed almost like the National Guard. Our first big deployment was 9/11. I was in Manhattan six days and spent most of my time on the debris pile. After it rained, there was a film over everything. I have responded to tornadoes in the Midwest and several hurricanes. Hurricane Katrina was probably the worst. Everybody's house was destroyed. Schools were destroyed. Puerto Rico was pretty bad. Every pole with wires on it got knocked down.

2. What are the most important skills and/or qualities for someone in your profession?

I am a little bit of an adrenaline junkie, and I like to learn new things. That is especially important in urban search and rescue, which took off after 9/11 but it is basically a new field.

3. What do you wish you had known going into this profession?

Firefighting is what we do the least of. Seventy-five to 80 percent of our calls are medical. Everybody has to be an EMT.

4. Are there many job opportunities in your profession? In what specific areas?

Since 9/11, it has become sort of a rock star job. Some cities and towns have a veteran's preference so military experience, including the Coast Guard, is a plus. Or get trained as a paramedic. It is almost a guarantee of getting a job in some states.

If you take courses or major in public administration or fire science, you will get higher pay along the way. My department paid for us to get college credit, so I just kept taking classes.

5. How do you see your profession changing in the next five years? How will technology impact that change, and what skills will be required?

I see more departments becoming part of bigger regionalized departments. It would be more efficient and cost effective. I would like to see technology make the job safer. A lot of technology developed by NASA would help protect firefighters.

6. **What do you enjoy most about your job? What do you enjoy least about your job?**

What I loved as a captain and shift commander was never knowing how your day was going to go. You might have something planned for the day, but you never get to the plan.

Sometimes you do your best work and have the worst results. I was only on the job three months and was not an EMT yet when I had to do CPR on a police lieutenant in my town. He did not make it, but that is when I realized, "I can do this job."

When you work thirty-two years as a firefighter, you have a lot of baggage. I was friends with twelve New York City firefighters who were killed on 9/11. I do not think about it a lot, but when something comes up on TV it puts me right in the moment.

7. **Can you suggest a valuable "try this" for students considering a career in your profession?**

Go to a firehouse. Ring the doorbell. Ask them what the job is like. Hang around on a Sunday. Just get a feel for what is going on. Or call and ask to be directed to the company lieutenant or captain. You would be surprised at how much time they will spend with you.

Famous First

In the 1884 book History of Philadelphia, 1609-1884, John Thomas Scharf and Thompson Westcott described the organization of the company:

The Union Fire Company was an association for mutual assistance. Each member agreed to furnish, at his own expense, six leather buckets and two stout linen bags, each marked with his name and the name of the company, which he was to bring to every fire. ... On an alarm of fire at night it was agreed that lights should be placed in the windows of houses of members near the fire "in order to prevent confusion, and to enable their friends to give them more speedy and effectual assistance.'

Source: https://en.wikipedia.org/wiki/Union_Fire_Company

MORE INFORMATION

For information about a career as a firefighter, contact your local fire department or visit

International Association of Fire Fighters
https://client.prod.iaff.org/

International Association of Women in Fire & Emergency Services
https://www.i-women.org/

U.S. Fire Administration
https://www.usfa.fema.gov/

National Fire Protection Association
https://www.nfpa.org/

For information about professional qualifications and a list of colleges and universities offering 2- or 4-year degree programs in fire science and fire prevention, visit

National Fire Academy, U.S. Fire Administration
https://www.nfpa.org/

For more information about emergency medical technicians and paramedics, visit

National Registry of Emergency Medical Technicians
https://www.nremt.org/rwd/public/

Sources

Bureau of Labor Statistics, U.S. Department of Labor, *Occupational Outlook Handbook*, Firefighters.

Fishing and Hunting Workers

CAREER OVERVIEW

What Fishing and Hunting Workers Do

The fish and wild animals that fishers and hunting workers catch and trap are used for food, bait, and other purposes.

Fishing and hunting workers catch and trap various types of animal life. The fish and wild animals they catch are for human food, animal feed, bait, and other uses.

Duties

Fishers and related fishing workers typically do the following:

- Locate fish with the use of fish-finding equipment
- Steer vessels and operate navigational instruments
- Maintain engines, fishing gear, and other onboard equipment by making minor repairs
- Sort, pack, and store the catch in holds with ice and other freezing methods
- Measure fish to ensure that they are of legal size
- Return undesirable or illegal catches to the water
- Guide nets, traps, and lines onto vessels by hand or with hoisting equipment
- Signal other workers to move, hoist, and position loads of the catch
- Hunters and trappers typically do the following:
- Locate wild animals with the use of animal-finding equipment
- Catch wild animals with weapons, such as rifles or bows, or with traps, such as snares
- Sort, pack, and store the catch with ice and other freezing methods
- Follow hunting regulations, which vary by state and always include a safety component
- Sell what they catch for food and decorative purposes

Fishers and related fishing workers

Fishers and fishing workers work in deep or shallow water. In deep water, they typically perform their duties on large fishing boats that are equipped for long stays at sea. Some process the catch on board and prepare the fish for sale.

Other fishers work in shallow water on small boats that often have a crew of only one or two. They might put nets across the mouths of rivers or inlets; use pots and traps to catch fish or shellfish, such as lobsters and crabs; or use dredges to gather other shellfish, such as oysters and scallops.

Some fishers harvest marine vegetation rather than fish. They use rakes and hoes to gather Irish moss and kelp.

The following are types of fishers and related fishing workers:

Fishing boat captains plan and oversee the fishing operation including the species of fish to be caught, the location of the best fishing grounds, the method of capture, trip length, and sale of the catch. They also supervise the crew and record daily activities in the ship's log.To plot a ship's course, fishing boat captains use electronic navigational equipment, including Global Positioning System (GPS) instruments. They also use radar and sonar to avoid obstacles above and below the water and to find fish.

Fishing deckhands perform the everyday tasks of baiting; setting lines or traps; hauling in and sorting the catch; and maintaining the boat and fishing gear. Deckhands also secure and remove mooring lines when docking or undocking the boat.

Fishers work in commercial fishing, which does not include recreational fishing.

Aquaculture—raising and harvesting fish and other aquatic life under controlled conditions in ponds or confined bodies of water—is a different field.

Hunters and trappers

Hunters and trappers locate wild animals with GPS instruments, compasses, charts, and whistles. They then catch or kill them with traps or weapons. Hunters and trappers sell the wild animals they catch, for either food, fur, or decorative purposes.

WORK ENVIRONMENT

Fishing and hunting workers work under various environmental conditions, depending on the region, body of water, and the kind of species sought.

Fishing and hunting workers held about 27,000 jobs in 2016. The largest employers of fishing and hunting workers were as follows:

Self-employed workers	61%
Fishing, hunting and trapping	35

Fishing and hunting operations are conducted under various environmental conditions, depending on the geographic region, body of water or land, and kinds of animals sought. Storms, fog, and wind may hamper fishing vessels or cause them to suspend fishing operations and return to port.

Although fishing gear has improved and operations have become more mechanized, netting and processing fish are nonetheless strenuous activities. Newer vessels have improved living quarters and amenities, but crews still experience the aggravations of confined quarters and the absence of family.

Injuries and Illnesses

Commercial fishing and hunting can be dangerous and can lead to workplace injuries or fatalities. Fishing and hunting workers often work under hazardous conditions. Transportation to a hospital or doctor is often not readily available for these workers because they can be out at sea or in a remote area.

And although fatalities are uncommon, fishing and hunting workers experience one of the highest rates of occupational fatalities of all occupations.

Most fatalities that happen to fishers and related fishing workers are from drowning. The crew must guard against the danger of injury from malfunctioning fishing gear, entanglement in fishing nets and gear, slippery decks, ice formation, or large waves washing over the deck. Malfunctioning navigation and communication equipment and other factors may lead to collisions, shipwrecks, or other dangerous situations, such as vessels becoming caught in storms.

Hunting accidents can occur because of the weapons and traps these workers use. Hunters and trappers minimize injury by wearing the appropriate gear and following detailed safety procedures. Specific safety guidelines vary by state.

Work Schedules

Fishing and hunting workers often endure long shifts and irregular work schedules. Commercial fishing trips may require workers to be away from their home port for several weeks or months.

Many fishers are seasonal workers, and those jobs are usually filled by students and by people from other occupations who are available for seasonal work, such as teachers. For example, employment of fishers in Alaska increases significantly during the summer months, which constitute the salmon season. During these times, fishers can expect to work long hours. Additionally, states may only allow hunters and trappers to hunt or trap during certain times of the year depending on the type of wild animals sought.

HOW TO BECOME A FISHING OR HUNTING WORKER

Fishing and hunting workers usually learn on the job. A formal educational credential is not required.

Education

A formal educational credential is not required for one to become fishing or hunting worker. However, fishers may improve their chances of getting a job by enrolling in a 2-year vocational–technical program. Some community colleges and universities offer fishery technology and related programs that include courses in seamanship, vessel operations, marine safety, navigation, vessel repair, and fishing gear technology. These programs are typically located near coastal areas and include hands-on experience.

Training

Most fishing and hunting workers learn on the job. They first learn how to sort and clean the animals they catch. Fishers would go on to learn how to operate the boat and fishing equipment.

Other Experience

Many prospective fishers start by finding work through family or friends, or simply by walking around the docks and asking for employment. Aspiring fishers also can look online for employment. Some larger trawlers and processing ships are run by big fishing companies with human resources departments to which new workers can apply. Operators of large commercial fishing vessels must complete a training course approved by the U.S. Coast Guard.

Most hunters and trappers have previous recreational hunting experience.

Licenses, Certifications, and Registrations

Captains of fishing boats and hunters and trappers must be licensed.

Crewmembers on certain fish-processing vessels may need a merchant mariner's document. The U.S. Coast Guard issues these documents, as well as licenses, to people who meet specific health, physical, and academic requirements.

States set licensing requirements for boats operating in state waters, defined as inland waters and waters within 3 miles of the coast.

Fishers need a permit to fish in almost any water. Permits are distributed by states for state waters and by regional fishing councils for federal waters. The permits specify the fishing season, the type and amount of fish that may be caught, and, sometimes, the type of permissible fishing gear.

Hunters and trappers need a state license to hunt in any land or forest. Licenses specify the hunting season, the type and amount of wild animals that may be caught, and the type of weapons or traps that can be used.

ADVANCEMENT

Experienced, reliable fishing boat deckhands can become boatswains, then second mates, first mates, and, finally, captains. Those who are interested in ship engineering may gain experience with maintaining and repairing ship engines to become licensed chief engineers on large commercial boats. In doing so, they must meet the Coast Guard's licensing requirements as well.

Almost all captains are self-employed, and most eventually own, or partially own, one or more fishing boats.

Important Qualities

Critical-thinking skills. Fishing and hunting workers must reach conclusions through sound reasoning and judgment. They determine how to improve their catch and must react appropriately to weather conditions.

Detail oriented. Fishing and hunting workers must be precise and accurate when measuring the quality of their catch or prey. They must also pay attention to detail when working with various fishing and hunting gear to guard against injury.

Listening skills. Because they take instructions from captains and other crewmembers or hunters, fishing and hunting workers need to communicate well and listen effectively.

Machine operation skills. Fishing and hunting workers must be able to operate and perform routine maintenance on complex fishing and navigation machinery, as well as weapons and traps.

Physical stamina. Fishing and hunting workers need endurance. They must be able to work long hours, often under strenuous conditions.

Physical strength. Fishing and hunting workers must use physical strength, along with hand dexterity and coordination, to perform difficult tasks repeatedly.

Famous First

Fishing as a means of obtaining food for survival as well as a business venture has existed since the Mesolithic period. Fishing and the fisherman influenced Ancient Egyptian religion where mullets were worshipped as a sign of the arriving flood season. Bastet was often manifested in the form of a catfish. In ancient Egyptian literature, the process that Amun used to create the world is associated with the tilapia's method of mouth-brooding

Source: https://en.wikipedia.org/wiki/Fisherman

WAGES

Median annual wages, May 2017

Total, all occupations: $37,690

Fishing and hunting workers: $28,530

Farming, fishing, and forestry occupations: $24,390

Note: All Occupations includes all occupations in the U.S. Economy. Source: U.S. Bureau of Labor Statistics, Occupational Employment Statistics

The median annual wage for fishing and hunting workers was $28,530 in May 2017. The lowest 10 percent earned less than $18,710, and the highest 10 percent earned more than $48,170.

Fishers are typically paid a percentage of the boat's overall catch, commonly referred to as a crew share. The more fish that are caught, the greater the crew share becomes. This can lead to unpredictable swings in pay from one season to another, as the overall catch can vary. More experienced crewmembers often receive a greater share compared to entry-level workers.

Trappers are typically paid per pelt, and the amount received can vary depending on the species and the quality of the fur. For example, trappers typically receive more for coyote pelts than for smaller species, such as muskrats.

Fishing and hunting workers endure strenuous outdoor work and long hours. Commercial fishing trips may require workers to be away from their home port for several weeks or months.

Many fishers are seasonal workers, and those jobs are usually filled by students and by people from other occupations who are available for seasonal work, such as teachers. For example, employment of fishers in Alaska increases significantly during the summer months, which constitute the salmon season. During these times, fishers can expect to work long hours. Additionally, states may only allow hunters and trappers to hunt or trap during certain times of the year.

JOB OUTLOOK

Percent change in employment, projected 2016-26

Fishing and hunting workers: 11%

Total, all occupations: 7%

Farming, fishing, and forestry occupations: 0%

Note: All Occupations includes all occupations in the U.S. Economy. Source: U.S. Bureau of Labor Statistics, Employment Projections program

Employment of fishing and hunting workers is projected to grow 11 percent from 2016 to 2026, faster than the average for all occupations. Fishing and hunting workers depend on the ability of fish stocks and wild animals to reproduce and grow. The demand for seafood should increase, as it is widely seen as a healthy choice of protein.

Governmental efforts to replenish fish stocks have led to some species being regulated under fishing quotas or catch shares. These quotas dictate how many fish each fisher may catch and keep. Additional quotas or catch shares can typically be purchased, but they are often very expensive. The implementation of additional catch share programs may reduce demand for fishers. However, new programs must undergo several years of research and public review before being approved.

Animal pelts will continue be used to manufacture fur coats, hats, and gloves, which may increase demand for trappers. However, the majority of fur used in clothing comes from ranches or farms that breed, maintain, and harvest desirable species, such as mink.

Job Prospects

Many job openings will result from the need to replace fishing and hunting workers who leave the occupation. Many workers leave because of the strenuous and hazardous nature of the job and the lack of a steady year-round income. The best prospects should be with large fishing operations and for seasonal employment.

Employment projections data for Fishing and hunting workers, 2016-26

Occupational Title	SOC Code	Employment, 2016	Projected Employment, 2026	Change, 2016-26	
				Percent	Numeric
Fishing and hunting workers	45-3000	27,000	29,900	11	2,900

Source: Bureau of Labor Statistics, Employment Projections program

Fast Fact

The North American Game Warden Museum, located near the U.S./Canadian border, shares the story of these professionals and honors those who have lost their lives in the line of duty. The museum is located in the International Peace Garden near Dunseith, North Dakota and Boissevain, in Manitoba province.
Source: gamewardenmuseum.com.

SIMILAR OCCUPATIONS

This table shows a list of occupations with job duties that are similar to those of fishing and hunting workers.

OCCUPATION	JOB DUTIES	ENTRY-LEVEL EDUCATION	2017 MEDIAN PAY
Water Transportation Workers	Water transportation workers operate and maintain vessels that take cargo and people over water. The vessels travel to and from foreign ports across the ocean and to domestic ports along the coasts, across the Great Lakes, and along the country's many inland waterways.	High school diploma or equivalent and on-the-job training for 6 months to a year	$55,590
Farmers, Ranchers, and Other Agricultural Managers	Farmers, ranchers, and other agricultural managers operate establishments that produce crops, livestock, and dairy products.	High school diploma or equivalent	$69,620

Conversation With . . .
JESSICA CONLEY

Park Ranger, 9 years

1. What was your individual career path in terms of education/training, entry-level job, or other significant opportunity?

I first became interested in environmental education through internships and programs I did growing up in middle school and high school, such as through the Chesapeake Bay Foundation. I knew I wanted to be in the environmental ed field, I just wasn't sure how. I earned a B.A. in environmental science from Messiah College in Pennsylvania, and had a number of jobs—from research biologist to managing a fish farm – when I was trying to decide what I wanted to do with my career. Then I started a family and earned a Master's of Education from American Intercontinental University. While I was working on my master's, I took a seasonal position as a naturalist. I worked for one year as a naturalist, then was hired as a civilian park ranger.

2. What are the most important skills and/or qualities for someone in your profession?

First and foremost, being clearheaded and calm in the face of emergency and crisis. We can literally be showing a 5-year-old leaves and how a tree grows and get a call for a medical emergency like heatstroke, then an hour later be telling someone to put dog on a leash. You also need to be flexible. You can't predict what will happen: a tree coming down, someone getting lost, or someone walking in and wanting information. Finally, it's important to be well-spoken and to have public speaking skills. You're interfacing with the public every single day.

3. What do you wish you had known going into this profession?

I wish I had realized it's more a way of life than a job. I'm on call a lot, and willing to jump in and help my co-workers. That's been a big adjustment for my family; they have to be the family of a park ranger.

4. Are there many job opportunities in your profession? In what specific areas?

I see turnover with retirement, for one, so while there are always positions coming open, they tend to come in waves. Also, I don't think everyone in the field realizes they are cut out for this before they begin. They usually figure out very quickly if it doesn't work out. There's not a lot of middle ground – you either love this, or figure it out quickly and leave.

5. How do you see your profession changing in the next five years? What role will technology play in those changes, and what skills will be required?

We're continually challenged with the resources necessary to manage the various needs of the park including operations, maintenance and programming. We must be creative with the funds we are given. Regarding technology, I think it can help us deliver services at lower cost. For example, we are offering trail maps online. Or, through the Dept. of Natural Resources app, you can make a reservation or learn to learn what's going on at a park at any given moment. Technology's important to get the word out to our visitors and help us do our job more effectively.

6. What do you enjoy most about your job? What do you enjoy least?

I love the unpredictable aspect of it. I love that if it's a gorgeous day I get to be outside. I get to work in place that people come to play, and be in one of Maryland's most beautiful places. What I like least is a harder question to answer. My family would certainly like it if I made more money; we don't get into this for the pay at all. I think a lot of people would complain about that. I don't have a lot of challenges to say about job; I love my job.

7. Can you suggest a valuable "try this" for students considering a career in your profession?

I think the best thing for someone to try would be a seasonal position. That gives you such a good idea of what goes on day in and day out in a park. Also, we recruit heavily from the Maryland Conservation Corps; its part of Americorps, a national program, so anyone should be able to access the program.

This conversation was originally published in Careers in Environment & Conservation *(Salem) in 2014.*

MORE INFORMATION

For more information about licensing of fishing boat captains and about requirements for merchant mariner documentation, visit

National Maritime Center, U.S. Coast Guard Headquarters
https://www.dco.uscg.mil/
national_maritime_center/

For more information about hunting licenses, visit

Where to Hunt
https://www.nssf.org/hunting/
where-to-hunt/

Sources

Bureau of Labor Statistics, U.S. Department of Labor, *Occupational Outlook Handbook*, Fishing and Hunting Workers.

Forensic Science Technicians

Snapshot

2017 Median Pay: $57,850 per year, $27.81 per hour

Typical Entry-Level Education: Bachelor's degree

Work Experience in a Related Occupation: None

On-the-Job Training: Moderate-term on-the-job training

Number of Jobs, 2016: 15,400

Job Outlook, 2016-26: 17% (Much faster than average)

Employment Change, 2016-26: 2,600

CAREER OVERVIEW

What Forensic Science Technicians Do

Forensic science technicians aid criminal investigations by collecting and analyzing evidence. Many technicians specialize in either crime scene investigation or laboratory analysis. Forensic science technicians perform chemical, biological, and physical analysis on evidence taken from crime scenes.

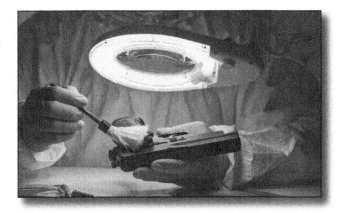

Duties

Forensic science technicians work in laboratories and on crime scenes. At crime scenes, forensic science technicians typically do the following:

- Analyze crime scenes to determine what evidence should be collected and how
- Take photographs of the crime scene and evidence
- Make sketches of the crime scene
- Record observations and findings, such as the location and position of evidence
- Collect evidence, including weapons, fingerprints, and bodily fluids
- Catalog and preserve evidence for transfer to crime labs
- Reconstruct crime scenes

In laboratories, forensic science technicians typically do the following:

- Perform chemical, biological, and microscopic analyses on evidence taken from crime scenes
- Explore possible links between suspects and criminal activity, using the results of DNA or other scientific analyses
- Consult with experts in specialized fields, such as toxicology (the study of poisons and their effect on the body) and odontology (a branch of forensic medicine that concentrates on teeth)

Forensic science technicians may be generalists who perform many or all of the duties listed above or they may specialize in certain techniques and sciences. Generalist forensic science technicians, sometimes called *criminalists* or *crime scene investigators*, collect evidence at the scene of a crime and perform scientific and technical analysis in laboratories or offices.

Forensic science technicians who work primarily in laboratories may specialize in the natural sciences or engineering. These workers, such as *forensic biologists* and *forensic chemists*, typically use chemicals and laboratory equipment such as microscopes when analyzing evidence. They also may use computers to examine DNA, substances, and other evidence collected at crime scenes. They often work to match evidence to people or other known elements, such as vehicles or weapons. Most forensic science technicians who perform laboratory analysis specialize in a specific type of evidence, such as DNA or ballistics.

Some forensic science technicians, called ***forensic computer examiners*** or ***digital forensics analysts***, specialize in computer-based crimes. They collect and analyze data to uncover and prosecute electronic fraud, scams, and identity theft. The abundance of digital data helps them solve crimes in the physical world as well. Computer forensics technicians must adhere to the same strict standards of evidence gathering found in general forensic science because legal cases depend on the integrity of evidence.

All forensic science technicians prepare written reports that detail their findings and investigative methods. They must be able to explain their reports to lawyers, detectives, and other law enforcement officials. In addition, forensic science technicians may be called to testify in court about their findings and methods.

WORK ENVIRONMENT

Forensic science technicians often work in crime labs.

Forensic science technicians held about 15,400 jobs in 2016. The largest employers of forensic science technicians were as follows:

Local government, excluding education and hospitals	57%
State government, excluding education and hospitals	29
Medical and diagnostic laboratories	3
Testing laboratories	2

Forensic science technicians may have to work outside in all types of weather, spend many hours in laboratories and offices, or do some combination of both. They often work with specialists and other law enforcement personnel. Many specialist forensic science technicians work only in laboratories.

Crime scene investigators may travel throughout their jurisdictions, which may be cities, counties, or states.

Work Schedules

Crime scene investigators may work staggered day, evening, or night shifts and may have to work overtime because they must always be available to collect or analyze evidence. Technicians working in laboratories usually work a standard workweek, although they may have to be on call outside of normal business hours if they are needed to work immediately on a case.

HOW TO BECOME A FORENSIC SCIENCE TECHNICIAN

Forensic science technicians typically need at least a bachelor's degree in a natural science, such as chemistry or biology, or in forensic science. On-the-job training is usually required both for those who investigate crime scenes and for those who work in labs.

Education

Forensic science technicians typically need at least a bachelor's degree in a natural science, such as chemistry or biology, or in forensic science. Forensic science programs may specialize in a specific area of study, such as toxicology, pathology, or DNA. Students who enroll in general natural science programs should make an effort to take classes related to forensic science. A list of schools that offer degrees in forensic science is available from the American Academy of Forensic Sciences. Many of those who seek to become forensic science technicians will have an undergraduate degree in the natural sciences and a master's degree in forensic science.

Many crime scene investigators who work for police departments are sworn police officers and have met educational requirements necessary for admittance into a police academy. Applicants for civilian crime scene investigator jobs should have a bachelor's degree in either forensic science, with a strong basic science background, or the natural sciences. For more information on police officers, see the profile on police and detectives.

Training

Forensic science technicians receive on-the-job training before they are ready to work on cases independently.

Newly hired crime scene investigators may work under experienced investigators while they learn proper procedures and methods for collecting and documenting evidence.

Forensic science technicians learn laboratory specialties on the job. The length of this training varies by specialty, but is usually less than a year. Technicians may need to pass a proficiency exam or otherwise be approved by a laboratory or accrediting body before they are allowed to perform independent casework.

Throughout their careers, forensic science technicians need to keep up with advances in technology and science that improve the collection or analysis of evidence.

Licenses, Certifications, and Registrations

A range of licenses and certifications is available to help credential, and aid in the professional development of, many types of forensic science technicians. Certifications and licenses are not typically necessary for entry into the occupation. Credentials can vary widely because standards and regulations vary considerably from one jurisdiction to another.

ADVANCEMENT

Important Qualities

Communication skills. Forensic science technicians write reports and testify in court. They often work with other law enforcement officials and specialists.

Critical-thinking skills. Forensic science technicians use their best judgment when matching physical evidence, such as fingerprints and DNA, to suspects.

Detail oriented. Forensic science technicians must be able to notice small changes in mundane objects to be good at collecting and analyzing evidence.

Math and science skills. Forensic science technicians need a solid understanding of statistics and natural sciences to be able to analyze evidence.

Problem-solving skills. Forensic science technicians use scientific tests and methods to help law enforcement officials solve crimes.

WAGES

Median annual wages, May 2017

Forensic science technicians: $57,850

Life, physical, and social science technicians: $45,780

Total, all occupations: $37,690

Note: All Occupations includes all occupations in the U.S. Economy. Source: U.S. Bureau of Labor Statistics, Occupational Employment Statistics

The median annual wage for forensic science technicians was $57,850 in May 2017. The lowest 10 percent earned less than $33,880, and the highest 10 percent earned more than $95,600.

In May 2017, the median annual wages for forensic science technicians in the top industries in which they worked were as follows:

Testing laboratories	$62,130
State government, excluding education and hospitals	59,240
Local government, excluding education and hospitals	58,140
Medical and diagnostic laboratories	40,210

Crime scene investigators may work staggered day, evening, or night shifts and may have to work overtime because they must always be available to collect or analyze evidence. Technicians working in laboratories usually work a standard workweek, although they may have to be on call outside of normal business hours if they are needed to work immediately on a case.

JOB OUTLOOK

Percent change in employment, projected 2016-26

Forensic science technicians: 17%

Life, physical, and social science technicians: 8%

Total, all occupations: 7%

Note: All Occupations includes all occupations in the U.S. Economy. Source: U.S. Bureau of Labor Statistics, Employment Projections program

Employment of forensic science technicians is projected to grow 17 percent from 2016 to 2026, much faster than the average for all occupations. However, because it is a small occupation, the fast growth will result in only about 2,600 new jobs over the 10-year period.

State and local governments are expected to hire additional forensic science technicians to process their high case loads. Additionally, scientific and technological advances are expected to increase the availability, reliability, and usefulness of objective forensic information used as evidence in trials. As a result, forensic science technicians will be able to provide even greater value than before, and more forensic science technicians will be needed to provide timely forensics information to law enforcement agencies and courts.

Job Prospects

Competition for jobs is expected to be strong. Applicants who have a master's degree should have the best opportunities.

Employment projections data for Forensic science technicians, 2016-26

Occupational Title	SOC Code	Employment, 2016	Projected Employment, 2026	Change, 2016-26	
				Percent	Numeric
Forensic science technicians	19-4092	15,400	18,000	17	2,600

Source: Bureau of Labor Statistics, Employment Projections program

SIMILAR OCCUPATIONS

This table shows a list of occupations with job duties that are similar to those of forensic science technicians.

OCCUPATION	JOB DUTIES	ENTRY-LEVEL EDUCATION	2017 MEDIAN PAY
Biological Technicians	Biological technicians help biological and medical scientists conduct laboratory tests and experiments.	Bachelor's degree	$43,800

OCCUPATION	JOB DUTIES	ENTRY-LEVEL EDUCATION	2017 MEDIAN PAY
Chemical Technicians	Chemical technicians use special instruments and techniques to help chemists and chemical engineers research, develop, produce, and test chemical products and processes.	Associate's degree	$47,280
Chemists and Materials Scientists	Chemists and materials scientists study substances at the atomic and molecular levels and analyze the ways in which the substances interact with one another. They use their knowledge to develop new and improved products and to test the quality of manufactured goods.	Bachelor's degree	$76,280
Environmental Science and Protection Technicians	Environmental science and protection technicians monitor the environment and investigate sources of pollution and contamination, including those affecting public health.	Associate's degree	$45,490
Fire Inspectors	Fire inspectors examine buildings in order to detect fire hazards and ensure that federal, state, and local fire codes are met. Fire investigators, another type of worker in this field, determine the origin and cause of fires and explosions. Forest fire inspectors and prevention specialists assess outdoor fire hazards in public and residential areas.	Postsecondary educational program for emergency medical technicians (EMTs) High school diploma or equivalent (forest fire inspectors and prevention specialists)	$56,670

OCCUPATION	JOB DUTIES	ENTRY-LEVEL EDUCATION	2017 MEDIAN PAY
Hazardous Materials Removal Workers	Hazardous materials (hazmat) removal workers identify and dispose of asbestos, lead, radioactive waste, and other hazardous materials. They also neutralize and clean up materials that are flammable, corrosive, or toxic.	High school diploma or equivalent	$41,400
Medical and Clinical Laboratory Technologists and Technicians	Medical laboratory technologists (commonly known as medical laboratory scientists) and medical laboratory technicians collect samples and perform tests to analyze body fluids, tissue, and other substances.	Bachelor's degree (technologist) High school diploma or equivalent (technician)	$51,770
Police and Detectives	Police officers protect lives and property. Detectives and criminal investigators, who are sometimes called agents or special agents, gather facts and collect evidence of possible crimes.	High school diploma or equivalent (police) Bachelor's degree (fish and game wardens) Bachelor's degree (federal agencies)	$62,960
Private Detectives and Investigators	Private detectives and investigators search for information about legal, financial, and personal matters. They offer many services, such as verifying people's backgrounds and statements, finding missing persons, and investigating computer crimes.	High school diploma or equivalent	$50,700

Conversation With . . .
JOY REHO

Case Management Supervisor, Forensic Lab
29 years in field

1. What was your individual career path in terms of education/training, entry-level job, or other significant opportunity?

When I went to college initially, I majored in liberal arts because I didn't know what I was going to pursue. After two years, I realized I enjoyed science. I majored in liberal arts and sciences with a concentration in biological sciences. After I received my bachelor's degree in biological sciences, I applied to and was accepted to a master's program in forensic science. My first job was at the state of Connecticut forensic lab in Forensic Serology, which is the study of blood and body fluids. After two years, I was promoted to Criminalist and two years after that, I was promoted to Lead Criminalist. For the last 24 years, I was a Supervisor in Forensic Biology. I recently became a supervisor in case management, which involves prioritizing cases, streamlining analyses and coordinating the workflow in the lab.

2. What are the most important skills and/or qualities for someone in your profession?

To be a successful criminalist, you must be very detail-oriented and have excellent organizational skills. You have to be a careful and accurate worker, because our work is scrutinized by attorneys in court. The results of our testing may exonerate someone or be the deciding factor in a conviction. The heavy case load necessitates a strong work ethic and the ability to work independently.

One misconception about forensic science is how quickly crimes can be solved. It takes more than a few hours to complete a case. This is dubbed the "CSI Effect." Popular TV shows depict lab personnel that are experts in every area. Typical forensic scientists are experts in one area of specialty, for example firearms, fingerprints, trace analysis, DNA, or blood and body fluid identification. No one is like Abby on NCIS or the scientists on Bones or CSI. Also, juries expect to see evidence examined in a crime lab, so even if there is a confession, the evidence needs to be tested.

3. What do you wish you had known going into this profession?

I wish I had known when I was still in school how much I would have to rely on strong math skills in my day-to-day job. You have to have a solid footing in statistics and molecular genetics. Additionally, I wish I had stronger computer skills when I started out.

4. What do you wish you had known going into this profession?

Yes, there are. One of the fields within forensic science that is seeing the most growth involves computer crimes. The field of molecular biology–and DNA in particular–is also burgeoning.

5. How do you see your profession changing in the next five years? What role will technology play in those changes, and what skills will be required?

Technology will definitely play a role in the changes that are coming. There will be more emphasis on robotics for DNA extraction because it allows a faster throughput of sampling and extraction. Additionally, newer techniques are more sensitive, allowing for a smaller sample size. Finally, computer forensics will only continue to become more commonplace and important in the next five or more years.

6. What do you enjoy most about your job? What do you enjoy least?

What I enjoy most about my job is the fulfillment I get from assisting police departments in solving crimes. It's a feeling of accomplishment when I use science to bring closure to victims. What I enjoy least is the volume of casework. It can really be overwhelming at times. There's a constant struggle for funding to obtain supplies and equipment that we need to do our job. This can be frustrating and time-consuming.

7. Can you suggest a valuable "try this" for students considering a career in your profession?

Students considering working as a criminalist could undertake a research project on an area of interest in forensic science. Are you interested in fingerprinting techniques? What about animal hair identification? Researching topics like this will help you discover how engaging you find the subject, and that, in turn, may help you figure out if this is really something you'd want to do for a career. You could prepare a display for a science fair and volunteer to show it at a Girl Scout or Boy Scout meeting. Are you able to clearly explain the topic?

Our lab has internships for college students. However, due to the nature of what we do, job shadowing is not an option. A major concern is contamination of the evidence by anyone near the evidence. Anyone entering the lab needs to provide a DNA sample that will be entered into the staff index of DNA profiles.

Famous First

Ambroise Paré, a French army surgeon, systematically studied the effects of violent death on internal organs. Two Italian surgeons, Fortunato Fidelis and Paolo Zacchia, studied changes that occurred in the structure of the body as the result of disease. By the late 18th century, writings on these topics began to appear, including *A Treatise on Forensic Medicine* and *Public Health* by Francois Immanuele Fodéré and *The Complete System of Police Medicine* by Johann Peter Frank

Source: https://en.wikipedia.org/wiki/Forensic_science#Origins_of_forensic_science_and_early_methods

Fast Fact

Forensic science provides scientifically based information that can be used at trial. Evidence collected at a crime scene or from a person is analyzed in a crime laboratory and then presented in court. Each crime scene is unique, and each case presents its own challenges

Source: www.nij.gov/topics.

MORE INFORMATION

For more information about forensic science technicians and related specialists, visit

**American Academy of
Forensic Sciences**
https://www.aafs.org/

**American Board of
Criminalistics**
http://www.criminalistics.com/

**American Board of
Medicolegal Death
Investigators**
https://abmdi.org/

**Association of Firearm and
Tool Mark Examiners**
https://afte.org/

**International Crime Scene
Investigators Association**
https://www.icsia.org/

Sources

Bureau of Labor Statistics, U.S. Department of Labor, *Occupational Outlook Handbook*, Forensic Science Technicians.

Health and Safety Engineers

Snapshot

2017 Median Pay: $88,510 per year, $42.55 per hour
Typical Entry-Level Education: Bachelor's degree
Work Experience in a Related Occupation: None
On-the-job Training: None
Number of Jobs, 2016: 25,900
Job Outlook, 2016-26: 9% (As fast as average)
Employment Change, 2016-26: 2,200

CAREER OVERVIEW

What Health and Safety Engineers Do

Health and safety in the workplace is a major concern of health and safety engineers.

Health and safety engineers develop procedures and design systems to protect people from illness and injury and property from damage. They combine knowledge of engineering and of health and safety to make sure that chemicals, machinery, software, furniture,

and other products will not cause harm to people or damage to property.

Duties

Health and safety engineers typically do the following:

- Maintain and apply knowledge of current health and safety policies, regulations, and industrial processes
- Review plans and specifications for new machinery and equipment to make sure that they meet safety requirements
- Identify and correct potential hazards by inspecting facilities, machinery, and safety equipment
- Evaluate the effectiveness of various industrial control mechanisms
- Ensure that buildings or products comply with health and safety regulations, especially after an inspection that required changes
- Install safety devices on machinery or direct the installation of these devices
- Review employee safety programs and recommend improvements

Health and safety engineers also investigate industrial accidents and injuries to determine their causes and to determine whether the incidents were avoidable or can be prevented in the future. They interview employers and employees to learn about work environments and incidents that lead to accidents or injuries. They also evaluate the corrections that were made to remedy violations found during health inspections.

Health and safety engineering is a broad field covering many activities. The following are examples of types of health and safety engineers:

Fire prevention and protection engineers conduct analyses and make recommendations regarding the potential fire hazards of buildings, materials, and transportation systems. They also design, install, and maintain fire prevention and suppression systems and inspect systems to ensure that they meet government safety regulations. Fire prevention and protection engineers must be licensed and must keep up with changes in fire codes and regulations.

Product safety engineers, sometimes called product compliance engineers, develop and conduct tests to make sure that various products are safe and comply with industry or government safety regulations. These engineers work on a wide range of products, from nuclear submarine reactors and robotics to cell phones and computer systems.

Systems safety engineers identify and analyze risks and hazards associated with system designs in order to make them safe while ensuring that the systems remain operational and effective. They work in many fields, including aerospace, and are moving into new fields, such as software safety, medical safety, and environmental safety.

WORK ENVIRONMENT

Health and safety engineers may need to spend time at worksites.

Health and safety engineers held about 25,900 jobs in 2016. The largest employers of health and safety engineers were as follows:

Manufacturing	25%
Construction	18
Government	13
Engineering services	7
Management, scientific, and technical consulting services	5

Health and safety engineers typically work in offices. However, they also must spend time at worksites when necessary, which sometimes requires travel.

Work Schedules

Most health and safety engineers work full time.

HOW TO BECOME A HEALTH AND SAFETY ENGINEER

Education

Entry-level jobs for health and safety engineers require a bachelor's degree, typically in environmental health and safety or in an engineering discipline, such as electrical, chemical, mechanical, industrial, or systems engineering. Bachelor's degree programs typically include classroom, laboratory, and field studies in applied engineering. Engineering students interested in becoming health and safety engineers also should take courses in occupational safety and health, industrial hygiene, ergonomics, or environmental safety. ABET accredits programs in engineering.

Many colleges and universities offer cooperative-education programs, which allow students to gain practical experience while completing their education.

A few colleges and universities offer 5-year accelerated programs through which students graduate with both a bachelor's and a master's degree. A master's degree allows engineers to enter the occupation at a higher level, from which they can develop and implement safety systems.

ADVANCEMENT

Important Qualities

Communication skills. Health and safety engineers must be able to interpret federal and state regulations and their intent so that they can propose proper designs for specific work environments. Health and safety engineers also prepare and present training materials to workers and must be able to describe new regulations and procedures to a variety of audiences.

Creativity. Health and safety engineers produce designs showing potential problems and remedies for them. They must be creative, in order to deal with situations that are unique to a project.

Critical-thinking skills. Health and safety engineers must be able to identify hazards to humans and property in the workplace or in the home before those hazards cause material damage or become a health threat.

Observational skills. Health and safety engineers must observe and learn how operations function so that they can identify risks to people and property. This requires the ability to think in terms of overall processes within an organization. Health and safety engineers can then recommend systemic changes to minimize risks.

Problem-solving skills. In designing solutions for entire organizational operations, health and safety engineers must take into account processes from more than one system at the same time. In addition, they must try to anticipate a range of human reactions to the changes they recommend.

Licenses, Certifications, and Registrations

Licensure is not required for entry-level positions as a health and safety engineer. A Professional Engineering (PE) license, which allows for higher levels of leadership and independence, can be acquired later in one's career. Licensed engineers are called professional engineers (PEs). A PE can oversee the work of other engineers, sign off on projects, and provide services directly to the public. State licensure generally requires

- A degree from an ABET-accredited engineering program
- A passing score on the Fundamentals of Engineering (FE) exam
- Relevant work experience, typically at least 4 years
- A passing score on the Professional Engineering (PE) exam

The initial FE exam can be taken after one earns a bachelor's degree. Engineers who pass this exam are commonly called engineers in training (EITs) or engineer interns (EIs). After meeting work experience requirements, EITs and EIs can take the second exam, called the Principles and Practice of Engineering (PE).

Each state issues its own licenses. Most states recognize licensure from other states, as long as the licensing state's requirements meet or exceed their own licensure requirements. Several states require continuing education for engineers to keep their licenses.

Health and safety engineers can earn professional certifications, including the following:

The Board of Certified Safety Professionals offers the Certified Safety Professional (CSP) certification, the Occupational Health and Safety Technologist (OHST) certification, and the new Associate Safety Professional (ASP) certification

The American Board of Industrial Hygiene awards the Certified Industrial Hygienist (CIH) certification

The American Society of Safety Engineers offers a Certificate in Safety Management (CSM)

The International Council on Systems Engineering offers a program leading to designation as a Certified Systems Engineering Professional (CSEP)

WAGES

Median annual wages, May 2017

Health and safety engineers, except mining safety engineers and inspectors: $92,220

Engineers: $88,510

Total, all occupations: $37,690

Note: All Occupations includes all occupations in the U.S. Economy. Source: U.S. Bureau of Labor Statistics, Occupational Employment Statistics

Pay

The median annual wage for health and safety engineers was $88,510 in May 2017. The lowest 10 percent earned less than $51,820, and the highest 10 percent earned more than $139,630.

In May 2017, the median annual wages for health and safety engineers in the top industries in which they worked were as follows:

Management, scientific, and technical consulting services	$98,720
Engineering services	93,910
Government	87,700
Manufacturing	85,940
Construction	80,600

Most health and safety engineers work full time.

JOB OUTLOOK

Percent change in employment, projected 2016-26

Health and safety engineers, except mining safety engineers and inspectors: 9%

Engineers: 8%

Total, all occupations: 7%

Note: All Occupations includes all occupations in the U.S. Economy. Source: U.S. Bureau of Labor Statistics, Employment Projections program

Employment of health and safety engineers is projected to grow 9 percent from 2016 to 2026, about as fast as the average for all occupations.

Health and safety engineers are employed mainly in construction, manufacturing, state and local government, and engineering and consulting firms. As buildings, products, and processes continue to become more complex and new regulations are created, these engineers will be needed to reduce costs, save lives, and produce safe consumer products.

Job Prospects

Employment projections data for Health and Safety Engineers, 2016-26

Occupational Title	SOC Code	Employment, 2016	Projected Employment, 2026	Change, 2016-26	
				Percent	Numeric
Health and safety engineers, except mining safety engineers and inspectors	17-2111	25,900	28,100	9	2,200

Source: Bureau of Labor Statistics, Employment Projections program

SIMILAR OCCUPATIONS

This table shows a list of occupations with job duties that are similar to those of health and safety engineers.

OCCUPATION	JOB DUTIES	ENTRY-LEVEL EDUCATION	2017 MEDIAN PAY
Construction and Building Inspectors	Construction and building inspectors ensure that construction meets local and national building codes and ordinances, zoning regulations, and contract specifications.	High school diploma or equivalent	$59,090

OCCUPATION	JOB DUTIES	ENTRY-LEVEL EDUCATION	2017 MEDIAN PAY
Fire Inspectors	Fire inspectors examine buildings in order to detect fire hazards and ensure that federal, state, and local fire codes are met. Fire investigators, another type of worker in this field, determine the origin and cause of fires and explosions. Forest fire inspectors and prevention specialists assess outdoor fire hazards in public and residential areas.	Postsecondary educational program for emergency medical technicians (EMTs) High school diploma or equivalent (forest fire inspectors and prevention specialists)	$56,670
Industrial Engineers	Industrial engineers find ways to eliminate wastefulness in production processes. They devise efficient systems that integrate workers, machines, materials, information, and energy to make a product or provide a service.	Bachelor's degree	$85,880
Mining and Geological Engineers	Mining and geological engineers design mines to safely and efficiently remove minerals such as coal and metals for use in manufacturing and utilities.	Bachelor's degree	$94,240
Occupational Health and Safety Specialists and Technicians	Occupational health and safety specialists and technicians collect data on and analyze many types of work environments and work procedures. Specialists inspect workplaces for adherence to regulations on safety, health, and the environment. Technicians work with specialists in conducting tests and measuring hazards to help prevent harm to workers, property, the environment, and the general public.	Bachelor's degree (specialist) High school diploma or equivalent (technician)	$67,720

Famous First

Traditionally, safety analysis techniques rely solely on skill and expertise of the safety engineer. In the last decade model-based approaches have become prominent. Model-based techniques try to derive relationships between causes and consequences from some sort of model of the system

Source: https://en.wikipedia.org/wiki/Safety_engineering

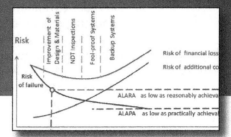

Fast Fact

A worker is injured every seven seconds. The most common workplace injury, at 34 percent, is overexertion – e.g., lifting, lowering, or repetitive motions.
Source: National Safety Council.

MORE INFORMATION

For information about general engineering education and career resources, visit

American Society for Engineering Education
http://www.asee.org/

American Society of Safety Engineers
https://www.assp.org/

Technology Student Association
https://tsaweb.org/

For more information about accredited engineering programs, visit

ABET
https://www.abet.org/

For more information about the Professional Engineer license, visit

National Council of Examiners for Engineering and Surveying
https://ncees.org/

National Society of Professional Engineers
https://www.nspe.org/

For information about protecting worker health, visit

American Industrial Hygiene Association
https://www.aiha.org//Pages/default.aspx

For information about certification, visit

American Board of Industrial Hygiene
http://www.abih.org/

American Society of Safety Engineers
https://www.assp.org/education/certificate-programs

Board of Certified Safety Professionals
https://www.bcsp.org/

International Council on Systems Engineering
https://www.incose.org/

Sources

Bureau of Labor Statistics, U.S. Department of Labor, *Occupational Outlook Handbook*, Health and Safety Engineers.

Health Educators and Community Health Workers

Snapshot

2017 Median Pay: $45,360 per year, $21.81 per hour

Typical Entry-Level Education: Health educators : bachelor's degree in health education or health promotion; master's or doctoral degree; Community health workers: high school diploma

Work Experience in a Related Occupation: None

On-the-job Training: Brief period of on-the-job training, covers core competencies, such as communication or outreach skills, and information about the specific health topics

Number of Jobs, 2016: 118,500

Job Outlook, 2016-26: 16% (Much faster than average)

Employment Change, 2016-26: 19,200

CAREER OVERVIEW

What Health Educators and Community Health Workers Do

Health educators and community health workers educate people about the availability of healthcare services.

Health educators teach people about behaviors that promote wellness. They develop and implement strategies to improve the health of individuals and communities. Community health workers provide a link between the community and healthcare professionals. They develop and implement strategies to improve the health of

individuals and communities. They collect data and discuss health concerns with members of specific populations or communities. Although the two occupations often work together, responsibilities of health educators and community health workers are distinct.

Duties

Health educators typically do the following:

- Assess the health needs of the people and communities they serve
- Develop programs, materials, and events to teach people about health topics
- Teach people how to manage existing health conditions
- Evaluate the effectiveness of programs and educational materials
- Help people find health services or information
- Provide training programs for community health workers or other health professionals
- Supervise staff who implement health education programs
- Collect and analyze data to learn about a particular community and improve programs and services
- Advocate for improved health resources and policies that promote health

Community health workers typically do the following:

- Discuss health concerns with community members
- Educate people about the importance and availability of healthcare services, such as cancer screenings
- Collect data
- Report findings to health educators and other healthcare providers
- Provide informal counseling and social support

- Conduct outreach programs
- Facilitate access to the healthcare services
- Advocate for individual and community needs

Health educators Also known as *health education specialists*, have different duties depending on their work setting. Most work in healthcare facilities, colleges, public health departments, nonprofits, and private businesses. People who teach health classes in middle and high schools are considered teachers.

The following are descriptions of duties for health educators, by work setting:

In *healthcare facilities*, health educators may work one-on-one with patients or with their families. They may be called patient navigators because they help consumers understand their health insurance options and direct people to outside resources, such as support groups or home health agencies. They teach patients about their diagnoses and about any necessary treatments or procedures. They lead hospital efforts in developing and administering surveys to identify major health issues and concerns of the surrounding communities and developing programs to meet those needs. Health educators also help organize health screenings, such as blood pressure checks, and classes on topics such as installing a car seat correctly. They also create programs to train medical staff to interact more effectively with patients.

In *colleges*, health educators create programs and materials on topics that affect young adults, such as smoking and alcohol use. They may train students to be peer educators and supervise the students' delivery of health information in person or through social media. Health educators also advocate for campus wide policies to promote health.

In *public health departments*, health educators administer public health campaigns on topics such as emergency preparedness, immunizations, proper nutrition, or stress management. They develop materials to be used by other public health officials. During emergencies, they may provide safety information to the public and the media. Some health educators work with other professionals to create public policies that support healthy behaviors and environments. They may also oversee grants and grant-funded programs to improve the health of the public. Some participate in statewide and local committees dealing with topics such as aging.

In *nonprofits*, health educators create programs and materials about health issues faced by the community that they serve. They help organizations obtain funding and other resources. They educate policymakers about ways to improve public health and work on securing grant funding for programs to promote health and disease awareness. Many nonprofits focus on a particular disease or audience, so health educators in these organizations limit programs to that specific topic or audience.

In *private businesses*, health educators identify common health problems among employees and create programs to improve health. They work to develop incentives for employees to adopt healthy behaviors, such as losing weight or controlling cholesterol. Health educators recommend changes in the workplace to improve employee health, such as creating smoke-free areas.

Community health workers have an in-depth knowledge of the communities they serve. Within their community, they identify health-related issues, collect data, and discuss health concerns with the people they serve. For example, they may help eligible residents of a neighborhood enroll in programs such as Medicaid or Medicare and explain the benefits that these programs offer. Community health workers address any barriers to care and provide referrals for such needs as food, housing, education, and mental health services.

Community health workers share information with health educators and healthcare providers so that health educators can create new programs or adjust existing programs or events to better suit the needs of the community. Community health workers also advocate for the health needs of community members. In addition, they conduct outreach to engage community residents, assist residents with health system navigation, and to improve care coordination.

WORK ENVIRONMENT

Community health workers held about 57,500 jobs in 2016. The largest employers of community health workers were as follows:

Individual and family services	18%
Government	16
Religious, grantmaking, civic, professional, and similar organizations	14
Hospitals; state, local, and private	10
Outpatient care centers	10

Health educators often work in hospitals, where they help patients understand and adjust to their diagnosis. Health educators held about 61,000 jobs in 2016. The largest employers of health educators were as follows:

Hospitals; state, local, and private	23%
Government	22
Religious, grantmaking, civic, professional, and similar organizations	9
Outpatient care centers	8
Individual and family services	7

Although most health educators work in offices, they may spend a lot of time away from the office to carry out programs or attend meetings.

Community health workers may spend much of their time in the field, communicating with community members, holding events, and collecting data.

Work Schedules

Most health educators and community health workers work full time. They may need to work nights and weekends to attend programs or meetings.

HOW TO BECOME A HEALTH EDUCATOR OR COMMUNITY HEALTH WORKER

Health educators need at least bachelor's degree. Some employers require the Certified Health Education Specialist (CHES) credential.

Community health workers need at least a high school diploma and must complete a brief period of on-the-job training. Some states have certification programs for community health workers.

Education

Health educators need at least a bachelor's degree in health education or health promotion. Students learn theories and methods of health behavior and health education and gain the knowledge and skills they will need to develop health education materials and programs. Most programs include an internship.

Some health educator positions require candidates to have a master's or doctoral degree. Graduate programs are commonly in community health education, school health education, public health education, or health promotion. A variety of undergraduate majors may be acceptable for entry to a master's degree program.

Community health workers need at least a high school diploma, although some jobs may require some postsecondary education. Education programs may lead to a 1-year certificate or a 2-year associate's degree and cover topics such as wellness, ethics, and cultural awareness.

Training

Community health workers typically complete a brief period of on-the-job training. Training often covers core competencies, such as communication or outreach skills, and information about the specific health topics that they will be focusing on. For example, community health workers who work with Alzheimer's patients may learn about how to communicate effectively with patients dealing with dementia.

Other Experience

Community health workers usually have some knowledge of a specific community, culture, medical condition, or disability. The ability to speak a foreign language may be helpful.

Licenses, Certifications, and Registrations

Some employers require health educators to obtain the Certified Health Education Specialist (CHES) credential, which is offered by the National Commission for Health Education Credentialing, Inc.

Candidates must pass an exam that is aimed at entry-level health educators who have completed at least a bachelor's degree. To maintain their certification, they must complete 75 hours of continuing education every 5 years. There is also the Master Certified Health Education Specialist (MCHES) credential for health educators with advanced education and experience.

Most states do not require community health workers to obtain certification, however, voluntary certification exists or is being considered or developed in a number of states. Requirements vary but may include completing an approved training program. For more information, contact your state's board of health, nursing, or human services.

ADVANCEMENT

Important Qualities

Analytical skills. Health educators collect and analyze data in order to evaluate programs and to determine the needs of the people they serve.

Instructional skills. Health educators and community health workers should be comfortable with public speaking so that they can lead programs, teach classes, and facilitate discussion with clients and families.

Interpersonal skills. Health educators and community health workers interact with many people from a variety of backgrounds. They must be good listeners and be culturally sensitive to respond to the needs of the people they serve.

Problem-solving skills. Health educators and community health workers must think creatively about how to improve the health of the community through health education programs. In addition, they may need to solve problems that arise in planning programs, such as changes to their budget or resistance from the community they are serving.

Writing skills. Health educators and community health workers develop written materials to convey health-related information. Health educators also write proposals to develop programs and apply for funding.

WAGES

Median annual wages, May 2017

Health educators: $53,940

Health educators and community health workers: $45,360

Counselors, social workers, and other community and social service specialists: $43,860

Community health workers: $38,370

Total, all occupations: $37,690

Note: All Occupations includes all occupations in the U.S. Economy. Source: U.S. Bureau of Labor Statistics, Occupational Employment Statistics

The median annual wage for community health workers was $38,370 in May 2017. The lowest 10 percent earned less than $25,150, and the highest 10 percent earned more than $64,500.

The median annual wage for health educators was $53,940 in May 2017. The lowest 10 percent earned less than $31,440, and the highest 10 percent earned more than $97,160.

In May 2017, the median annual wages for community health workers in the top industries in which they worked were as follows:

Hospitals; state, local, and private	$46,350
Religious, grantmaking, civic, professional, and similar organizations	41,110
Government	40,740
Individual and family services	36,470
Outpatient care centers	35,370

In May 2017, the median annual wages for health educators in the top industries in which they worked were as follows:

Hospitals; state, local, and private	$63,510
Government	55,420
Outpatient care centers	51,130
Religious, grantmaking, civic, professional, and similar organizations	48,640
Individual and family services	40,360

Most health educators and community health workers work full time. They may need to work nights and weekends to attend programs or meetings.

JOB OUTLOOK

Percent change in employment, projected 2016-26

Community health workers: 18%

Health educators and community health workers: 16%

Counselors, social workers, and other community and social service specialists: 16%

Health educators: 14%

Total, all occupations: 7%

Note: All Occupations includes all occupations in the U.S. Economy. Source: U.S. Bureau of Labor Statistics, Employment Projections program

Overall employment of health educators and community health workers is projected to grow 16 percent from 2016 to 2026, much faster than the average for all occupations. Growth will be driven by efforts to improve health outcomes and to reduce healthcare costs by teaching people healthy behaviors and explaining how to use available healthcare services.

Governments, healthcare providers, social services providers want to find ways to improve the quality of care and health outcomes, while reducing costs. This should increase demand for health educators and community health workers because they teach people how to live healthy lives and how to avoid costly diseases and medical procedures.

Job Prospects

Community health workers who have completed a formal education program and those who have experience working with a specific population may have more favorable job prospects. In addition, opportunities may be better for candidates who speak a foreign language and understand the culture of the community that they intend to serve.

Employment projections data for Health Educators and Community Health Workers, 2016-26

Occupational Title	SOC Code	Employment, 2016	Projected Employment, 2026	Change, 2016-26	
				Percent	Numeric
Health educators and community health workers	–	118,500	137,700	16	19,200
Health educators	21-1091	61,000	69,900	14	8,800
Community health workers	21-1094	57,500	67,800	18	10,400

Source: Bureau of Labor Statistics, Employment Projections program

SIMILAR OCCUPATIONS

This table shows a list of occupations with job duties that are similar to those of health educators and community health workers.

OCCUPATION	JOB DUTIES	ENTRY-LEVEL EDUCATION	2017 MEDIAN PAY
Dietitians and Nutritionists	Dietitians and nutritionists are experts in the use of food and nutrition to promote health and manage disease. They advise people on what to eat in order to lead a healthy lifestyle or achieve a specific health-related goal.	Bachelor's degree	$59,410

OCCUPATION	JOB DUTIES	ENTRY-LEVEL EDUCATION	2017 MEDIAN PAY
Epidemiologists	Epidemiologists are public health professionals who investigate patterns and causes of disease and injury in humans. They seek to reduce the risk and occurrence of negative health outcomes through research, community education, and health policy.	Master's degree	$69,660
High School Teachers	High school teachers help prepare students for life after graduation. They teach academic lessons and various skills that students will need to attend college and to enter the job market.	Bachelor's degree	$59,170
Middle School Teachers	Middle school teachers educate students, typically in sixth through eighth grades. They help students build on the fundamentals they learned in elementary school and prepare them for the more difficult curriculum they will face in high school.	Bachelor's degree	$57,720
Postsecondary Teachers	Postsecondary teachers instruct students in a wide variety of academic and technical subjects beyond the high school level. They may also conduct research and publish scholarly papers and books.	PhD (master's degree may be adequate to teach at community colleges)	$76,000
School and Career Counselors	School counselors help students develop the academic and social skills needed to succeed in school. Career counselors help people choose careers and follow a path to employment.	Master's degree	$55,410

OCCUPATION	JOB DUTIES	ENTRY-LEVEL EDUCATION	2017 MEDIAN PAY
Social and Human Service Assistants	Social and human service assistants provide client services, including support for families, in a wide variety of fields, such as psychology, rehabilitation, and social work. They assist other workers, such as social workers, and they help clients find benefits or community services.	High school diploma or equivalent	$33,120
Social Workers	Social workers help people solve and cope with problems in their everyday lives. Clinical social workers also diagnose and treat mental, behavioral, and emotional issues.	Bachelor's degree in social work (BSW) with supervised fieldwork or an internship for direct-service work Master's degree in social work (MSW) with supervised practicum or an internship, clinical work for clinical work	$47,980
Substance Abuse, Behavioral Disorder, and Mental Health Counselors	Substance abuse, behavioral disorder, and mental health counselors advise people who suffer from alcoholism, drug addiction, eating disorders, mental health issues, or other mental or behavioral problems. They provide treatment and support to help clients recover from addiction or modify problem behaviors.	Bachelor's degree	$43,300
Marriage and Family Therapists	Marriage and family therapists help people manage and overcome problems with family and other relationships.	Master's degree	$48,790

Conversation With . . .
KATHIE A. COX, CHES

Public Health Educator II, PIO Health Department
Scotland County, NC
Health Educator, 19 years

1. What was your individual career path in terms of education/training, entry-level job, or other significant opportunity?

I started college at the University of Southern Mississippi determined to become my family's first female attorney, but wound up going to school part time, working full time, getting married, and moving to rural North Carolina. I went back to a community college and switched my major to psychology, hoping to help people with behavioral and mental health issues. But I landed in public health and community health education after I moved on to the University of North Carolina at Pembroke and met the chair of that department. I was inspired by her. I earned my BS, completed an internship at the local hospital, and was fortunate to find my passion. The hospital hired me right after graduation. I was responsible for employee wellness, grant-funded programs, community health and events—and learned a lot from my supervisor.

After five years, I moved to the county health department. Job responsibilities in public health are quite different from private settings like hospitals because you have to meet certain standards. I wore a number of hats and hit the ground running.

Today, I am responsible for both developing programming and for researching evidence-based programming that I implement and evaluate. A lot of community health and public health involves communicating with the public.

My job is to help improve the public's health by promoting healthy behaviors. I encourage people to make healthy choices through behavioral change and I educate them about how to make informed decisions regarding such things as heat-related illness. For example, do they know the signs and symptoms of the three health-related illnesses—heat stress, exhaustion, and heat stroke? Do they know heat stroke is deadly? We do a lot of information-sharing through media and social media, and we do community events at, say, a church's Community Day.

Professionally, I participate in ongoing continuing education. For instance, I'll complete my Chronic Care Professional Certification this year; it's one of a number of certifications I hold in different specialties.

2. **What are the most important skills and/or qualities for someone in your profession?**

   Communication—language and writing skills—as well as people skills. Some people just don't have that. You need to be passionate, as any good teacher is. You need to show that you are compassionate and have empathy. You need to be able to engage individuals and diverse groups in order to educate them about positive lifestyle changes. People are at different levels where change is concerned. It takes practice and creativity to help people change.

3. **What do you wish you had known going into this profession?**

   The wide range of opportunity. A health educator can work in a number of areas —business and industry, schools, hospitals—and educate in areas ranging from nutrition to diabetes. You often can make very good money, depending on the agency, or your specialty.

4. **Are there many job opportunities in your profession? In what specific areas?**

   Many. Health educators are increasingly employed across business and industry; hospitals; doctors' offices; insurance agencies; and local, state, and federal public health offices. There are different certifications for different specialties. It's important to consider travel and the work setting, as well as the job responsibilities, when you're looking for a job. Most of that is learned through experience and not education.

5. **How do you see your profession changing in the next five years as it relates to fitness and/or sports injuries? What role will technology play, and what skills will be required?**

   Social media is critical to engage younger people, and you've got to have up-to-date computer skills. Prevention will be key to health and fitness. Thinking outside the box to face challenges will continue to be important.

6. **What do you enjoy most about your job? What do you enjoy least about your job?**

   I most enjoy working with people. I'm a talker, I'm a teacher, and encouraging people also encourages me to work on the changes I need to make. A lot of people need support; a buddy system.

   I least enjoy all the specific requirements involved in public health that keep me at my desk rather than out in the community. This is not a five-day-a-week; 9-to-5 job. Health educators work weekday evenings, many Saturdays and some Sundays.

7. **Can you suggest a valuable "try this" for students considering a career in your profession?**

Shadow a health educator, volunteer at a local public health agency or hospital, and get an internship. Internships are important not only to gain hands-on experience, but to determine whether or not a profession is a good "fit."

This conversation was originally published in 2014.

Famous First

The British bacteriologist Almroth Edward Wright developed a typhoid vaccine at the Army Medical School in Netley, Hampshire. It was used successfully by the British during the Boer War in South Africa at a time when typhoid often killed more soldiers than were lost during battle. Wright further convinced the British Army that 10 million vaccine doses should be produced for the troops being sent to the Western Front, saving up to half a million lives during World War I. As a result, the British Army casualties due to combat exceeded those from disease.

Source: https://en.wikipedia.org/wiki/Typhoid_fever#History

Fast Fact

Community health centers act as primary health care providers to nearly 25 million people in the United States

Source: intercare.org

MORE INFORMATION

Society for Public Health Education
https://www.sophe.org/

American Public Health Association
https://www.apha.org/

For more information about the Certified Health Education Specialist (CHES) credential, visit

National Commission for Health Education Credentialing, Inc.
https://www.nchec.org/

Sources

Bureau of Labor Statistics, U.S. Department of Labor, *Occupational Outlook Handbook*, Health Educators and Community Health Workers.

Homeland Security

People who work in homeland security anticipate, prepare for, prevent, and react to everything from pandemics to hurricanes to terrorism. These workers help to reduce our Nation's vulnerabilities and to minimize the damage from catastrophic events. Due to the nature of their work, those involved with homeland security might have to meet certain criteria not generally required of other workers. For example, many applicants for homeland security jobs must undergo security clearances or background checks. Workers need security clearances because of the sensitive information with which they may come into contact. Applicants should understand that

this can mean a longer waiting period before being offered a job. Another common requirement for homeland security employment is that applicants be U.S. citizens. But beyond these basic parameters, opportunities exist for people of varying interests, skills, and backgrounds.

VARIED EMPLOYERS

Homeland security is a dynamic and diverse career field. Like security threats themselves, the work required to protect the Nation is constantly changing. That work cuts across numerous disciplines, creating job possibilities for people with nearly any level of education and experience. Options exist both for those who like to be in the forefront and for those who prefer to work in the background. Homeland security work is available in the air, on land, and at sea. There are jobs in every State, in the District of Columbia, and abroad. Many homeland security jobs are with State, Federal, or local governments. But there are plenty of other opportunities in private companies and nonprofit organizations. In 2001, the U.S. Department of Homeland Security was created to promote homeland security and to coordinate homeland security efforts among other government agencies and private industry. With multiple locations in and around Washington, D.C., and throughout the country, the Department of Homeland Security employed about 240,000 workers in 2019—making it one of the largest Federal agencies.

U.S. DEPARTMENT OF HOMELAND SECURITY

Jobs at the Homeland Security Department are many and varied. They include air marshals, program analysts, and Coast Guard officers, to name a few. Along with these Federal positions, the Department also has a significant number of contractor positions. For example, the workers who administer physical examinations for its agents and officers are often employed by contract firms. And the

Department's efforts are supported by advisory councils, national laboratories, and research and development centers.

This list shows some of the occupations found within the U.S. Department of Homeland Security. The list is not all-inclusive; there are many other occupations in the Department. Moreover, just because an occupation is listed under a particular Division of the Department does not mean that the occupation exists only in that Division. For example, criminal investigators are employed not only in the Transportation Security Administration and the U.S. Secret Service, as shown below, but also in the Immigration and Customs Enforcement Division and in the Office of the Inspector General. Similarly, although engineers are only listed under the Science and Technology Directorate and the U.S. Coast Guard, engineers are also employed by the Information Analysis and Infrastructure Protection Directorate and the Federal Emergency Management Agency.

Citizenship and Immigration Services

Asylum officer
Immigration officer

Customs and Border Protection

Border Patrol agent
Import specialist

Federal Emergency Management Agency

Federal coordinating officer
Program specialist (fire; national security; response, recovery, preparedness, and mitigation)

Federal Law Enforcement Training Center

Law enforcement specialist (instruction)

Immigration and Customs Enforcement

Detention and deportation officer
Police officer
Immigration enforcement agent
Security specialist

Information Analysis and Infrastructure Protection Directorate

Protective security advisor
Intelligence operations specialist
IT specialist (information security)
Security specialist
Telecommunications specialist

Office of the Inspector General

Attorney
Auditor

Science and Technology Directorate

Biological scientist
Chemist
Computer scientist
Engineer
Physicist

Secretarial Offices

Human resources specialist
Policy analyst

Transportation and Security Administration

Criminal investigator
Intelligence operations specialist
Program and management analyst
Transportation security screener

U.S. Coast Guard

Contract specialist
Engineer

U.S. Secret Service

Criminal investigator

OTHER FEDERAL AGENCIES

Many other Federal workers have responsibilities related to securing the Nation. Workers at the Central Intelligence Agency and elsewhere, for example, help to identify potential threats. The U.S. Department of Labor sends inspectors to ensure that fire fighters and others who might be exposed to hazardous conditions wear sufficiently protective gear. And the U.S. Department of State's Bureau of Diplomatic Security has special agents who advise U.S. ambassadors in foreign countries and protect foreign dignitaries in the United States.

STATE AND LOCAL GOVERNMENTS

State and local governments also employ large numbers of people who do homeland security work. For example, many of the Nation's first responders—emergency medical technicians, paramedics, fire fighters, police, and other workers who arrive at the scene of a threat or incident—are State and local government employees.

Public buildings and facilities—such as municipal waterworks—often need workers to handle safety and security-related issues. And all States, as well as many cities and counties, have an emergency management agency or similar organization to coordinate crisis services and look at ways to ensure homeland security at the State and local levels.

PRIVATE INDUSTRY AND NONPROFITS

Businesses—both for-profit and not-for-profit—also do homeland security work. Security is one of the biggest areas of private sector employment. Many companies hire security workers to protect against possible threats to employees, customers, and physical and electronic assets. Corporations also rely on workers to develop contingency plans detailing how to handle possible disruptions to their business. Moreover, some businesses employ workers who develop and sell products and services related to homeland security.

Nonprofit organizations are another source of homeland security employment. A nonprofit environmental organization, for example, might examine the best ways to clean up a site that has been contaminated by a chemical or biological agent. And educational institutions employ people who teach and conduct research on a number of issues related to homeland security.

Fast Fact

Ben Gurion Airport in Israel is considered to be the world's most secure airport, even though it deals with a high volume of terrorist threats

Source: Travel + Leisure

Conversation With . . .
JACK RAMSY

Recruiting Program Manager
U.S. Customs and Border Protection
12 years in field

1. What was your individual career path in terms of education/training, entry-level job, or other significant opportunity?

I was in the military, a Navy diver. When I retired, I was looking for something different to do. I already had my graduate degree and I wanted to go into law enforcement. I worked as a college campus police officer for a year. But U.S. Customs looked like the place to go at the time, and I was hired as a customs inspector.

2. What are the most important skills and/or qualities for someone in your profession?

You've got to be willing to become part of a dynamic team that works in a very fast paced environment. Every day represents new challenges. You have to be technologically astute. Everything we do has some type of technology behind it. You've got to be flexible. You have to be able to think on your feet, be able to determine if someone is telling you the truth or not. You have to be open to all ideas, accepting of all cultures.

3. What do you wish you had known going into this profession?

For the new person coming in, I think they need to know they have to be in better shape than they thought. There are physical fitness standards going into this job. The application process is a year long. Because it's a national security position, it requires a thorough background investigation and a polygraph test. There are medical exams, a physical fitness test, structured interviews, both video and face-to-face. If you're hired, you're accepted into the training academy, which is 17-19 weeks long.

4. What do you wish you had known going into this profession?

Right now, we're getting ready to hire an additional 2,000 customs patrol and border officers, nationwide. The biggest need is on the borders. Most of those jobs will go to our busiest ports.

5. How do you see your profession changing in the next five years? What role will technology play in those changes, and what skills will be required?

The technology is getting better every year. Customs and Border Patrol is constantly upgrading its technology to keep up with what's really happening out there. Everything from biometrics to non-intrusive inspection systems using gamma x-ray systems so we can do vehicle and cargo inspections faster and more efficiently.

You've got to be a technology user. Learning new systems is part of the job. There's always training on new systems, new tools being introduced, and maintaining your training. And everyone has to do it, front the entry level officer all the way up to senior officer.

6. Do you have any general advice or additional professional insights to share with someone in your profession? What is the most fulfilling part of your job, and what is the most frustrating?

The most fulfilling part of the job is the job itself. What we do makes a difference. Customs and Border Patrol Officers not only enforce the customs and immigration laws, but we also enforce the laws for 40 other federal agencies. It's always changing, there's always something new to learn, there's always something different that can happen.

It's a job that makes a difference and it's one that attracts a certain individual. If you can stand on your feet and pass the background check, we'll make you a good officer.

7. Can you suggest a valuable "try this" for students considering a career in your profession?

We have a lot of student intern opportunities around the country. Speak to a recruiter. Speak to an officer who actually works at a port of entry. They'll tell you how it is. It takes a long time to get this job, but it extremely worth it.

Information Security Analysts

CAREER OVERVIEW

What Information Security Analysts Do

Information security analysts install software, such as firewalls, to protect computer networks. They work to protect a company's computer systems

Information security analysts plan and carry out security measures to protect an organization's computer networks and

systems. Their responsibilities are continually expanding as the number of cyberattacks increases.

Duties

Information security analysts typically do the following:

- Monitor their organization's networks for security breaches and investigate a violation when one occurs
- Install and use software, such as firewalls and data encryption programs, to protect sensitive information
- Prepare reports that document security breaches and the extent of the damage caused by the breaches
- Conduct penetration testing, which is when analysts simulate attacks to look for vulnerabilities in their systems before they can be exploited
- Research the latest information technology (IT) security trends
- Develop security standards and best practices for their organization
- Recommend security enhancements to management or senior IT staff
- Help computer users when they need to install or learn about new security products and procedures

IT security analysts are heavily involved with creating their organization's disaster recovery plan, a procedure that IT employees follow in case of emergency. These plans allow for the continued operation of an organization's IT department. The recovery plan includes preventive measures such as regularly copying and transferring data to an offsite location. It also involves plans to restore proper IT functioning after a disaster. Analysts continually test the steps in their recovery plans.

Information security analysts must stay up to date on IT security and on the latest methods attackers are using to infiltrate computer systems. Analysts need to research new security technology to decide what will most effectively protect their organization.

WORK ENVIRONMENT

Many analysts work in IT departments and manage the security of their companies computer networks.

Information security analysts held about 100,000 jobs in 2016. The largest employers of information security analysts were as follows:

Computer systems design and related services	28%
Finance and insurance	19
Management of companies and enterprises	9
Information	8
Administrative and support services	6

Many information security analysts work with other members of an information technology department, such as network administrators or computer systems analysts.

Work Schedules

Most information security analysts work full time. Information security analysts sometimes have to be on call outside of normal business hours in case of an emergency. About 1 in 4 worked more than 40 hours per week in 2016.

Fast Fact

Here are some worrisome numbers: 8 in 10 adults in the U.S. are concerned about businesses' ability to protect their financial and personal information, and cybercrime cost U.S. consumers $19.4 billion of their own money in 2017.
Source: American Institute of CPAs.

HOW TO BECOME AN INFORMATION SECURITY ANALYST

There are a number of information security certifications available, and many employers prefer candidates to have certification.

Most information security analyst positions require a bachelor's degree in a computer-related field. Employers usually prefer analysts to have experience in a related occupation.

Education

Information security analysts usually need at least a bachelor's degree in computer science, information assurance, programming, or a related field.

Some employers prefer applicants who have a Master of Business Administration (MBA) in information systems. Programs offering the MBA in information systems generally require 2 years of study beyond the undergraduate level and include both business and computer-related courses.

Work Experience in a Related Occupation

Information security analysts generally need to have previous experience in a related occupation. Many analysts have experience in an information technology department, often as a network or computer systems administrator. Some employers look for people who have already worked in fields related to the one in which they are hiring. For example, if the job opening is in database security, they may look for a database administrator. If they are hiring in systems security, a computer systems analyst may be an ideal candidate.

Licenses, Certifications, and Registrations

There are a number of information security certifications available, and many employers prefer candidates to have certification, which validates the knowledge and best practices required from information security analysts. Some are general information security certificates, such as the Certified Information Systems Security Professional (CISSP), while others have a more narrow focus, such as penetration testing or systems auditing.

ADVANCEMENT

Information security analysts can advance to become chief security officers or another type of computer and information systems manager.

Important Qualities

Analytical skills. Information security analysts must carefully study computer systems and networks and assess risks to determine how security policies and protocols can be improved.

Detail oriented. Because cyberattacks can be difficult to detect, information security analysts must pay careful attention to computer systems and watch for minor changes in performance.

Ingenuity. Information security analysts must anticipate information security risks and implement new ways to protect their organizations' computer systems and networks.

Problem-solving skills. Information security analysts must respond to security alerts and uncover and fix flaws in computer systems and networks.

WAGES

Median annual wages, May 2017

Information security analysts: $95,510

Computer occupations: $84,580

Total, all occupations: $37,690

Note: All Occupations includes all occupations in the U.S. Economy. Source: U.S. Bureau of Labor Statistics, Occupational Employment Statistics

The median annual wage for information security analysts was $95,510 in May 2017. The lowest 10 percent earned less than $55,560, and the highest 10 percent earned more than $153,090.

In May 2017, the median annual wages for information security analysts in the top industries in which they worked were as follows:

Computer systems design and related services	$98,100
Finance and insurance	97,680
Information	96,250
Administrative and support services	91,510
Management of companies and enterprises	90,940

Most information security analysts work full time. Information security analysts sometimes have to be on call outside of normal business hours in case of an emergency. About 1 in 4 worked more than 40 hours per week in 2016.

JOB OUTLOOK

Percent change in employment, projected 2016-26

Information security analysts: 28%

Computer occupations: 13%

Total, all occupations: 7%

Note: All Occupations includes all occupations in the U.S. Economy. Source: U.S. Bureau of Labor Statistics, Employment Projections program

Employment of information security analysts is projected to grow 28 percent from 2016 to 2026, much faster than the average for all occupations.

Demand for information security analysts is expected to be very high. Cyberattacks have grown in frequency, and analysts will be needed to come up with innovative solutions to prevent hackers from stealing critical information or creating problems for computer networks.

Banks and financial institutions, as well as other types of corporations, will need to increase their information security capabilities in the face of growing cybersecurity threats. In addition, as the healthcare industry expands its use of electronic medical records, ensuring patients' privacy and protecting personal data are becoming more important. More information security analysts are likely to be needed to create the safeguards that will satisfy patients' concerns.

Employment of information security analysts is projected to grow 56 percent in computer systems design and related services from 2016 to 2026. The increasing adoption of cloud services by small and medium-sized businesses and a rise in cybersecurity threats will create demand for managed security services providers in this industry.

Job Prospects

Job prospects for information security analysts should be good. Information security analysts with related work experience will have the best prospects. For example, an applicant with experience as a database administrator would have better prospects in database security than someone without that experience.

Employment projections data for Information Security Analysts, 2016-26

Occupational Title	SOC Code	Employment, 2016	Projected Employment, 2026	Change, 2016-26	
				Percent	Numeric
Information security analysts	15-1122	100,000	128,500	28	28,500

Source: Bureau of Labor Statistics, Employment Projections program

SIMILAR OCCUPATIONS

This table shows a list of occupations with job duties that are similar to those of information security analysts.

OCCUPATION	JOB DUTIES	ENTRY-LEVEL EDUCATION	2017 MEDIAN PAY
Computer and Information Research Scientists	Computer and information research scientists invent and design new approaches to computing technology and find innovative uses for existing technology. They study and solve complex problems in computing for business, medicine, science, and other fields.	Master's degree	$114,520
Computer and Information Systems Managers	Computer and information systems managers, often called information technology (IT) managers or IT project managers, plan, coordinate, and direct computer-related activities in an organization. They help determine the information technology goals of an organization and are responsible for implementing computer systems to meet those goals.	Bachelor's degree	$139,220
Computer Network Architects	Computer network architects design and build data communication networks, including local area networks (LANs), wide area networks (WANs), and Intranets. These networks range from small connections between two offices to next-generation networking capabilities such as a cloud infrastructure that serves multiple customers.	Bachelor's degree	$104,650

OCCUPATION	JOB DUTIES	ENTRY-LEVEL EDUCATION	2017 MEDIAN PAY
Computer Programmers	Computer programmers write and test code that allows computer applications and software programs to function properly. They turn the program designs created by software developers and engineers into instructions that a computer can follow.	Bachelor's degree	$82,240
Computer Support Specialists	Computer support specialists provide help and advice to computer users and organizations. These specialists either support computer networks or they provide technical assistance directly to computer users.	High school diploma or equivalent (some companies require associate's or bachelor's degree)	$52,810
Computer Systems Analysts	Computer systems analysts, sometimes called systems architects, study an organization's current computer systems and procedures, and design solutions to help the organization operate more efficiently and effectively. They bring business and information technology (IT) together by understanding the needs and limitations of both.	Bachelor's degree	$88,270
Database Administrators	Database administrators (DBAs) use specialized software to store and organize data, such as financial information and customer shipping records. They make sure that data are available to users and secure from unauthorized access.	Bachelor's degree	$87,020
Network and Computer Systems Administrators	Computer networks are critical parts of almost every organization. Network and computer systems administrators are responsible for the day-to-day operation of these networks.	Bachelor's degree	$81,100

OCCUPATION	JOB DUTIES	ENTRY-LEVEL EDUCATION	2017 MEDIAN PAY
Software Developers	Software developers are the creative minds behind computer programs. Some develop the applications that allow people to do specific tasks on a computer or another device. Others develop the underlying systems that run the devices or that control networks.	Bachelor's degree	$103,560
Web Developers	Web developers design and create websites. They are responsible for the look of the site. They are also responsible for the site's technical aspects, such as its performance and capacity, which are measures of a website's speed and how much traffic the site can handle. In addition, web developers may create content for the site.	Associate's degree	$67,990

Famous First

The Fourth Amendment to the U.S. Constitute alludes to the right to privacy. This amendment can be traced back to English legal doctrine. In Semayne's case (1604), Sir Edward Coke stated: "The house of every one is to him as his castle and fortress, as well for his defence against injury and violence as for his repose." Semayne's Case acknowledged that the King did not have unrestricted authority to intrude on his subjects' dwellings, but did establish that government agents could conduct searches and seizures when their purpose was lawful and a warrant had been obtained.

Source: https://en.wikipedia.org/wiki/Fourth_Amendment_to_the_United_States_Constitution

Conversation With . . .

RYDER JEFFERSON MOSES

Vice President of Information Security
Electronic Payment Processor, Mid-Atlantic Region
IT, 32 years; Cybersecurity, 5 years

1. **What was your individual career path in terms of education/training, entry-level job, or other significant opportunity?**

I graduated with a biology degree in 1981 to limited employment opportunities, so I fixed computers and printers because I have good mechanical aptitude. I realized that what really grabbed my attention was networks, data transmission, and telecommunications carrier services between computers. This was before the internet. As my career in network engineering progressed, I experienced, first-hand, the evolution of data transmission protocols for both private and public (internet) networks.

I wound up working as a contractor on government networks, and decided to go back to school so I had the academic credentials to back up the work I'd been doing for 10 years. I got my master's in Telecommunications Management; today I would recommend a degree in information security, which wasn't available at that time.

I went on to work for a company that supports banks in the electronic payment processing industry. As that business grew—dramatically—and credit card processing migrated toward the internet, it became vulnerable to hackers who stole information to produce counterfeit credit cards. This was in the early 2000s, and the increased use of the internet gave rise to new encryption methods for data transmission. As I spent more time implementing encryption methods, I was working closely with people in the developing field of information security.

As encryption grew more sophisticated, the hackers became more sophisticated at uncovering vulnerabilities, which led to the creation of a security standard to force banks, merchants, and processors to improve data protection methods. In my most recent role, I helped explain to merchants the need to implement these measures to meet the Payment Card Industry Data Security Standards. I also helped merchants make changes to support chip-enabled payment cards.

2. **What are the most important skills and/or qualities for someone in your profession?**

Critical thinking skills, an analytical approach to risk assessment, and a fundamental understanding of cryptography and data transmissions protocols, because you need the ability to do an end-to-end assessment of the data processing environment. Also, you need a clean background check with no arrests and an absolute dedication to integrity. You aren't going to get a join information security if potential employers have any reason to suspect they can't trust you.

3. What do you wish you had known going into this profession?

The fact that you will be on call 24/7, 365 days because you need to drop whatever you're doing and devote all your attention to any kind of data compromise. I once left a company meeting to help decode transaction data in real time after a guy who'd just gotten out of jail for committing credit card fraud stole a dial-up terminal and started doing fraudulent credit card transactions from his house. I was on a conference call with law enforcement sitting in a van across from his house as I manually decoded his fraudulent transactions so they could catch him in the act.

4. Are there many job opportunities in your profession? In what specific areas?

Definitely. Every merchant who accepts credit and debit cards needs technical personnel to assess vulnerabilities and implement measures to protect themselves, the cardholders, and the banks. Many industries face growing information security requirements, including banks, electronic funds processing companies, stock brokerages, hospitals, government agencies, and colleges.

5. How do you see your profession changing in the next five years, and what skills will be required?

In this business, the technology—and the use of technology by the bad guys—evolves at a rapid pace. You have to constantly update your knowledge and skills, and continuously monitor systems and networks for emerging trends in vulnerability exploitation.

6. What do you enjoy most about your job? What do you enjoy least about your job?

I enjoy the satisfaction of knowing I'm helping to protect financial data and reduce the risk of financial losses to cardholders, merchants, and banks. I also enjoy explaining very technical security requirements in terms that everyone can understand. This field pays well, and I enjoy that.

I don't like being on call. I don't like security breaches, and the stress levels associated with protecting the country's commerce infrastructure while knowing that information security is only effective until the bad guys find another vulnerability to exploit.

7. **Can you suggest a valuable "try this" for students considering a career in your profession?**

Internships are a great way to learn about networks and data transmission technologies. There's also, certainly, a lot of information online. Look into things like Cisco router training. Also, the military is worth considering because they have training opportunities due to the critical requirements for keeping data secure.

This conversation was originally published in Careers in Information Technology *(Salem) 2016.*

Conversation With . . .
GREGORY WHITE, PhD

Cybersecurity director, 15 years

Gregory White is the director of the Center for Infrastructure Assurance and Security for the University of Texas in San Antonio, Texas.

1. What was your individual career path in terms of education/training, entry-level job, or other significant opportunity?

When I went to Brigham Young University (BYU) in Provo, Utah, I thought I was going to be a medical doctor. This had been my thought since middle school, even though my father had taught me FORTRAN on an old teletype machine back in fifth grade. He was rooting for computer science because he knew I liked it.

At BYU, I was automatically put into the pre-med chemistry track. It turned out chemistry and I did not get along. At age seventeen, away from home for the first time, I did not realize I could switch to a microbiology track because I did not talk to an academic advisor. I changed majors two more times before I ended up going into computer programming and earning a bachelor of science in computer science. It turned out my father was right.

An ROTC scholarship paid for my last two years of college. I entered the Air Force upon graduation and, after four years doing computer programming, they sent me to get a master's degree in computer engineering at the Air Force Institute of Technology in Dayton, Ohio. My thesis was on artificial intelligence and war gaming. I was then sent to San Antonio where the Air Force was forming a new computer security office.

At the time I went into computer security professionally, the internet was starting to appear. IBM personal computers had been introduced a few years earlier and people wanted to connect to others. The Air Force understood that its rules and regulations did not cover this new environment and intelligence sources were taking advantage of it.

The Morris Worm brought the Internet to its knees in 1988. After that, the people who tried to respond had a big meeting and from that came the computer emergency response team concept. I worked in the network security branch of the Air Force Cryptologic Support Center, which was part of the Air Force Electronic Security Command. I went on to advanced computer communication officer school, then to teach at the Air Force Academy where I helped introduce security into the curriculum. After a few years, the Air Force sent me for a PhD in computer science at Texas A&M. My dissertation was in security intrusion detection. I went back to the academy and was responsible for creating its first undergraduate information warfare lab.

After nineteen years, I separated from the Air Force and went into the reserves. An opportunity had arisen to work in San Antonio with colleagues who created SecureLogix, Corp. I was vice president of services and chief technical officer there, and I also began teaching at UT San Antonio. An effort was underway to establish a cybersecurity program here. I came to the university fulltime in the fall of 2001.

Some of the things we are trying to teach people today are the same things we were trying to convince folks of twenty or more years ago. The natural thing for a computer scientist to do is to look at the problem of cybersecurity from a technical standpoint—all you need to do is build a secure system—but it's not just a technical problem.

Security is prevention, detection, and response. You have to assume the attackers are going to try to get in and it is critical to detect and respond. Our center has a big focus on helping communities and small and medium businesses understand what they need to be doing. That's a weak link. I guarantee there's a utility company somewhere in this country that is not protected.

On the education side, we have to start a culture of security. When I grew up, we knew that Smokey wanted us to prevent fires and McGruff told me to take a bite out of crime. Nobody is telling kids to take a bite out of cybercrime.

2. What are the most important skills and/or qualities for someone in your profession?

Intellectual curiosity. Someone who takes apart the phone. Bonus points if you can get it back together and it works. I need someone who says, "I wonder what would happen if…?"

3. What do you wish you had known going into this position?

This is not a job where you are going to get a degree and rest on your laurels. This field changes very quickly.

4. Are there many job opportunities in your profession? In what specific areas?

Many. The estimate of open security positions by 2023, depending on what study you read, ranges from a few hundred thousand to two million. Those are unfilled positions worldwide.

5. How do you see your profession changing in the next five years? How will technology impact that change, and what skills will be required?

Any time new technology is introduced you have to be on top of it because there will be security flaws and issues. It takes a lot of time; you must constantly read, go to conferences, and take classes. This will continue. Here at my center, we believe that we do not just need a larger security workforce; we need security in the workforce. Everybody needs to know his or her responsibilities.

6. What do you enjoy most about your job? What do you enjoy least about your job?

I like it because it does not get boring. There are times when it would be nice to slow down a little.

7. Can you suggest a valuable "try this" for students considering a career in your profession?

We produce something here called Cyber Threat Defender, designed to give people a basic understanding of cybersecurity. Find it at cyberthreatdefender.com. I also would encourage middle or high school students to participate in the CyberPatriot competition, which you can learn about at uscyberpatriot.org.

MORE INFORMATION

For more information about computer careers, visit

**Association for Computing
Machinery**
https://www.acm.org/

IEEE Computer Society
https://www.computer.org/

**Computing Research
Association**
https://cra.org/

For information about opportunities for women pursuing information
technology careers, visit

**National Center for Women &
Information Technology**
https://www.ncwit.org/

Sources

Bureau of Labor Statistics, U.S. Department of Labor, *Occupational Outlook Handbook*, Information Security
Analysts.

Occupational Health and Safety Specialists and Technicians

Snapshot

2017 Median Pay: $67,720 per year, $32.56 per hour
Typical Entry-Level Education: Bachelor's degree (specialist), High school diploma or equivalent (technician)
Work Experience in a Related Occupation: None
On-the-job Training: Moderate-term on-the-job training or combination of related work experience and training
Number of Jobs, 2016: 101,800
Job Outlook, 2016-26: 8% (As fast as average)
Employment Change, 2016-26: 8,600

CAREER OVERVIEW

What Occupational Health and Safety Specialists and Technicians Do

Occupational health and safety specialists inspect workplaces for adherence to regulations on safety, health, and the environment. They collect data on and analyze many types of work environments and work procedures. Specialists inspect workplaces for adherence to regulations on safety, health, and the environment. Technicians work with specialists in conducting tests and measuring hazards to help prevent harm to workers, property, the environment, and the general public.

Duties

Occupational health and safety specialists and technicians typically do the following:

- Inspect, test, and evaluate workplace environments, equipment, and practices to ensure that they follow safety standards and government regulations
- Prepare written reports on their findings
- Design and implement workplace processes and procedures that help protect workers from hazardous work conditions
- Evaluate programs on workplace health and safety
- Educate employers and workers about workplace safety by preparing and providing training programs
- Demonstrate the correct use of safety equipment
- Investigate incidents and accidents to identify what caused them and how they might be prevented

Occupational health and safety specialists examine the workplace for environmental or physical factors that could affect employee health, safety, comfort, and performance. They may examine factors such as lighting, equipment, materials, and ventilation. Technicians may check to make sure that workers are using required protective gear, such as masks and hardhats.

Some develop and conduct employee safety and training programs. These programs cover a range of topics, such as how to use safety equipment correctly and how to respond in an emergency.

WORK ENVIRONMENT

Occupational health and safety technicians often work with complex equipment to test and evaluate workplace environments and equipment.

Occupational health and safety specialists held about 83,700 jobs in 2016. The largest employers of occupational health and safety specialists were as follows:

Government	26%
Manufacturing	15
Construction	8
Management, scientific, and technical consulting services	6
Hospitals; state, local, and private	4

Occupational health and safety technicians held about 18,100 jobs in 2016. The largest employers of occupational health and safety technicians were as follows:

Government	17%
Manufacturing	15
Construction	9
Management, scientific, and technical consulting services	8
Hospitals; state, local, and private	7

Occupational health and safety specialists and technicians work in a variety of settings, such as offices or factories. Their jobs often involve considerable fieldwork and travel. They may be exposed to strenuous, dangerous, or stressful conditions. They use gloves, helmets, respirators, and other personal protective and safety equipment to minimize the risk of illness and injury.

Work Schedules

Most occupational health and safety specialists and technicians work full time. Some may work weekends or irregular hours in emergencies.

HOW TO BECOME AN OCCUPATIONAL HEALTH AND SAFETY SPECIALIST OR TECHNICIAN

Specialists and technicians carry out and evaluate programs on workplace safety and health.

Occupational health and safety specialists typically need a bachelor's degree in occupational health and safety or in a related scientific or technical field. Occupational health and safety technicians typically enter the occupation through one of two paths: on-the-job training or postsecondary education, such as an associate's degree or certificate.

Education

Occupational health and safety specialists typically need a bachelor's degree in occupational health and safety or a related scientific or technical field, such as engineering, biology, or chemistry. For some positions, a master's degree in industrial hygiene, health physics, or a related subject is required. In addition to science courses, typical courses include ergonomics, writing and communications, occupational safety management, and accident prevention.

Employers typically require technicians to have at least a high school diploma. High school students interested in this occupation should complete courses in English, mathematics, chemistry, biology, and physics.

Some employers prefer to hire technicians who have earned an associate's degree or certificate from a community college or vocational school. These programs typically take 2 years or less. They include courses in respiratory protection, hazard communication, and material-handling and storage procedures.

Important Qualities

Ability to use technology. Occupational health and safety specialists and technicians must be able to use advanced technology. They often work with complex testing equipment.

Communication skills. Occupational health and safety specialists and technicians must be able to communicate safety instructions and concerns to employees and managers. They frequently prepare written reports and prepare and deliver safety training to other workers.

Detail oriented. Occupational health and safety specialists and technicians need to understand and follow safety standards and complex government regulations.

Physical stamina. Occupational health and safety specialists and technicians must be able to stand for long periods and be able to travel regularly. Some work in environments that can be uncomfortable, such as tunnels or mines.

Problem-solving skills. Occupational health and safety specialists and technicians must be able to solve problems in order to design and implement workplace processes and procedures that help protect workers from hazardous conditions.

Licenses, Certifications, and Registrations

Although certification is voluntary, many employers encourage it. Certification is available through several organizations, depending on the field in which the specialists work. Specialists must have graduated from an accredited educational program and have work experience to be eligible to take most certification exams. To keep their certification, specialists usually are required to complete periodic continuing education.

Occupational safety and health specialists and technicians can earn professional certifications including the following:

The Board of Certified Safety Professionals offers the following certifications:

- Certified Safety Professional (CSP) certification
- Associate Safety Professional (ASP)
- Occupational Health and Safety Technologist (OHST)
- Construction Health and Safety Technician (CHST)

The American Board of Industrial Hygiene awards a certification known as a Certified Industrial Hygienist (CIH)

Training

Occupational health and safety technicians usually receive on-the-job training. They learn about specific laws and inspection procedures, and learn to conduct tests and recognize hazards. The length of training varies with the employee's level of experience, education, and industry in which he or she works.

Some technicians enter the occupation through a combination of related work experience and training. They may take on health and safety tasks at the company where they are employed. For example, an employee may volunteer to complete annual workstation inspections for an office in which he or she already works.

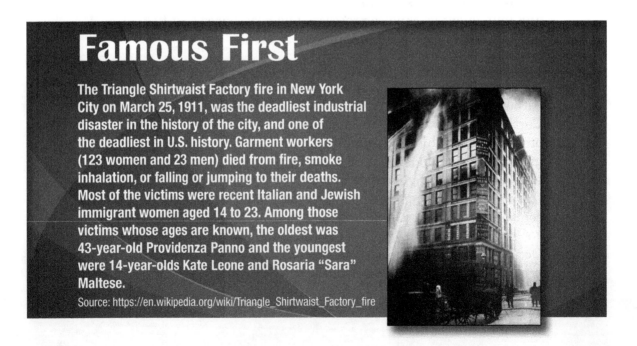

Famous First

The Triangle Shirtwaist Factory fire in New York City on March 25, 1911, was the deadliest industrial disaster in the history of the city, and one of the deadliest in U.S. history. Garment workers (123 women and 23 men) died from fire, smoke inhalation, or falling or jumping to their deaths. Most of the victims were recent Italian and Jewish immigrant women aged 14 to 23. Among those victims whose ages are known, the oldest was 43-year-old Providenza Panno and the youngest were 14-year-olds Kate Leone and Rosaria "Sara" Maltese.

Source: https://en.wikipedia.org/wiki/Triangle_Shirtwaist_Factory_fire

WAGES

Median annual wages, May 2017

Occupational health and safety specialists: $71,780

Occupational health and safety specialists and technicians: $67,720

Other healthcare practitioners and technical occupations: $60,710

Occupational health and safety technicians: $49,960

Total, all occupations: $37,690

Note: All Occupations includes all occupations in the U.S. Economy. Source: U.S. Bureau of Labor Statistics, Occupational Employment Statistics

The median annual wage for occupational health and safety specialists was $71,780 in May 2017. The lowest 10 percent earned less than $41,670, and the highest 10 percent earned more than $105,840.

The median annual wage for occupational health and safety technicians was $49,960 in May 2017. The lowest 10 percent earned less than $31,650, and the highest 10 percent earned more than $82,190.

In May 2017, the median annual wages for occupational health and safety specialists in the top industries in which they worked were as follows:

Hospitals; state, local, and private	$73,270
Manufacturing	72,590
Construction	71,370
Government	69,530
Management, scientific, and technical consulting services	66,550

In May 2017, the median annual wages for occupational health and safety technicians in the top industries in which they worked were as follows:

Construction	$57,580
Government	49,960
Manufacturing	47,880
Hospitals; state, local, and private	45,120
Management, scientific, and technical consulting services	44,130

Most occupational health and safety specialists and technicians work full time. Some specialists may work weekends or irregular hours in emergencies.

JOB OUTLOOK

Percent change in employment, projected 2016-26

Other healthcare practitioners and technical occupations: 12%

Occupational health and safety technicians: 10%

Occupational health and safety specialists and technicians: 8%

Occupational health and safety specialists: 8%

Total, all occupations: 7%

Note: All Occupations includes all occupations in the U.S. Economy. Source: U.S. Bureau of Labor Statistics, Employment Projections program

Employment of occupational health and safety specialists is projected to grow 8 percent from 2016 to 2026, about as fast as the average for all occupations. Employment of occupational health and safety technicians is projected to grow 10 percent from 2016 to 2026, faster than the average for all occupations.

Specialists and technicians will be needed to work in a variety of industries and government agencies to ensure that employers are adhering to both existing and new regulations. In addition, specialists will be necessary because insurance costs and workers' compensation costs have become a concern for many employers and insurance companies. An aging population is remaining in the workforce longer than past generations did, and older workers usually have a greater proportion of workers' compensation claims.

Job Prospects

Applicants for jobs as occupational health and safety specialists or technicians with a background in the sciences, experience in more than one area of health and safety, or certification will have the best prospects.

Employment projections data for Occupational health and safety specialists and technicians, 2016-26

Occupational Title	SOC Code	Employment, 2016	Projected Employment, 2026	Change, 2016-26	
				Percent	Numeric
Occupational health and safety specialists and technicians	29-9010	101,800	110,400	8	8,600
Occupational health and safety specialists	29-9011	83,700	90,500	8	6,800
Occupational health and safety technicians	29-9012	18,100	19,900	10	1,800

Source: Bureau of Labor Statistics, Employment Projections program

OCCUPATION	JOB DUTIES	ENTRY-LEVEL EDUCATION	2017 MEDIAN PAY
Health and Safety Engineers	Health and safety engineers develop procedures and design systems to protect people from illness and injury and property from damage. They combine knowledge of engineering and of health and safety to make sure that chemicals, machinery, software, furniture, and other products will not cause harm to people or damage to property.	Bachelor's degree	$88,510
Environmental Science and Protection Technicians	Environmental science and protection technicians monitor the environment and investigate sources of pollution and contamination, including those affecting public health.	Associate's degree	$45,490

MORE INFORMATION

For more information about credentialing in industrial hygiene, visit

American Board of Industrial Hygiene   http://www.abih.org/

For more information about occupations in safety, a list of safety and related academic programs, and credentialing, visit

Board of Certified Safety Professionals
https://www.bcsp.org/

For more information about occupational health and safety, visit

U.S. Department of Labor, Occupational Safety and Health Administration (OSHA)
https://www.osha.gov/

Centers for Disease Control and Prevention, National Institute for Occupational Safety and Health (NIOSH)
https://www.cdc.gov/niosh/

To find job openings for occupational health and safety positions in the federal government, visit

USAJOBS
https://www.usajobs.gov/

Sources

Bureau of Labor Statistics, U.S. Department of Labor, *Occupational Outlook Handbook*, Occupational Health and Safety Specialists and Technicians.

Police and Detectives

Snapshot

2017 Median Pay: $62,960 per year, $30.27 per hour

Typical Entry-Level Education: High school diploma or equivalent (police), Bachelor's degree (fish and game wardens), Bachelor's degree (federal agencies)

Work Experience in a Related Occupation: PPolice officer (detective), 3 years of professional work experience in areas ranging from computer science to accounting (FBI special agent)

On-the-job Training: Moderate-term on-the-job training

Number of Jobs, 2016: 807,000

Job Outlook, 2016-26: 7% (As fast as average)

Employment Change, 2016-26: 53,400

CAREER OVERVIEW

What Police and Detectives Do

Police officers, detectives, and game wardens enforce laws to protect people and their property. Detectives and criminal investigators, who are sometimes called *agents* or *special agents*, gather facts and collect evidence of possible crimes.

Duties

Police officers, detectives, and criminal investigators typically do the following:

- Respond to emergency and nonemergency calls
- Patrol assigned areas
- Conduct traffic stops and issue citations
- Search for vehicle records and warrants using computers in the field
- Obtain warrants and arrest suspects
- Collect and secure evidence from crime scenes
- Observe the activities of suspects
- Write detailed reports and fill out forms
- Prepare cases and testify in court

Job duties differ by employer and function, but all police and detectives write reports and keep detailed records that will be needed if they testify in court. Most carry law enforcement tools, such as radios, handcuffs, and guns.

The following are examples of types of police and detectives:

Detectives and criminal investigators are uniformed or plainclothes investigators who gather facts and collect evidence for criminal cases. They conduct interviews, examine records, observe the activities of suspects, and participate in raids and arrests. Detectives usually specialize in investigating one type of crime, such as homicide or fraud. Detectives are typically assigned cases on a rotating basis and work on them until an arrest and trial are completed or until the case is dropped.

Fish and game wardens enforce fishing, hunting, and boating laws. They patrol fishing and hunting areas, conduct search and rescue operations, investigate complaints and accidents, and educate the public about laws pertaining to the outdoors. Federal fish and game wardens are often referred to as Federal Wildlife Officers.

Police and sheriff's patrol officers are the most common type of police and detectives, and have general law enforcement duties. They wear uniforms that allow the public to easily recognize them as police officers. They have regular patrols and also respond to emergency and nonemergency calls. During patrols, officers look for signs of criminal activity and may conduct searches and arrest suspected criminals.

Some police officers work only on a specific type of crime, such as narcotics. Officers, especially those working in large departments, may work in special units, such as horseback, motorcycle, canine corps, and special weapons and tactics (SWAT). Typically, officers must work as patrol officers for a certain number of years before they may be appointed to a special unit.

Transit and railroad police patrol railroad yards and transit stations. They protect property, employees, and passengers from crimes such as thefts and robberies. They remove trespassers from railroad and transit properties and check IDs of people who try to enter secure areas.

WORK ENVIRONMENT

Police and detectives held about 807,000 jobs in 2016. Employment in the detailed occupations that make up police and detectives was distributed as follows:

Police and sheriff's patrol officers	684,200
Detectives and criminal investigators	110,900
Fish and game wardens	7,000
Transit and railroad police	4,900

The largest employers of police and detectives were as follows:

Local government, excluding education and hospitals	78%
State government, excluding education and hospitals	11
Federal government	7
Educational services; state, local, and private	3

Police and detective work can be physically demanding, stressful, and dangerous. Officers must be alert and ready to react throughout their entire shift. Officers regularly work at crime and accident scenes and encounter suffering and the results of violence. Although a career in law enforcement may be stressful, many officers find it rewarding to help members of their communities.

Some federal agencies, such as the Federal Bureau of Investigation and U.S. Secret Service, require extensive travel, often on short notice. These agents may relocate a number of times over the course of their careers. Some special agents, such as U.S. Border Patrol agents, may work outdoors in rugged terrain and in all kinds of weather.

Injuries and Illnesses

Police and sheriff's patrol officers and transit and railroad police have some of the highest rates of injuries and illnesses of all occupations. They may face physical injuries during conflicts with criminals and other high-risk situations.

Work Schedules

Police and detectives usually work full time. Paid overtime is common, and shift work is necessary because the public must be protected at all times.

HOW TO BECOME A POLICE OFFICER OR DETECTIVE

Police and detectives must use good judgment and have strong communication skills when gathering facts about a crime.

Education requirements range from a high school diploma to a college degree. Most police and detectives must graduate from their agency's training academy before completing a period of on-the-job training. Candidates must be U.S. citizens, usually at least 21 years old, and able to meet rigorous physical and personal qualification standards. A felony conviction or drug use may disqualify a candidate.

Education

Police and detective applicants must have at least a high school diploma or equivalent, although many federal agencies and some police departments require some college coursework or a college degree. Many community colleges, 4-year colleges, and universities offer programs in law enforcement and criminal justice. Knowledge of a foreign language is an asset in many federal agencies and geographical regions.

Fish and game wardens typically need a bachelor's degree; desirable fields of study include wildlife science, biology, or natural resources management.

Federal agencies such as the Federal Bureau of Investigation also typically require prospective detectives and investigators to have a bachelor's degree.

Many applicants for entry-level police jobs have taken some college classes, and a significant number are college graduates.

Training

Candidates for appointment usually attend a training academy before becoming an officer. Training includes classroom instruction in state and local laws and constitutional law, civil rights, and police ethics. Recruits also receive training and supervised experience in areas such as patrol, traffic control, firearm use, self-defense, first aid, and emergency response.

Federal law enforcement agents undergo extensive training, usually at the U.S. Marine Corps base in Quantico, Virginia, or at a Federal Law Enforcement Training Center.

Work Experience in a Related Occupation

Detectives normally begin their careers as police officers before being promoted to detective.

FBI special agent applicants typically must have at least 3 years of professional work experience in areas ranging from computer science to accounting.

Other Experience

Some police departments have cadet programs for people interested in a career in law enforcement who do not yet meet age requirements for becoming an officer. These cadets do clerical work and attend classes until they reach the minimum age requirement and can apply for a position with the regular force. Military or police experience may be considered beneficial for potential cadets.

Cadet candidates must be U.S. citizens, usually be at least 21 years old, have a driver's license, and meet specific physical qualifications. Applicants may have to pass physical exams of vision, hearing, strength, and agility, as well as written exams. Previous work or military experience is often seen as a plus. Candidates typically go through a series of interviews and may be asked to take lie detector and drug tests. A felony conviction may disqualify a candidate.

ADVANCEMENT

Police officers usually become eligible for promotion after a probationary period. Promotions to corporal, sergeant, lieutenant, and captain usually are made according to scores on a written examination and on-the-job performance. In large departments, promotion may enable an officer to become a detective or to specialize in one type of police work, such as working with juveniles.

Important Qualities

Communication skills. Police and detectives must be able to speak with people when gathering facts about a crime and to express details about a given incident in writing.

Empathy. Police officers need to understand the perspectives of a wide variety of people in their jurisdiction and have a willingness to help the public.

Good judgment. Police and detectives must be able to determine the best way to solve a wide array of problems quickly.

Leadership skills. Police officers must be comfortable with being a highly visible member of their community, as the public looks to them for assistance in emergency situations.

Perceptiveness. Officers, detectives, and fish and game wardens must be able to anticipate a person's reactions and understand why people act a certain way.

Physical stamina. Officers and detectives must be in good physical shape, both to pass required tests for entry into the field, and to keep up with the daily rigors of the job.

Physical strength. Police officers must be strong enough to physically apprehend offenders.

WAGES

Median annual wages, May 2017

Police and detectives: $62,960

Law enforcement workers: $54,520

Total, all occupations: $37,690

Note: All Occupations includes all occupations in the U.S. Economy. Source: U.S. Bureau of Labor Statistics, Occupational Employment Statistics

The median annual wage for police and detectives was $62,960 in May 2017. The lowest 10 percent earned less than $35,780, and the highest 10 percent earned more than $105,230.

Median annual wages for police and detectives in May 2017 were as follows:

Detectives and criminal investigators	$79,970
Transit and railroad police	70,280
Police and sheriff's patrol officers	61,050
Fish and game wardens	56,410

In May 2017, the median annual wages for police and detectives in the top industries in which they worked were as follows:

Federal government	$84,660
State government, excluding education and hospitals	65,880
Local government, excluding education and hospitals	61,340
Educational services; state, local, and private	52,080

Uniformed officers, detectives, agents, and wardens usually work full time. Paid overtime is common. Shift work is necessary because the public must be protected at all times.

Other Compensation and Benefits

Many agencies provide officers with an allowance for uniforms, as well as extensive benefits and the option to retire at an age that is younger than the typical retirement age. Some police departments offer additional pay for bilingual officers or those with college degrees.

Union Membership

Most police and detectives belonged to a union in 2016.

Fast Fact

The first female police officer in the United States was Marie Owens, who was a Chicago cop in the 1890s.

Source: Chicago Tribune.

Famous First

The pattern for modern police investigative work follows the pattern used to solve the murders committed by Jack the Ripper in London. A large team of policemen conducted house-to-house inquiries to gather forensic materials. Suspects were identified, traced, and either examined or eliminated from the inquiry. More than 2,000 people were interviewed, "upwards of 300" people were investigated, and 80 people were detained. The investigation was initially conducted by the Metropolitan Police Whitechapel (H) Division Criminal Investigation Department (CID) headed by Detective Inspector Edmund Reid. Detective Inspectors Frederick Abberline, Henry Moore, and Walter Andrews were sent from Central Office at Scotland Yard to assist.

Source: https://en.wikipedia.org/wiki/Jack_the_Ripper#Criminal_profiling

JOB OUTLOOK

Percent change in employment, projected 2016-26

Total, all occupations: 7%

Police and detectives: 7%

Law enforcement workers: 1%

Note: All Occupations includes all occupations in the U.S. Economy. Source: U.S. Bureau of Labor Statistics, Employment Projections program

Employment of police and detectives is projected to grow 7 percent from 2016 to 2026, about as fast as the average for all occupations.

While a continued desire for public safety is expected to result in a need for more officers, demand for employment is expected to vary depending on location, driven largely by local and state budgets. Even with crime rates falling in recent years, demand for police services to maintain and improve public safety is expected to continue.

Job Prospects

Job applicants may face competition because of relatively low rates of turnover. Applicants with a bachelor's degree and law enforcement or military experience, especially investigative experience, as well as those who speak more than one language, should have the best job opportunities.

Because the level of government spending determines the level of employment for police and detectives, the number of job opportunities can vary from year to year and from place to place.

Employment projections data for Police and detectives, 2016-26

Occupational Title	SOC Code	Employment, 2016	Projected Employment, 2026	Change, 2016-26	
				Percent	Numeric
Police and detectives	—	807,000	860,300	7	53,400
Detectives and criminal investigators	33-3021	110,900	115,900	5	5,000
Fish and game wardens	33-3031	7,000	7,300	4	300
Police and sheriff's patrol officers	33-3051	684,200	731,900	7	47,800
Transit and railroad police	33-3052	4,900	5,300	6	300

Source: Bureau of Labor Statistics, Employment Projections program

SIMILAR OCCUPATIONS

This table shows a list of occupations with job duties that are similar to those of police and detectives.

OCCUPATION	JOB DUTIES	ENTRY-LEVEL EDUCATION	2017 MEDIAN PAY
Correctional Officers and Bailiffs	Correctional officers are responsible for overseeing individuals who have been arrested and are awaiting trial or who have been sentenced to serve time in jail or prison. Bailiffs are law enforcement officers who maintain safety and order in courtrooms.	High school diploma or equivalent	$43,510
EMTs and Paramedics	Emergency medical technicians (EMTs) and paramedics care for the sick or injured in emergency medical settings. People's lives often depend on the quick reaction and competent care provided by these workers. EMTs and paramedics respond to emergency calls, performing medical services and transporting patients to medical facilities.	Postsecondary nondegree award	$33,380
Firefighters	Firefighters control and put out fires and respond to emergencies where life, property, or the environment is at risk.	Postsecondary nondegree award	$49,080
Private Detectives and Investigators	Private detectives and investigators search for information about legal, financial, and personal matters. They offer many services, such as verifying people's backgrounds and statements, finding missing persons, and investigating computer crimes.	High school diploma or equivalent	$50,700

OCCUPATION	JOB DUTIES	ENTRY-LEVEL EDUCATION	2017 MEDIAN PAY
Probation Officers and Correctional Treatment Specialists	Probation officers and correctional treatment specialists provide social services to assist in rehabilitation of law offenders in custody or on probation or parole.	Bachelor's degree	$51,410
Security Guards and Gaming Surveillance Officers	Security guards and gaming surveillance officers patrol and protect property against theft, vandalism, and other illegal activity.	High school diploma or equivalent	$26,960
Emergency Management Directors	Emergency management directors prepare plans and procedures for responding to natural disasters or other emergencies. They also help lead the response during and after emergencies, often in coordination with public safety officials, elected officials, nonprofit organizations, and government agencies.	Bachelor's degree	$72,760
Forensic Science Technicians	Forensic science technicians aid criminal investigations by collecting and analyzing evidence. Many technicians specialize in various types of laboratory analysis.	Bachelor's degree	$57,850
Fire Inspectors	Fire inspectors examine buildings in order to detect fire hazards and ensure that federal, state, and local fire codes are met. Fire investigators, another type of worker in this field, determine the origin and cause of fires and explosions. Forest fire inspectors and prevention specialists assess outdoor fire hazards in public and residential areas.	Postsecondary educational program for emergency medical technicians (EMTs) High school diploma or equivalent (forest fire inspectors and prevention specialists)	$56,670

Conversation With . . .
JAMAAL LITTLEJOHN

Homicide detective, 5 years

Jamal Littlejohn is a homicide detective in the police department of Fayetteville, North Carolina.

1. What was your individual career path in terms of education/training, entry-level job, or other significant opportunity?

My father was active duty in the U.S. Army and my mother worked for Womack Army Medical Center at Fort Bragg, NC, as a licensed practical nurse. Growing up the only son of three children, I was my father's number one fan. I admired his work ethic and dedication to the military and our family. After completing only one semester at Fayetteville State University, I joined the Army Reserves in December 2007.

I attended basic training and AIT (Advanced Individual Training) in Fort Leonard Wood, Missouri, then entered the Military Police Corps in May 2008.During my first year as a reservist, I worked with a unit on Fort Bragg where we served garrison support for the military police units. During monthly drills and three weeks of annual training, I served as a military police officer.

In July 2009, I applied for and was accepted to the Fayetteville Police Academy in North Carolina. My wife and I had discussed the pros and cons of my becoming a police officer. A deciding factor was to put myself in a position to impact people of the community where I grew up. After graduating, I completed fourteen weeks of field training, which consisted of on-the-road training with an experienced office where I learned how to effectively enforce state law and interact with citizens.

I made a personal decision to work as a patrol officer for at least five years before transitioning to another unit within the department because I felt that would put me in a position to see and experience different incidents. It has always been my opinion that if I perfected my job at the lowest level, I would perform higher as I moved through the ranks.

In March 2015, I transferred to work as a detective in the aggravated assault unit and worked cases where citizens were victims of violent felony assaults. During this time, I used the communication skills I had perfected as a patrol officer to interview witnesses and suspects. After only five months in the aggravated assault unit, I transferred to the homicide unit, where I have worked for four years.

Numerous schools and training events helped me better serve the community while working death investigations. These include a general investigations course and PLI (Police Law Institute), as well as Vernon Geberth's Practical Homicide and Advanced Practical Homicide courses. Also, I have attended conferences as a member of the North Carolina Homicide Investigators Association.

I have been lead investigator on approximately seventeen homicide cases, and assisted on more than seventy-five. The unit has had only one unsolved homicide since December 2015.

2. What are the most important skills and/or qualities for someone in your profession?

Basic communication skills. On a daily basis, a homicide detective meets people on their worst days. You have to be able to show empathy and patience for the family because they just lost a loved one while also gathering pertinent information to solve the case for them. Depending on the circumstances surrounding a death, I have experienced family and friends withhold information to protect the deceased love one. It is important to make family, friends, and witnesses feel comfortable enough to give all the necessary information to solve the case as swiftly and efficiently as possible.

3. What do you wish you had known going into this profession?

How much one positive or negative contact with someone could change the way people view the entire profession. I was raised to treat everyone equally, and I carry that in my job. I am able to communicate with victims, witnesses, and suspects on the same level. My job as a patrol officer became harder after national incidents such as the shootings of Trayvon Martin and Michael Brown. Those and similar incidents changed people's opinions and made the way many people viewed law enforcement worse.

Growing up, I had very few positive experiences with local police officers. As a child, my older sister was approached by an officer as she walked with me from her friend's house. The officer asked my sister, who was sixteen at the time, "Do you want to get locked up?" I remember being angry; I was only five years old. As a teenager, I believed law enforcement officers could show up and conduct "regular business" because they felt like it and do this without any explanation to those they encountered. But, sitting and learning about why police officers did certain things was a life changer during my training to become one.

Now, even as a homicide detective, I spend the early part of some investigations building trust in order to move the case forward. That becomes easy with effective communication and sticking by my word. Along with other members of the homicide unit, I never make unrealistic promises to people. But, we do promise to put 100% into the investigation and provide answers to the families we serve.

4. Are there many job opportunities in your profession? In what specific areas?

One can work as a patrol officer or study to be promoted to detective where job opportunities include investigating property, robberies, or even juvenile and sex crimes. However, there are also numerous opportunities to work in law enforcement and investigate crimes on the federal level with the FBI, Secret Service, DEA, and others.

5. **How do you see your profession changing in the next five years? How will technology impact that change, and what skills will be required?**

I can only imagine how much technology could change my job. For instance, over the last four years in my unit, we have learned to identify suspects using phone records and social media. Those records also assisted detectives by tracking the current and previous locations of the victim and/or suspect.

6. **What do you enjoy most about your job? What do you enjoy least about your job?**

Mainly what I enjoy is solving cases and getting justice for the families affected. The real satisfaction, for me, comes in court when the suspect either is convicted or pleads guilty to the crimes committed.

I least enjoy the long hours we work. As seen on television, the first forty-eight hours of an investigation are the most important when it comes to finding a lead on the case. There is usually no pause or break for the first fifteen to twenty hours of a case. On multiple occasions, there have been times I have worked 20+ hours and gotten off work just to be called in for another investigation.

7. **Can you suggest a valuable "try this" for students considering a career in your profession?**

Volunteer at a local police department.Most have a ride along program where students can apply to ride with a patrol officer for a shift to see what the job is like on a daily basis. Internships within most departments are also available for college students.

Conversation With . . .
JEFF LEDFORD

Chief of Police
Law Enforcement, 26 years

Jamal Littlejohn is a homicide detective in the police department of Fayetteville, Jeff Ledford is the Chief of Police for the Shelby Police Department in Shelby, North Carolina.

1. What was your individual career path in terms of education/training, entry-level job, or other significant opportunity?

My first official training in law enforcement was in the police academy, specifically Basic Law Enforcement Training (BLET) at Gaston College in Dallas, NC. I chose law enforcement because I was drawn to the community service part of the job. I wanted to help people regardless of their issues.

After graduating, the Shelby Police Department hired me, and I began my career as all new recruits do, in the patrol division. I took several training classes to grow as an officer, such as radar operator, how to use breath alcohol testing instruments, and comparison and blood spatter analysis. Sometimes, veteran officers not only told me how to handle a situation better, but also showed me. I believe that much of the success I have had is directly attributed to those who helped me learn in my younger years.

As I progressed though my career, I realized that to excel I would need to pursue academics. I completed my bachelor's degree in criminal justice through University of Columbia and Gardner-Webb University.

I served as my agency's first full-time crime scene technician for several years in the patrol division, before a promotion to sergeant. Then, I served in administration as well as criminal investigations. Next, I became a lieutenant with the Problem Solving Unit, overseeing that and the Vice/Narcotics Unit. I was then promoted to the rank of captain as the Operations Commander, overseeing Shelby police's Patrol Division.

In 2004, my current chief retired and during the transition of preparing for a new chief, I was appointed as our agency's interim chief. This gave me an insight into the role's duties and helped me decide if that was a role I wanted someday. I knew I wanted to be chief but at the time, I felt too young and needed more experience.

I was selected Chief of Police for Shelby in 2008. I was honored. Every experience and training opportunity I had helped me to be successful in my current role.

2. What are the most important skills and/or qualities for someone in your profession?

One of the most important: humility. Focus on "who" you are more than "what" you are. While you lead the organization, you will only be able to lead people if they respect you. Realizing you are just like the other officers in your organization, but with a different set of responsibilities, will take you a long way.

Another important quality: relating to people. Leading an organization is predominately taking care of people and will help you more than anything as a leader. Being able to take care of people mindfully will help more than anything in a leadership role. Taking time every day to ensure the people you are responsible for are doing well and meeting all of their needs is important. It is fitting to say that if a person interacting with the public is not in a good place or has something bothering him/her, the service they deliver will not be the best it can be.

A final quality is being a cheerleader. While this sounds like an odd quality to have, it fits! Your job is to lead your organization and promote your agency in the best possible light to your staff and the community. You must always keep your staff upbeat and excited about their jobs because when they meet customers on the street, they will portray a positive image.

Also, keep the community excited about its police force. You must convey to the public that they are safe. Through good and bad times, they can rely on officers to take care of them, providing services they need.

3. What do you wish you had known going into this profession?

If people told me the things I would face when I was new to the profession, I would not have believed them. Some things you just have to experience for yourself. For example, if someone told me twenty years ago that law enforcement would have to work to keep up its public perception and acceptance, I would not have believed it.

However, I wish I had known how much the experienced people around would teach me. I was fortunate to have a lot of great people around me as I progressed through my career. The people who paved the way for all of us are a wealth of information. One lesson I learned was if you take care of your officers and staff inside the building, they will take care of the customer outside the building.

Also, I wish I had known the job's impact on my family. I have a wife, a son, and a daughter. My children are growing up in the era of social media, which means they have heard and read some really bad things about officers. Neither of them has ever really mentioned it to me, but I know it has to be hard on them. My wife deals with my job pulling me in different directions, but she also deals with walking me out every day knowing I may not return. It has to be difficult to be married to an officer. Families deserve as much credit as the officers.

Being chief, my family has to share me with the entire city of more than 20,000 people. Everyone expects you to be at his or her events and simultaneously, you have a family who expects you to make time for them, too. Time commitment is one of the biggest challenges for a chief and something everyone should discuss it with his or her family before accepting the position.

4. Are there many job opportunities in your profession? In what specific areas?

Turnover in law enforcement is becoming more of an issue. Agencies are looking for qualified people who have the drive and commitment to do the jobs. Finding people who are looking for a career helping others while understanding the dangers involved is becoming more difficult. Social media and the news often highlight the negative side of law enforcement, which could turn people away. Also, there are shows about law enforcement portraying it as a fun and low stress job. An applicant needs to look deeper into the profession before making that commitment.

The positions available include being a K9 officer, detective, vice agent to a traffic officer, or a state or federal government agent. State jobs include highway patrol, state investigator, or even North Carolina Wildlife Resources Commission. Federal jobs could range from being an FBI agent to a U.S. Marshal.

5. How do you see your profession changing in the next five years? How will technology impact that change, and what skills will be required?

We have seen more technology implemented over the past several years, a continuing trend. Many companies now offer products allowing us to do our jobs more efficiently and effectively through technology.

One of the biggest changes we have seen in our profession is social media, a great tool for law enforcement. We tell our story, connect with people, and inform people of an emergency or an event instantly. As an agency, we promote what we are doing and show people what we do that may not receive news coverage.

Social media can help us and be detrimental. Oftentimes, people will have limited facts or a tainted view of something and put it out. This can cause chaos and is something we have to be mindful of at all times. Officers now do their jobs every day knowing they are being filmed and reported on. Social media is here to stay, so we must change how we do business and learn to work with the medium to the agency's and public's benefit.

6. What do you enjoy most about your job? What do you enjoy least about your job?

Interacting with people in the department or the community and getting to know people and be part of their lives. Knowing I have impacted their lives in some small way is very rewarding, whether walking through a community and meeting people on their front porches or being around our headquarters and having a conversation with a member of our staff about his or her latest family vacation.

What I enjoy least is seeing tragedy and loss of life. Through the years, I have seen many young lives taken as a result of senseless violence. Nothing is harder than having to tell a parent their child is not coming home. No matter what the circumstance is, it never gets easier and each story is unique in its own way.

Tragedy and loss of life is not just confined to the community. In 2016, our agency was dealt the worst blow. We lost one of our own to violence—a K9 officer who served our city for more than 10 years. As a chief, it is the worst possible scenario you can face. While I always knew this could happen, I was not prepared to receive that call. To this day, we are dealing with the effects both mentally and as an agency. As chief, I realize each member of our organization is my responsibility. Losing one of them is a feeling of failure that cannot be described. It is something you have to learn to put into perspective and deal with every day while keeping your focus on taking care of the agency. It will change you, but only you can control in what way that change impacts you.

7. Can you suggest a valuable "try this" for students considering a career in your profession?

Research what the job truly entails. Do not consider TV show portrayals or the perceptions on the news or social media. Ask your local agencies if they have a ride-along program where you can ride and talk with an officer first-hand about what the job is like.

Secondly, remember all agencies conduct very thorough background investigations. Young people will make mistakes; it is a part of growing up. However, the decisions a young person makes can affect them for years to come. It is hard to deal with peer pressure, but knowing you are looking for a career in public service is a good incentive to make sure every decision you make takes you one step closer to that goal.

Lastly, find out what the job is about. Understand the risks involved, the lifestyle, and the impact it can have on your family. I truly believe law enforcement is the noblest profession in the world. To serve your community and protect those who cannot protect themselves is a feeling of accomplishment that cannot be described. It takes a special person to serve in law enforcement, and we will need people to continue to protect our cities, our states, and our country. We are always looking for the right people who are sometimes described as "the best of the best."

MORE INFORMATION

For more information about federal law enforcement, visit

Bureau of Alcohol, Tobacco, Firearms and Explosives
https://www.atf.gov/

Drug Enforcement Administration
https://www.dea.gov/

Federal Bureau of Investigation
https://www.fbi.gov/

U.S. Customs and Border Protection
https://www.cbp.gov/

U.S. Department of Homeland Security
https://www.dhs.gov/

U.S. Fish & Wildlife Service
https://www.fws.gov/

U.S. Marshals Service
https://www.usmarshals.gov/

U.S. Secret Service
https://www.secretservice.gov/

Sources

Bureau of Labor Statistics, U.S. Department of Labor, *Occupational Outlook Handbook*, Police and Detectives.

Police, Fire, and Ambulance Dispatchers

Snapshot

2017 Median Pay: $39,640 per year, $19.06 per hour
Typical Entry-Level Education: High school diploma or equivalent
Work Experience in a Related Occupation: None
On-the-job Training: Moderate-term on-the-job training
Number of Jobs, 2016: 98,600
Job Outlook, 2016-26: 8% (As fast as average)
Employment Change, 2016-26: 8,200

CAREER OVERVIEW

What Police, Fire, and Ambulance Dispatchers Do

Police, fire, and ambulance dispatchers, also called *public safety telecommunicators*, answer emergency and nonemergency calls.

Duties

Police, fire, and ambulance dispatchers typically do the following:

- Answer 9-1-1 emergency telephone and alarm system calls
- Determine the type of emergency and its location and decide the appropriate response on the basis of agency procedures
- Relay information to the appropriate first-responder agency
- Coordinate the dispatch of emergency response personnel to accident scenes
- Give basic over-the-phone medical instructions before emergency personnel arrive
- Monitor and track the status of police, fire, and ambulance units
- Synchronize responses with other area communication centers
- Keep detailed records of calls

Dispatchers answer calls from people who need help from police, firefighters, emergency services, or a combination of the three. They take emergency, nonemergency, and alarm system calls.

Dispatchers must stay calm while collecting vital information from callers to determine the severity of a situation and the location of those who need help. They then communicate this information to the appropriate first-responder agencies.

Dispatchers keep detailed records of the calls that they answer. They use computers to log important facts, such as the nature of the incident and the caller's name and location. Most computer systems detect the location of cell phones and landline phones automatically.

Dispatchers often must instruct callers on what to do before responders arrive. Many dispatchers are trained to offer medical help over the phone. For example, they might help the caller provide first aid at the scene until emergency medical services arrive. At other times they may advise callers on how to remain safe while waiting for assistance.

WORK ENVIRONMENT

Dispatchers work in communication centers, often called public safety answering points (PSAPs).

Police, fire, and ambulance dispatchers held about 98,600 jobs in 2016. The largest employers of police, fire, and ambulance dispatchers were as follows:

Local government, excluding education and hospitals	80%
State government, excluding education and hospitals	6
Ambulance services	6
Colleges, universities, and professional schools; state, local, and private	3
Hospitals; state, local, and private	2

Dispatchers typically work in communication centers, often called public safety answering points (PSAPs). Some dispatchers work for unified communication centers, where they answer calls for all types of emergency services, while others may work specifically for police or fire departments.

Work as a dispatcher can be stressful. Dispatchers often work long shifts, take many calls, and deal with troubling situations. Some calls require them to assist people who are in life-threatening situations, and the pressure to respond quickly and calmly can be demanding.

Work Schedules

Most dispatchers work 8- to 12-hour shifts, but some agencies require even longer ones. Overtime is common in this occupation.

Because emergencies can happen at any time, dispatchers are required to work some shifts during evenings, weekends, and holidays.

HOW TO BECOME A POLICE OFFICER OR DETECTIVE

Most police, fire, and ambulance dispatchers have a high school diploma. Many states and localities require dispatchers to have training and certification.

In addition, candidates must pass a written exam and a typing test. In some instances, applicants may need to pass a background check, lie detector and drug tests, and tests for hearing and vision.

Some jobs require a driver's license, and experience using computers and in customer service can be helpful. The ability to speak Spanish is also desirable in this occupation.

Education

Most dispatchers are required to have a high school diploma.

Training

Training requirements vary by state. The Association of Public-Safety Communications Officials (APCO International) provides a list of states requiring training and certification.

Some states require 40 or more hours of initial training, and some require continuing education every 2 to 3 years. Other states do not mandate any specific training, leaving individual localities and agencies to structure their own requirements and conduct their own courses.

Some agencies have their own programs for certifying dispatchers; others use training from a professional association. The Association of Public-Safety Communications Officials (APCO International), the National Emergency Number Association (NENA), and the International Academies of Emergency Dispatch (IAED) have established a number of recommended standards and best practices that agencies often use as a guideline for their own training programs.

Training is usually conducted in a classroom and on the job, and may be followed by a probationary period of about 1 year. However, the period may vary by agency, as there is no national standard governing training or probation.

Training covers a wide variety of topics, such as local geography, agency protocols, and standard procedures. Dispatchers are also taught how to use specialized equipment, such as two-way radios and computer-aided dispatch software. Computer systems that dispatchers use consist of several monitors that display call information, maps, any relevant criminal history, and video, depending on the location of the incident. Dispatchers often receive specialized training to prepare for high-risk incidents, such as child abductions and suicidal callers.

Licenses, Certifications, and Registrations

Many states require dispatchers to be certified. The Association of Public-Safety Communications Officials (APCO) provides a list of states requiring training and certification. One certification is the Emergency Medical Dispatcher (EMD) certification, which enables dispatchers to give medical assistance over the phone.

Dispatchers may choose to pursue additional certifications, such as the National Emergency Number Association's Emergency Number Professional (ENP) certification or APCO's Registered Public-Safety Leader (RPL) certification, which demonstrate their leadership skills and knowledge of the profession.

ADVANCEMENT

Training and additional certifications can help dispatchers become senior dispatchers or supervisors. Additional education and related work experience may be helpful in advancing to management-level positions.

Important Qualities

Ability to multitask. Dispatchers must stay calm in order to simultaneously answer calls, collect vital information, coordinate responders, use mapping software and camera feeds, and assist callers.

Communication skills. Dispatchers work with law enforcement, emergency response teams, and civilians. They must be able to communicate the nature of an emergency effectively and coordinate the appropriate response.

Decisionmaking skills. When people call for help, dispatchers must be able to quickly determine the response dictated by procedures.

Empathy. Dispatchers must be willing and able to help callers who have a wide range of needs. They must be calm, polite, and sympathetic, while also collecting relevant information quickly.

Listening skills. Dispatchers must listen carefully to collect relevant details, even though some callers might have trouble speaking because of anxiety or stress.

Typing skills. Dispatchers type the details of calls into computers, and speed and accuracy is of the essence when responding to emergencies.

WAGES

Median annual wages, May 2017

Police, fire, and ambulance dispatchers: $39,640

Total, all occupations: $37,690

Material recording, scheduling, dispatching, and distributing workers: $31,100

Note: All Occupations includes all occupations in the U.S. Economy. Source: U.S. Bureau of Labor Statistics, Occupational Employment Statistics

The median annual wage for police, fire, and ambulance dispatchers was $39,640 in May 2017. The lowest 10 percent earned less than $25,920, and the highest 10 percent earned more than $62,680.

In May 2017, the median annual wages for police, fire, and ambulance dispatchers in the top industries in which they worked were as follows:

State government, excluding education and hospitals	$45,710
Local government, excluding education and hospitals	39,650
Colleges, universities, and professional schools; state, local, and private	37,820
Hospitals; state, local, and private	36,460
Ambulance services	36,170

Most dispatchers work 8- to 12-hour shifts, but some agencies require even longer ones. Overtime is common in this occupation.

Because emergencies can happen at any time, dispatchers are required to work some shifts on evenings, weekends, and holidays.

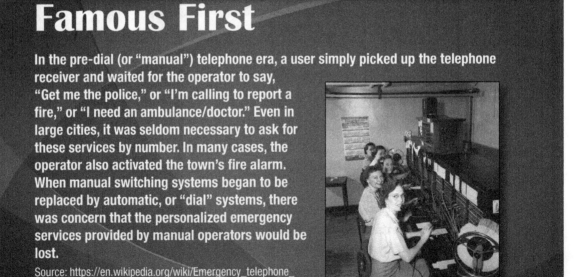

Famous First

In the pre-dial (or "manual") telephone era, a user simply picked up the telephone receiver and waited for the operator to say, "Get me the police," or "I'm calling to report a fire," or "I need an ambulance/doctor." Even in large cities, it was seldom necessary to ask for these services by number. In many cases, the operator also activated the town's fire alarm. When manual switching systems began to be replaced by automatic, or "dial" systems, there was concern that the personalized emergency services provided by manual operators would be lost.

Source: https://en.wikipedia.org/wiki/Emergency_telephone_number

JOB OUTLOOK

Percent change in employment, projected 2016-26

Police, fire, and ambulance dispatchers: 8%

Total, all occupations: 7%

Material recording, scheduling, dispatching, and distributing workers: 2%

Note: All Occupations includes all occupations in the U.S. Economy. Source: U.S. Bureau of Labor Statistics, Employment Projections program

Employment of police, fire, and ambulance dispatchers is projected to grow 8 percent from 2016 to 2026, about as fast as the average for all occupations.

Although state and local government budget constraints may limit the number of dispatchers hired in the coming decade, population growth and the commensurate increase in 9-1-1 call volume is expected to increase the employment of dispatchers.

Job Prospects

Overall job prospects should be favorable because the work of a dispatcher remains stressful and demanding, leading some applicants to seek other types of work.

The majority of job openings will come from the need to replace dispatchers who transfer to other occupations or leave the labor force.

**Employment projections data for
Police, Fire, and Ambulance Dispatchers, 2016-26**

Occupational Title	SOC Code	Employment, 2016	Projected Employment, 2026	Change, 2016-26	
				Percent	Numeric
Police, fire, and ambulance dispatchers	43-5031	98,600	106,700	8	8,200

Source: Bureau of Labor Statistics, Employment Projections program

SIMILAR OCCUPATIONS

This table shows a list of occupations with job duties that are similar to those of police, fire, and ambulance dispatchers.

OCCUPATION	JOB DUTIES	ENTRY-LEVEL EDUCATION	2017 MEDIAN PAY
Air Traffic Controllers	Air traffic controllers coordinate the movement of aircraft to maintain safe distances between them.	Associate's degree	$124,540
Customer Service Representatives	Customer service representatives interact with customers to handle complaints, process orders, and provide information about an organization's products and services.	High school diploma or equivalent	$32,890

OCCUPATION	JOB DUTIES	ENTRY-LEVEL EDUCATION	2017 MEDIAN PAY
EMTs and Paramedics	Emergency medical technicians (EMTs) and paramedics care for the sick or injured in emergency medical settings. People's lives often depend on the quick reaction and competent care provided by these workers. EMTs and paramedics respond to emergency calls, performing medical services and transporting patients to medical facilities.	Postsecondary nondegree award	$33,380
Power Plant Operators, Distributors, and Dispatchers	Power plant operators, distributors, and dispatchers control the systems that generate and distribute electric power.	High school diploma or equivalent	$80,440
Security Guards and Gaming Surveillance Officers	Security guards and gaming surveillance officers patrol and protect property against theft, vandalism, and other illegal activity.	High school diploma or equivalent	$26,960

Fast Fact

About half of the 84 million calls made to New York City's 9-1-1 are mistakes.

Source: boredomtherapy.com

Conversation With . . .
DON HANCOCK

Emergency Dispatcher, 14 years

1. What was your individual career path in terms of education/training, entry-level job, or other significant opportunity?

I became an EMT in 1993 and a CPR/first aid instructor for a major hotel chain. Later, while working for a private ambulance company providing treatment and transportation, I assisted office personnel and began cross training and filling in as a dispatcher.

2. What are the most important skills and/or qualities for someone in your profession?

A dispatcher's most important skill is the ability to multitask while gathering crucial details. You should be an effective communicator and an active listener. You should also possess a strong, commanding voice. You have to be able to tolerate a quick change of pace. One moment you are sitting bored in a dimly lit office and then the phone will ring with a person screaming for help. You have to calm the caller while quickly ascertaining where and what type of emergency they are experiencing. Then you have to get the appropriate resources dispatched to the caller's location. Situations can further be complicated by multiple callers for the same incident or similar incidents in nearby locations. This is where being detail oriented and a good listener become extremely important.

3. What do you wish you had known going into this profession?

I wish I knew about the impact it would have on my cardiovascular health. The combination of stress and a sedentary career is not good for the heart. It's also important to be prepared for calls from people you know or may even be related to. Further, remember the requirement of confidentiality and do not violate it.

4. What do you wish you had known going into this profession?

Yes, there are many opportunities in the dispatch career path. Many departments are continuing to phase sworn personnel (police officers or firefighters) out of the communication centers. Also there seems to be a recent interest in regional dispatch centers.

5. How do you see your profession changing in the next five years? What role will technology play in those changes, and what skills will be required?

With all the technology in this field, it is no longer possible to have an officer or firefighter cross-trained to "fill in" on the desk. The job is no longer a matter of simply sitting in the room and picking up the phone. The average telecommunicator sits in front of and controls four to six computer screens. Those are connected to two or three computers and running between 10 to 20 different applications.

Further, the next generation 911 systems (commonly referred to as NexGen) will receive text and video to 911 in the near future. Along with the words, sounds and screams we are currently exposed to as professionals, there will be visual images viewed, interpreted and stored for possible further court action. This certainly will be instrumental in situations with language barriers.

6. Do you have any general advice or additional professional insights to share with someone in your profession? What is the most fulfilling part of your job, and what is the most frustrating?

Listen carefully, and then listen more. Try not to rush callers and speak slowly and clearly. Rushing a caller may mean missing an important detail.

The most fulfilling part of my job is helping people. I know it sounds corny but when you have a scared caller at 3 a.m. who has heard an unusual noise, it's fulfilling to talk to and calm them while waiting for help to arrive.

The most frustrating part of my job is dealing with tempers and rage. Although, in some disturbances, I have been able to talk with the aggressor and at a minimum, distract him while units respond. Not to mention that keeping the aggressor on the phone also allows the victim to flee the situation. Also in a few situations, the aggressor has made statements implicating him or herself.

7. Can you suggest a valuable "try this" for students considering a career in your profession?

Similar to a police ride along, get to know a dispatcher and come in and sit with him or her. Watch how they occupy their downtime and pay attention to how they stay prepared for that next call. Listening to a scanner can be helpful, but it shows only a small portion of the tasks we are responsible for.

This conversation was originally published in Careers in Healthcare *(Salem) in 2014.*

MORE INFORMATION

For more information about police, fire, and ambulance dispatcher training and certification, visit

Association of Public-Safety Communications Officials
https://www.apcointl.org/

International Academies of Emergency Dispatch
https://www.emergencydispatch.org/

International Municipal Signal Association
http://www.imsasafety.org/

National Emergency Number Association
https://www.nena.org/default.aspx

Sources

Bureau of Labor Statistics, U.S. Department of Labor, *Occupational Outlook Handbook*, Police, Fire, and Ambulance Dispatchers.

Private Detectives and Investigators

Snapshot

2017 Median Pay: $50,700 per year, $24.38 per hour
Typical Entry-Level Education: High school diploma or equivalent
Work Experience in a Related Occupation: Less than 5 years
On-the-Job Training: Moderate-term on-the-job training
Number of Jobs, 2016: 41,400
Job Outlook, 2016-26: 11% (Faster than average)
Employment Change, 2016-26: 4,400

CAREER OVERVIEW

What Private Detectives and Investigators Do

Private detectives and investigators must properly collect and document evidence so that it may be used in a court of law.

Private detectives and investigators search for information about legal, financial, and personal matters. They offer many services, such as verifying people's backgrounds and statements, finding missing persons, and investigating computer crimes.

Duties

Private detectives and investigators typically do the following:

- Interview people to gather information
- Search online, public, and court records to uncover clues
- Conduct surveillance
- Collect evidence for clients
- Check for civil judgments and criminal history

Private detectives and investigators offer many services for individuals, attorneys, and businesses. Examples include performing background checks, investigating employees for possible theft from a company, proving or disproving infidelity in a divorce case, and helping to locate a missing person.

Private detectives and investigators use a variety of tools when researching the facts in a case. Much of their work is done with a computer, allowing them to obtain information such as telephone numbers, details about social networks, descriptions of online activities, and records of a person's prior arrests. They make phone calls to verify facts and interview people when conducting a background investigation.

Detectives also conduct surveillance when investigating a case. They may watch locations, such as a person's home or office, often from a hidden position. Using cameras and binoculars, detectives gather information on people of interest.

Detectives and investigators must be mindful of the law when conducting investigations. Because they lack police authority, their work must be done with the same authority as a private citizen. As a result, detectives and investigators must have a good understanding of federal, state, and local laws, such as privacy laws, and other legal issues affecting their work. Otherwise, evidence they collect may not be useable in court and they could face prosecution.

Skip tracers specialize in locating people whose whereabouts are unknown. For example, debt collectors may employ them to locate people who have unpaid bills.

WORK ENVIRONMENT

Many private detectives and investigators spend time away from their desks while conducting surveillance in the field.

Private detectives and investigators held about 41,400 jobs in 2016. The largest employers of private detectives and investigators were as follows:

Investigation, guard, and armored car services	31%
Self-employed workers	31
Government	8
Finance and insurance	5
Retail trade	5

Private detectives and investigators work in many environments, depending on the case. Some spend more time in offices, researching cases on computers and making phone calls. Others spend more time in the field, conducting interviews or performing surveillance. In addition, private detectives and investigators may have to work outdoors or from a vehicle, in all kinds of weather, in order to obtain the information their client needs.

Although investigators often work alone, some work with others while conducting surveillance or carrying out large, complicated assignments.

Work Schedules

Private detectives and investigators often work irregular hours because they conduct surveillance and contact people outside of normal work hours. They may work early mornings, evenings, weekends, and holidays.

HOW TO BECOME A PRIVATE DETECTIVE OR INVESTIGATOR

Although most learn on the job, many private detectives and investigators have a law enforcement background.

Private detectives and investigators typically need several years of work experience and a high school diploma. In addition, the vast majority of states require private detectives and investigators to have a license.

Education

Education requirements vary greatly with the job, but most jobs require a high school diploma. Some, though, may require a 2- or 4-year degree in a field such as criminal justice.

Training

Most private detectives and investigators learn through on-the-job training, typically lasting between several months and a year.

Although new investigators must learn how to gather information, additional training depends on the type of firm that hires them. For example, investigators may learn to conduct remote surveillance, reconstruct accident scenes, or investigate insurance fraud. Corporate investigators hired by large companies may receive formal training in business practices, management structure, and various finance-related topics.

Work Experience in a Related Occupation

Private detectives and investigators must typically have previous work experience, usually in law enforcement, the military, or federal intelligence. Those in such jobs, who are frequently able to retire after 20 or 25 years of service, may become private detectives or investigators in a second career.

Other private detectives and investigators may have previously worked as bill and account collectors, claims adjusters, paralegals, or process servers.

Licenses, Certifications, and Registrations

Most states require private detectives and investigators to have a license. Check with your state for more information; Professional Investigator Magazine has links to most states' licensing requirements. Because laws often change, jobseekers should verify the licensing laws related to private investigators with the state and locality in which they want to work.

Candidates may also obtain certification, although it is not required for employment. Still, becoming certified through professional organizations can demonstrate competence and may help candidates advance in their careers.

For investigators who specialize in negligence or criminal defense investigation, the National Association of Legal Investigators offers the Certified Legal Investigator certification. For other investigators, ASIS International offers the Professional Certified Investigator certification.

Important Qualities

Communication skills. Private detectives and investigators must listen carefully and ask appropriate questions when interviewing a person of interest.

Decisionmaking skills. Private detectives and investigators must be able to think on their feet and make quick decisions, based on the limited information that they have at a given time.

Inquisitiveness. Private detectives and investigators must want to ask questions and search for the truth.

Patience. Private detectives and investigators may have to spend long periods conducting surveillance while waiting for an event to occur. Investigations may take a long time, and they may not provide a resolution quickly—or at all.

Resourcefulness. Private detectives and investigators must work persistently with whatever leads they have, no matter how limited, to determine the next step toward their goal. They sometimes need to anticipate what a person of interest will do next.

WAGES

Median annual wages, May 2017

Private detectives and investigators: $50,700

Total, all occupations: $37,690

Other protective service workers: $27,150

Note: All Occupations includes all occupations in the U.S. Economy. Source: U.S. Bureau of Labor Statistics, Occupational Employment Statistics

The median annual wage for private detectives and investigators was $50,700 in May 2017. The lowest 10 percent earned less than $28,780, and the highest 10 percent earned more than $86,730.

In May 2017, the median annual wages for private detectives and investigators in the top industries in which they worked were as follows:

Government	$56,700
Finance and insurance	56,090
Investigation, guard, and armored car services	48,920
Retail trade	45,300

Private detectives and investigators often work irregular hours because they conduct surveillance and contact people outside of normal work hours. They may work early mornings, evenings, weekends, and holidays.

JOB OUTLOOK

Percent change in employment, projected 2016-26

Private detectives and investigators: 11%

Total, all occupations: 7%

Other protective service workers: 7%

Note: All Occupations includes all occupations in the U.S. Economy. Source: U.S. Bureau of Labor Statistics, Employment Projections program

Employment of private detectives and investigators is projected to grow 11 percent from 2016 to 2026, faster than the average for all occupations.

Continued lawsuits, fraud and other crimes, and interpersonal mistrust create demand for investigative services, particularly by the legal services industry.

Background checks will continue to be a source of work for some investigators, as online investigations are not always sufficient.

Job Prospects

Strong competition for jobs can be expected because private detective and investigator careers attract many qualified people, including relatively young retirees from law enforcement and the military.

Candidates with related work experience, as well as those with strong interviewing skills and familiarity with computers, may find more job opportunities than others.

Employment projections data for
Private Detectives and Investigators, 2016-26

Occupational Title	SOC Code	Employment, 2016	Projected Employment, 2026	Change, 2016-26	
				Percent	Numeric
Private detectives and investigators	33-9021	41,400	45,800	11	4,400

Source: Bureau of Labor Statistics, Employment Projections program

Famous First

The world's most famous fictional detective, Sherlock Holmes, appeared in print in 1887's *A Study in Scarlet*. The Strand Magazine published a series of stories, beginning with "A Scandal in Bohemia" in 1891. By 1927, four novels and 56 short stories had been published. All but one are set in the Victorian or Edwardian eras, between about 1880 and 1914. Most of the stories begin at 221B Baker Street, London, Holmes's residence.

Source: https://en.wikipedia.org/wiki/Sherlock_Holmes

Fast Fact

The word "detective" was first used in 1843 to describe a crimesolver, but the first literary detective arrived two years earlier, when C. Auguste Dupin appeared in Edgar Allan Poe's 1841 short story, Murders in The Rue Morgue
Source: https://www.express.co.uk

SIMILAR OCCUPATIONS

This table shows a list of occupations with job duties that are similar to those of private detectives and investigators.

OCCUPATION	JOB DUTIES	ENTRY-LEVEL EDUCATION	2017 MEDIAN PAY
Accountants and Auditors	Accountants and auditors prepare and examine financial records. They ensure that financial records are accurate and that taxes are paid properly and on time. Accountants and auditors assess financial operations and work to help ensure that organizations run efficiently.	Bachelor's degree	$69,350
Bill and Account Collectors	Bill and account collectors try to recover payment on overdue bills. They negotiate repayment plans with debtors and help them find solutions to make paying their overdue bills easier.	High school diploma or equivalent	$35,330
Claims Adjusters, Appraisers, Examiners, and Investigators	Claims adjusters, appraisers, examiners, and investigators evaluate insurance claims. They decide whether an insurance company must pay a claim, and if so, how much.	High school diploma or equivalent	$64,690
Financial Examiners	Financial examiners ensure compliance with laws governing financial institutions and transactions. They review balance sheets, evaluate the risk level of loans, and assess bank management.	Bachelor's degree	$81,690

Security Guards and Gaming Surveillance Officers	Security guards and gaming surveillance officers patrol and protect property against theft, vandalism, and other illegal activity.	High school diploma or equivalent	$26,960
Paralegals and Legal Assistants	Paralegals and legal assistants perform a variety of tasks to support lawyers, including maintaining and organizing files, conducting legal research, and drafting documents.	Associate's degree	$50,410
Fire Inspectors	Fire inspectors examine buildings in order to detect fire hazards and ensure that federal, state, and local fire codes are met. Fire investigators, another type of worker in this field, determine the origin and cause of fires and explosions. Forest fire inspectors and prevention specialists assess outdoor fire hazards in public and residential areas.	Postsecondary educational program for emergency medical technicians (EMTs) High school diploma or equivalent (forest fire inspectors and prevention specialists)	$56,670
Police and Detectives	Police officers protect lives and property. Detectives and criminal investigators, who are sometimes called agents or special agents, gather facts and collect evidence of possible crimes.	High school diploma or equivalent (police) Bachelor's degree (fish and game wardens) Bachelor's degree (federal agencies)	$62,960
Forensic Science Technicians	Forensic science technicians aid criminal investigations by collecting and analyzing evidence. Many technicians specialize in various types of laboratory analysis.	Bachelor's degree	$57,850

MORE INFORMATION

For more information about private detectives and investigators, including information on certification, visit

National Association of Legal Investigators
https://www.nalionline.org/

ASIS International
https://www.asisonline.org/

Sources

Bureau of Labor Statistics, U.S. Department of Labor, *Occupational Outlook Handbook*, Private Detectives and Investigators.

Probation Officers and Correctional Treatment Specialists

Snapshot

2017 Median Pay: $51,410 per year, $24.71 per hour
Typical Entry-Level Education: Bachelor's degree
Work Experience in a Related Occupation: None
On-the-job Training: Short-term on-the-job training
Number of Jobs, 2016: 91,300
Job Outlook, 2016-26: 6% (As fast as average)
Employment Change, 2016-26: 5,200

CAREER OVERVIEW

What Probation Officers and Correctional Treatment Specialists Do

Correctional treatment specialists counsel law offenders and create rehabilitation plans for them to follow when they are no longer in prison.

Probation officers and correctional treatment specialists provide social services to assist in rehabilitation of law offenders in custody or on probation or parole.

Duties

Probation officers and correctional treatment specialists typically do the following:

- Interview with probationers and parolees, their friends, and their relatives in an office or at a residence to assess progress
- Evaluate probationers and parolees to determine the best course of rehabilitation
- Provide probationers and parolees with resources, such as job training
- Test offenders for drugs and offer substance abuse counseling
- Complete prehearing investigations and testify in court regarding offender's backgrounds
- Write reports and maintain case files on offenders

The following are examples of types of probation officers and correctional treatment specialists:

Probation officers, who are sometimes referred to as community supervision officers, supervise people who have been placed on probation instead of sent to prison. They work to ensure that the probationer is not a danger to the community and to help in their rehabilitation through frequent visits with the probationer. Probation officers write reports that detail each probationer's treatment plan and their progress since being put on probation. Most work exclusively with either adults or juveniles.

Parole officers work with people who have been released from prison and are serving parole, helping them re-enter society. Parole officers monitor post-release parolees and provide them with information on various resources, such as substance abuse counseling or job training, to aid in their rehabilitation. By doing so, the officers try to change the parolee's behavior and thus reduce the risk of that person committing another crime and having to return to prison.

Both probation and parole officers supervise probationers and parolees through personal contact with them and their families (also known as community supervision). Probation and parole officers require regularly scheduled contact with parolees and probationers by telephone or through office visits, and they also check on them at their homes or places of work. When making home visits, probation and parole officers take into account the safety of the neighborhood in which the probationers and parolees live and any mental health considerations that may be pertinent. Probation and parole officers also oversee drug testing and electronic monitoring of those under supervision. In some states, workers perform the duties of both probation and parole officers.

Pretrial services officers investigate a pretrial defendant's background to determine if the defendant can be safely allowed back into the community before his or her trial date. Officers must assess the risk and make a recommendation to a judge, who decides on the appropriate sentencing (in settled cases with no trial) or bond amount. When pretrial defendants are allowed back into the community, pretrial officers supervise them to make sure that they stay within the terms of their release and appear at their trials.

Correctional treatment specialists, also known as case managers or correctional counselors, advise probationers and parolees and develop rehabilitation plans for them to follow. They may evaluate inmates using questionnaires and psychological tests. They also work with inmates, parole officers, and staff of other agencies to develop parole and release plans. For example, they may plan education and training programs to improve probationers' job skills.

Correctional treatment specialists write case reports that cover the inmate's history and the likelihood that he or she will commit another crime. When inmates are eligible for release, the case reports are given to the appropriate parole board. The specialist may help set up counseling for the parolees and their families, find substance abuse or mental health treatment options, aid in job placement, and find housing. Correctional treatment specialists also explain the terms and conditions of the prisoner's release and keep detailed written accounts of each parolee's progress.

The number of cases a probation officer or correctional treatment specialist handles at one time depends on the needs of individuals under supervision and the risks associated with each individual.

Higher risk probationers usually command more of an officer's time and resources. Caseload size also varies by agency.

Improved tests for drug screening and electronic devices to monitor clients help probation officers and correctional treatment specialists supervise and counsel probationers.

WORK ENVIRONMENT

Extensive travel and paperwork can also contribute to more hours of work.

Probation officers and correctional treatment specialists held about 91,300 jobs in 2016. The largest employers of probation officers and correctional treatment specialists were as follows:

State government, excluding education and hospitals	54%
Local government, excluding education and hospitals	43
Social assistance	1

Probation officers and correctional treatment specialists work with probationers and parolees. While supervising individuals, they may interact with others, such as family members and friends of their clients, who may be upset or difficult to work with. Workers may be assigned to fieldwork in high-crime areas or in institutions where there is a risk of violence.

Probation officers and correctional treatment specialists may have court deadlines imposed by the statute of limitations. In addition, many officers travel to perform home and employment checks and property searches. Because of the hostile environments they may encounter, some may carry a firearm or pepper spray for protection.

All of these factors, in addition to the challenge some officers experience in dealing with probationers and parolees who violate the terms of their release, can contribute to a stressful work environment.

Although the high stress levels can make the job difficult at times, this work can also be rewarding. Many officers and specialists receive personal satisfaction from counseling members of their community and helping them become productive citizens.

Work Schedules

Although many officers and specialists work full time, the demands of the job sometimes lead to working overtime and variable hours. For example, many agencies rotate an on-call officer position. When these workers are on-call, they must respond to any issues with probationers, parolees, or law enforcement 24 hours a day.

Extensive travel and paperwork can also contribute to more hours of work.

HOW TO BECOME A PROBATION OFFICER OR CORRECTIONAL TREATMENT SPECIALIST

Probation officers may go on to specialize in a certain type of casework, such as working with juvenile law offenders.

Probation officers and correctional treatment specialists usually need a bachelor's degree. In addition, most employers require candidates to pass competency exams, drug testing, and a criminal background check.

A valid driver's license is often required, and most agencies require applicants to be at least 21 years old.

Education

A bachelor's degree in social work, criminal justice, behavioral sciences, or a related field is usually required. Requirements vary by jurisdiction.

Training

Most probation officers and correctional treatment specialists must complete a training program sponsored by their state government or the federal government, after which they may have to pass a certification test. In addition, they may be required to work as trainees for up to 1 year before being offered a permanent position.

Some probation officers and correctional treatment specialists specialize in a certain type of casework. For example, an officer may work only with domestic violence probationers or deal only with substance abuse cases. Some may work only cases involving juvenile offenders. Officers receive the appropriate specific training so that they are better prepared to help that type of probationer.

Other Experience

Although job requirements vary, work experience obtained by way of internships in courthouses or with probationers in the criminal justice field can be helpful for some positions.

ADVANCEMENT

Advancement to supervisory positions is primarily based on experience and performance. A master's degree in criminal justice, social work, or psychology may be required for advancement.

Important Qualities

Communication skills. Probation officers and correctional treatment specialists must be able to effectively interact with probationers, probationers' family members, lawyers, judges, treatment providers, and law enforcement.

Critical-thinking skills. Probation officers and correctional treatment specialists must be able to assess the needs of individual probationers before determining the best resources for helping them.

Decisionmaking skills. Probation officers and correctional treatment specialists must consider the best rehabilitation plan for offenders.

Emotional stability. Probation officers and correctional treatment specialists cope with hostile individuals or otherwise upsetting circumstances on the job.

Organizational skills. Probation officers and correctional treatment specialists manage multiple cases at the same time.

WAGES

Median annual wages, May 2017

Probation officers and correctional treatment specialists: $51,410

Counselors, social workers, and other community and social service specialists: $43,860

Total, all occupations: $37,690

Note: All Occupations includes all occupations in the U.S. Economy. Source: U.S. Bureau of Labor Statistics, Occupational Employment Statistics

The median annual wage for probation officers and correctional treatment specialists was $51,410 in May 2017. The lowest 10 percent earned less than $33,920, and the highest 10 percent earned more than $90,880.

In May 2017, the median annual wages for probation officers and correctional treatment specialists in the top industries in which they worked were as follows:

Local government, excluding education and hospitals	$54,990
State government, excluding education and hospitals	50,030
Social assistance	34,450

Although many officers and specialists work full time, the demands of the job sometimes lead to working overtime and variable hours. For example, many agencies rotate an on-call officer position. When these workers are on-call, they must respond to any issues with probationers or law enforcement 24 hours a day.

Extensive travel and paperwork can also contribute to more hours of work.

Union Membership

Compared with workers in all occupations, probation officers and correctional treatment specialists had a higher percentage of workers who belonged to a union in 2016.

JOB OUTLOOK

Percent change in employment, projected 2016-26

Counselors, social workers, and other community and social service specialists: 16%

Total, all occupations: 7%

Probation officers and correctional treatment specialists: 6%

Note: All Occupations includes all occupations in the U.S. Economy. Source: U.S. Bureau of Labor Statistics, Employment Projections program

Employment of probation officers and correctional treatment specialists is projected to grow 6 percent from 2016 to 2026, about as fast as the average for all occupations.

Employment growth depends primarily on the amount of state and local government funding for corrections, especially the amount allocated to probation and parole systems.

Because community corrections is viewed as an economically viable alternative to incarceration in some cases, demand for probation officers and correctional treatment specialists should continue. Parole officers will continue to be needed to supervise individuals who will be released from prison in the future.

Job Prospects

Many job openings will result from the need to replace those who leave the occupation each year due to the heavy workloads and high job-related stress. Job opportunities should be plentiful for those who qualify. The ability to speak Spanish is also desirable in this occupation and may present better job prospects.

Employment projections data for
Probation Officers and Correctional Treatment Specialists,
2016-26

Occupational Title	SOC Code	Employment, 2016	Projected Employment, 2026	Change, 2016-26	
				Percent	Numeric
Probation officers and correctional treatment specialists	21-1092	91,300	96,500	6	5,200

Source: Bureau of Labor Statistics, Employment Projections program

Famous First

Names given to probation officers and correctional treatment specialists vary from country to count. These are uniformed officials are responsible for the supervision, safety, and security of prisoners in a prison or jail. They are known by the term prison officer, corrections officer, correctional officer, detention officer, or penal officer. Historically, terms such as jailer (also spelled jailor or gaoler), jail guard, prison guard, and turnkey have also been used.

Source: https://en.wikipedia.org/wiki/Prison_officer

SIMILAR OCCUPATIONS

This table shows a list of occupations with job duties that are similar to those of probation officers and correctional treatment specialists.

OCCUPATION	JOB DUTIES	ENTRY-LEVEL EDUCATION	2017 MEDIAN PAY
Correctional Officers and Bailiffs	Correctional officers are responsible for overseeing individuals who have been arrested and are awaiting trial or who have been sentenced to serve time in jail or prison. Bailiffs are law enforcement officers who maintain safety and order in courtrooms.	High school diploma or equivalent	$43,510
Police and Detectives	Police officers protect lives and property. Detectives and criminal investigators, who are sometimes called agents or special agents, gather facts and collect evidence of possible crimes.	High school diploma or equivalent (police) Bachelor's degree (fish and game wardens) Bachelor's degree (federal agencies)	$62,960
Social and Human Service Assistants	Social and human service assistants provide client services, including support for families, in a wide variety of fields, such as psychology, rehabilitation, and social work. They assist other workers, such as social workers, and they help clients find benefits or community services.	High school diploma or equivalent	$33,120

OCCUPATION	JOB DUTIES	ENTRY-LEVEL EDUCATION	2017 MEDIAN PAY
Social Workers	Social workers help people solve and cope with problems in their everyday lives. Clinical social workers also diagnose and treat mental, behavioral, and emotional issues.	Bachelor's degree in social work (BSW) with supervised fieldwork or an internship for direct-service work Master's degree in social work (MSW) with supervised practicum or an internship, clinical work for clinical work	$47,980
Substance Abuse, Behavioral Disorder, and Mental Health Counselors	Substance abuse, behavioral disorder, and mental health counselors advise people who suffer from alcoholism, drug addiction, eating disorders, mental health issues, or other mental or behavioral problems. They provide treatment and support to help clients recover from addiction or modify problem behaviors.	Bachelor's degree	$43,300

Fast Fact

Probation has grown dramatically in the United States: from 1.1 million people on probation in 1980 to 3.9 million in 2014.
Source: Brennan Center for Justice

> # *Conversation With . . .*
> # *PAM PIERCE*
> Probation Officer, 21 years

1. What was your individual career path in terms of education/training, entry-level job, or other significant opportunity?

I have my undergraduate degree in criminal justice. Once I got through college, I said, "I'm going to go play." I worked two summers down on Cape Cod at a hotel and then in the winter, I'd go skiing in Aspen and waitress at night. I worked at a travel agency and went to Sweden, backpacked through Europe. I worked as a nanny in the Florida Keys.

My first job in this field was in a locked unit for the Massachusetts Department of Youth Services (DYS). Then I became a DYS case worker, handling juvenile offenders who had been committed to the state. The work is very similar to what probation officers do. After six years, I became a probation officer and dealt with juvenile offenders, up to age 18. Now I am an adult probation officer.

2. What are the most important skills and/or qualities for someone in your profession?

You have to have patience. You have to be a good listener. I think you have to be fair. You should be able to read people as well, so you know what you're dealing with. You have to be firm and consistent: "These are the rules and this is what you have to do." And you can't take things personally. It gets very frustrating when you get people who should be in recovery and they continue to drink or they continue to do drugs. Or they go back to certain people they shouldn't be around, people who are hurting them or mistreating them. I try to tell them, "Stop. Think about this." But it's their life. You can't tell them what to do. You can only encourage them to get help or counseling.

3. What do you wish you had known going into this profession?

I wish I knew how to type because everything has to be documented. You have to keep notes on everything and you have to be clear. If you can type, it's a lot easier. I just never learned how to type in high school. I waste a lot of time hunting and pecking.

4. **Are there many job opportunities in your profession? In what specific areas?**

I don't think so. We need more people, but there's a hiring freeze. It's a very difficult job to get now in Massachusetts. It's a very popular job. That's one reason they're looking at people with master's degrees now.

We used to be the second highest paid probation department in the country. The benefits are very good. People pretty much don't leave this job once they get it.

5. **How do you see your profession changing in the next five years? What role will technology play in those changes, and what skills will be required?**

The big focus now is trying to track and reduce the rate of recidivism. One of the keys to doing that, I think, is jobs. If you get kids good jobs, they wouldn't be back out on the street.

GPS is a major technological advance that's helping. People are on the ankle bracelet and we're able to track and monitor them. There's also a new computer system where anyone in the state (with the right clearance) can read someone else's notes (on a given client.) And because of the National Crime Information Center, we have access to more information about offenders. But the crux of the job won't change. Probation involves a lot of human interaction, building a rapport with the defendants and their families. It involves trying to get people to think about how they can improve their lives.

6. **What do you enjoy most about your job? What do you enjoy least?**

I enjoy trying to make a difference in people's lives and help them turn their lives around. When it happens, it's really quite a joyous thing. It's nice when you see someone in court and find out they're not there for themselves. I tell them, "Hey, life's not so bad being Mr. Average and just kind of going along, is it?"

What I like least is the paperwork. It cuts into the amount of time you can spend with people. Also, worrying and staying on top of the caseload.

7. **Can you suggest a valuable "try this" for students considering a career in your profession?**

I would suggest what I did years ago. I went in and sat in the courtroom and watched what went on. I watched what the judge did. I watched what everyone's role was. Also, try to do an internship through the court with a probation officer, not just the front desk, so you can sit in on their interviews and office visits.

This conversation was originally published in Careers in Law, Criminal Justice & Emergency Services *(Salem) in 2014.*

MORE INFORMATION

For more information about probation officers and correctional treatment specialists, visit

American Probation and Parole Association
http://www.appa-net.org/eweb/

Discover Corrections
http://www.discovercorrections.com/

For more information about criminal justice job opportunities in your area, contact the departments of corrections, criminal justice, or probation for individual states.

Sources

Bureau of Labor Statistics, U.S. Department of Labor, *Occupational Outlook Handbook*, Probation Officers and Correctional Treatment Specialists.

Registered Nurses

Snapshot

2017 Median Pay: $70,000 per year, $33.65 per hour
Typical Entry-Level Education: Bachelor's degree
Career Cluster: Health science
On-the-job Training: None
Number of Jobs, 2016: 2,955,200
Job Outlook, 2016-26: 15% (Much faster than average)
Employment Change, 2016-26: 438,100

CAREER OVERVIEW

Registered nurses (RNs) provide and coordinate patient care, educate patients and the public about various health conditions, and provide advice and emotional support to patients and their family members.

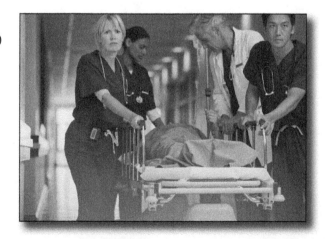

Duties

Registered nurses typically do the following:

- Assess patients' conditions
- Record patients' medical histories and symptoms
- Observe patients and record the observations
- Administer patients' medicines and treatments
- Set up plans for patients' care or contribute information to existing plans
- Consult and collaborate with doctors and other healthcare professionals
- Operate and monitor medical equipment
- Help perform diagnostic tests and analyze the results
- Teach patients and their families how to manage illnesses or injuries
- Explain what to do at home after treatment

Most registered nurses work as part of a team with physicians and other healthcare specialists. Some registered nurses oversee licensed practical nurses, nursing assistants, and home health aides.

Registered nurses' duties and titles often depend on where they work and the patients they work with. For example, an oncology nurse may work with cancer patients or a geriatric nurse may work with elderly patients. Some registered nurses combine one or more areas of practice. For example, a pediatric oncology nurse works with children and teens who have cancer.

Many possibilities for working with specific patient groups exist. The following list includes just a few examples:

Addiction nurses care for patients who need help to overcome addictions to alcohol, drugs, and other substances.

Cardiovascular nurses care for patients with heart disease and people who have had heart surgery.

Critical care nurses work in intensive-care units in hospitals, providing care to patients with serious, complex, and acute illnesses and injuries that need very close monitoring and treatment.

Genetics nurses provide screening, counseling, and treatment for patients with genetic disorders, such as cystic fibrosis.

Neonatology nurses take care of newborn babies.

Nephrology nurses care for patients who have kidney-related health issues stemming from diabetes, high blood pressure, substance abuse, or other causes.

Public health nurses promote public health by educating people on warning signs and symptoms of disease or managing chronic health conditions. They may also run health screenings, immunization clinics, blood drives, or other community outreach programs.

Rehabilitation nurses care for patients with temporary or permanent disabilities. Some nurses do not work directly with patients, but they must still have an active registered nurse license. For example, they may work as nurse educators, healthcare consultants, public policy advisors, researchers, hospital administrators, salespeople for pharmaceutical and medical supply companies, or as medical writers and editors.

Clinical nurse specialists (CNSs) are a type of advanced practice registered nurse (APRN). They provide direct patient care in one of many nursing specialties, such as psychiatric-mental health or pediatrics. CNSs also provide indirect care, by working with other nurses and various other staff to improve the quality of care that patients receive. They often serve in leadership roles and may educate and advise other nursing staff. CNSs also may conduct research and may advocate for certain policies.

WORK ENVIRONMENT

Registered nurses held about 3.0 million jobs in 2016. The largest employers of registered nurses were as follows:

Hospitals; state, local, and private	61%
Ambulatory healthcare services	18
Nursing and residential care facilities	7
Government	5
Educational services; state, local, and private	3

Ambulatory healthcare services includes industries such as physicians' offices, home healthcare, and outpatient care centers. In addition, some nurses serve in the military. Nurses who work in home health travel to patients' homes, while public health nurses may travel to community centers, schools, and other sites.

Some nurses move frequently, traveling in the United States and throughout the world to help care for patients in places where there are not enough healthcare workers.

Injuries and Illnesses

Registered nurses may spend a lot of time walking, bending, stretching, and standing. They are vulnerable to back injuries because they often must lift and move patients.

The work of registered nurses may put them in close contact with people who have infectious diseases, and they frequently come in contact with potentially harmful and hazardous drugs and other substances. Therefore, registered nurses must follow strict, standardized guidelines to guard against diseases and other dangers, such as radiation, accidental needle sticks, or the chemicals used to create a sterile and clean environment.

Work Schedules

Because patients in hospitals and nursing care facilities need round-the-clock care, nurses in these settings usually work in shifts, covering all 24 hours. They may work nights, weekends, and holidays. They may be on call, which means that they are on duty and must be available to work on short notice. Nurses who work in offices, schools, and other places that do not provide 24-hour care are more likely to work regular business hours.

HOW TO BECOME A REGISTERED NURSE

Registered nurses usually take one of three education paths: a Bachelor of Science degree in nursing (BSN), an associate's degree in nursing (ADN), or a diploma from an approved nursing program. Registered nurses must be licensed.

Education

In all nursing education programs, students take courses in anatomy, physiology, microbiology, chemistry, nutrition, psychology, and other social and behavioral sciences, as well as in liberal arts. BSN programs typically take 4 years to complete; ADN and diploma programs usually take 2 to 3 years to complete. Diploma programs are typically offered by hospitals or medical centers, and there are far fewer diploma programs than there are BSN and ADN programs. All programs include supervised clinical experience.

Bachelor's degree programs usually include additional education in the physical and social sciences, communication, leadership, and critical thinking. These programs also offer more clinical experience in nonhospital settings. A bachelor's degree or higher is often necessary for administrative positions, research, consulting, and teaching.

Generally, licensed graduates of any of the three types of education programs (bachelor's, associate's, or diploma) qualify for entry-level positions as a staff nurse. However, employers—particularly those in hospitals—may require a bachelor's degree.

Registered nurses with an ADN or diploma may go back to school to earn a bachelor's degree through an RN-to-BSN program. There are also master's degree programs in nursing, combined bachelor's and master's programs, and accelerated programs for those who wish to enter the nursing profession and already hold a bachelor's degree in another field. Some employers offer tuition reimbursement.

Clinical nurse specialists (CNSs) must earn a master's degree in nursing and typically already have 1 or more years of work experience as an RN or in a related field. CNSs who conduct research typically need a doctoral degree.

Licenses, Certifications, and Registrations

In all states, the District of Columbia, and U.S. territories, registered nurses must have a nursing license. To become licensed, nurses must graduate from an approved nursing program and pass the National Council Licensure Examination (NCLEX-RN).

Other requirements for licensing, such as passing a criminal background check, vary by state. Each state's board of nursing provides specific requirements. For more information on the NCLEX-RN and a list of state boards of nursing, visit the National Council of State Boards of Nursing.

Nurses may become certified through professional associations in specific areas, such as ambulatory care, gerontology, and pediatrics, among others. Although certification is usually voluntary, it demonstrates adherence to a higher standard, and some employers require it.

In addition, registered nursing positions may require certification in cardiopulmonary resuscitation (CPR), basic life support (BLS) certification, and/or advanced cardiac life support (ACLS).

CNSs must satisfy additional state licensing requirements, such as earning specialty certifications. Contact state boards of nursing for specific requirements.

ADVANCEMENT

Important Qualities

Critical-thinking skills. Registered nurses must assess changes in the health status of patients, such as determining when to take corrective action and when to make referrals.

Communication skills. Registered nurses must be able to communicate effectively with patients in order to understand their concerns and assess their health conditions. Nurses need to clearly explain instructions, such as how to take medication. They must work in teams with other health professionals and communicate the patients' needs.

Compassion. Registered nurses should be caring and empathetic when looking after patients.

Detail oriented. Registered nurses must be responsible and detail oriented because they must make sure that patients get the correct treatments and medicines at the right time.

Emotional stability. Registered nurses need emotional resilience and the ability to manage their emotions to cope with human suffering, emergencies, and other stresses.

Organizational skills. Nurses often work with multiple patients with various health needs. Organizational skills are critical to ensure that each patient is given appropriate care.

Physical stamina. Nurses should be comfortable performing physical tasks, such as moving patients. They may be on their feet for most of their shift.

Most registered nurses begin as staff nurses in hospitals or community health settings. With experience, good performance, and continuous education, they can move to other settings or be promoted to positions with more responsibility.

In management, nurses can advance from assistant clinical nurse manager, charge nurse, or head nurse to more senior-level administrative roles, such as assistant director or director of nursing, vice president of nursing, or chief nursing officer. Increasingly, management-level nursing positions require a graduate degree in nursing or health services administration. Administrative positions require leadership, communication skills, negotiation skills, and good judgment.

Some nurses move into the business side of healthcare. Their nursing expertise and experience on a healthcare team equip them to manage ambulatory, acute, home-based, and chronic care businesses. Employers—including hospitals, insurance companies, pharmaceutical manufacturers, and managed care organizations, among others— need registered nurses for jobs in health planning and development, marketing, consulting, policy development, and quality assurance.

Some RNs may become nurse anesthetists, nurse midwives, or nurse practitioners, which, along with clinical nurse specialists, are types of advanced practice registered nurses (APRNs). APRN positions require a master's degree, and many have a doctoral degree. APRNs may provide primary and specialty care, and in many states they may prescribe medications.

Other nurses work as postsecondary teachers or researchers in colleges and universities, which typically requires a Ph.D.

WAGES

Median annual wages, May 2017

Health diagnosing and treating practitioners: $79,480

Registered nurses: $70,000

Total, all occupations: $37,690

Note: All Occupations includes all occupations in the U.S. Economy. Source: U.S. Bureau of Labor Statistics, Occupational Employment Statistics

The median annual wage for registered nurses was $70,000 in May 2017. The lowest 10 percent earned less than $48,690, and the highest 10 percent earned more than $104,100. In May 2017, the median annual wages for registered nurses in the top industries in which they worked were as follows:

Government	$75,900
Hospitals; state, local, and private	72,070
Ambulatory healthcare services	66,300
Nursing and residential care facilities	62,320
Educational services; state, local, and private	60,300

Because patients in hospitals and nursing care facilities need round-the-clock care, nurses in these settings usually work in shifts, covering all 24 hours. They may work nights, weekends, and holidays. They may be on call, which means that they are on duty and must be available to work on short notice. Nurses who work in offices, schools, and other places that do not provide 24-hour care are more likely to work regular business hours.

Famous First

Despite equal opportunity legislation, nursing has continued to be a female-dominated profession. Exceptions include Francophone Africa—Benin, Burkina Faso, Cameroon, Chad, Congo, Côte d'Ivoire, the Democratic Republic of Congo, Djibouti, Guinea, Gabon, Mali, Mauritania, Niger, Rwanda, Senegal, and Togo—all of which have more male than female nurses. In some European countries, such as Spain, Portugal, Czech Republic and Italy, over 20% of nurses are male. In the United Kingdom, 11% of nurses and midwives registered with the Nursing and Midwifery Council (NMC) are male. The number of male-registered nurses in the United States between 1980 and 2000s doubled.

Source: https://en.wikipedia.org/wiki/Nursing

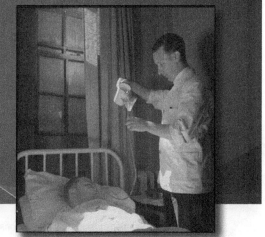

JOB OUTLOOK

Percent change in employment, projected 2016-26

Health diagnosing and treating practitioners: 16%

Registered nurses: 15%

Total, all occupations: 7%

Note: All Occupations includes all occupations in the U.S. Economy. Source: U.S. Bureau of Labor Statistics, Employment Projections program

Employment of registered nurses is projected to grow 15 percent from 2016 to 2026, much faster than the average for all occupations. Growth will occur for a number of reasons.

Demand for healthcare services will increase because of the aging population, given that older people typically have more medical problems than younger people. Nurses also will be needed to educate and care for patients with various chronic conditions, such as arthritis, dementia, diabetes, and obesity.

The financial pressure on hospitals to discharge patients as soon as possible may result in more people being admitted to long-term care facilities and outpatient care centers, and greater need for healthcare at home. Job growth is expected in facilities that provide long-term rehabilitation for stroke and head injury patients, and in facilities that treat people with Alzheimer's disease. In addition, because many older people prefer to be treated at home or in residential care facilities, registered nurses will be in demand in those settings.

Growth is also expected to be faster than average in outpatient care centers, where patients do not stay overnight, such as those which provide same-day chemotherapy, rehabilitation, and surgery.

In addition, an increased number of procedures, as well as more sophisticated procedures previously done only in hospitals, are being performed in ambulatory care settings and physicians' offices.

Job Prospects

Overall, job opportunities for registered nurses are expected to be good because of employment growth and the need to replace workers who retire over the coming decade. However, the supply of new nurses entering the labor market has increased in recent years. This increase has resulted in competition for jobs in some areas of the country. Generally, registered nurses with a Bachelor of Science degree in nursing (BSN) will have better job prospects than those without one. Employers also may prefer candidates who have some related work experience or certification in a specialty area, such as gerontology.

Employment projections data for Registered Nurses, 2016-26

Occupational Title	Employment, 2016	Projected Employment, 2026	Change, 2016-26	
			Percent	Numeric
Registered nurses	2,955,200	3,393,200	15	438,100

Source: Bureau of Labor Statistics, Employment Projections program

SIMILAR OCCUPATIONS

This list shows occupations with job duties that are similar to those of registered nurses.

OCCUPATION	JOB DUTIES
Dental Hygienists	Dental hygienists clean teeth, examine patients for signs of oral diseases such as gingivitis, and provide other preventive dental care. They also educate patients on ways to improve and maintain good oral health.
Diagnostic Medical Sonographers and Cardiovascular Technologists and Technicians, Including Vascular Technologists	Diagnostic medical sonographers and cardiovascular technologists and technicians, including vascular technologists, also called diagnostic imaging workers, operate special imaging equipment to create images or to conduct tests. The images and test results help physicians assess and diagnose medical conditions.
EMTs and Paramedics	Emergency medical technicians (EMTs) and paramedics care for the sick or injured in emergency medical settings. People's lives often depend on the quick reaction and competent care provided by these workers. EMTs and paramedics respond to emergency calls, performing medical services and transporting patients to medical facilities.
Licensed Practical and Licensed Vocational Nurses	Licensed practical nurses (LPNs) and licensed vocational nurses (LVNs) provide basic nursing care. They work under the direction of registered nurses and doctors.
Nurse Anesthetists, Nurse Midwives, and Nurse Practitioners	Nurse anesthetists, nurse midwives, and nurse practitioners, also referred to as advanced practice registered nurses (APRNs), coordinate patient care and may provide primary and specialty healthcare. The scope of practice varies from state to state.
Physician Assistants	Physician assistants, also known as PAs, practice medicine on teams with physicians, surgeons, and other healthcare workers. They examine, diagnose, and treat patients.

OCCUPATION	JOB DUTIES
Social Workers	Social workers help people solve and cope with problems in their everyday lives. Clinical social workers also diagnose and treat mental, behavioral, and emotional issues.
Respiratory Therapists	Respiratory therapists care for patients who have trouble breathing—for example, from a chronic respiratory disease, such as asthma or emphysema. Their patients range from premature infants with undeveloped lungs to elderly patients who have diseased lungs. They also provide emergency care to patients suffering from heart attacks, drowning, or shock.

Fast Fact

Linda Richards and Agnes Elizabeth Jones helped to create a number of nursing schools throughout the U.S. and Japan during the mid to late 1800's.

Source: The Nursing School Hub, https://www.nursingschoolhub.com/history-nursing/

Conversation With . . .
JEFF SOLHEIM

MSN, RN, CEN, TCRN, CFRN, FAEN, FAAN
Emergency Nurses Association President, 2018

Jeff Solheim has been a nurse for thirty years and is the founder of Solheim Enterprises in Portland, Oregon.

1. What was your individual career path in terms of education/training, entry-level job, or other significant opportunity?

I always had a desire to do this work, and three paths intersected. My father had a friend who was the administrator of a nursing home, so my high school job was working in a nursing home caring for older patients. Also, I was diagnosed with cancer at fifteen. I successfully battled it for a year but, unfortunately, due to treatments back in the day, I developed a secondary cancer that I continue to deal with. Finally, it just happened there was a nursing program near the town where I lived. So, being a patient and watching what nurses did, it all came together. That's how I chose nursing.

I graduated with an associate degree in nursing from Medicine Hat College in Alberta, Canada, and immediately got a job as a staff nurse taking care of patients directly in the intensive care unit. After a few years, an opportunity arose in the emergency department (ED), and I transferred to that area. During that time, I knew I had an interest in leadership, so I earned a certificate in healthcare. After three years in the ED, I accepted a leadership position in south Texas and relocated. There, I managed a telemetry unit and shortly thereafter was given responsibility to manage the ICU and ED.

During this time, I picked up a job as a flight nurse on weekends. There are two types of flight nursing: one is on a helicopter. In Texas, a large and rural state, say a farmer is injured in the field. It's much quicker to dispatch a helicopter than to try to get a ground ambulance out there. The helicopter lands right at the scene, and we stabilize the patient. I did this on the side for many, many years. More recently, I do the second type, international flight nursing. If somebody is overseas on vacation or working and needs to be repatriated back to the United States, a flying intensive care unit is deployed. It's a very specialized subset of emergency nursing and difficult to enter. I also am a cruise ship nurse several weeks a year. That's the great thing about emergency nursing: you can work in a prison, the ED, flights, and many other places. It's a great, versatile career.

Cases can be very difficult. I'll never forget the family who ran out of gas and was pushing their car along the side of the road, the father standing in the door steering and the wife and two teens in back pushing. A stolen, speeding vehicle hit the back of the car, and the three family members in back were pinned at high speed and suffered traumatic amputations. The father was not injured. Imagine trying to be comforter-in-chief while we two flight nurses triaged quickly and administered care.

I was in hospital administration for quite a few years. During this time, I was invited to the governor's office to help write legislation for trauma care in the state of Texas. This provided an opportunity to be a nurse in the governor's office and work on health care policy. Once that was over, I started my own consulting firm to assist states in setting up trauma systems, became a speaker and educator, and grew my company, which helps people become better nurses.

I worked with an associate degree for much of my career but felt the need to continue my education. Several years ago, I returned to school and earned my bachelor's and master's degrees in nursing at Western Governors University in Utah.

During 2018, I served as president of the Emergency Nurses Association. My job entailed representing and guiding our profession around the world. I've traveled almost a half-million miles. My other responsibility was to guide and lead the changes that impact the profession when we set standards for care.

My term recently ended, and I'm considering my options for what's next.

2. What are the most important skills and/or qualities for someone in your profession?

One of the greatest skills you must possess for emergency nursing is flexibility. Say I'm working at bedside with a child with a laceration, next to someone with severe abdominal pain who may have appendicitis, and I stop to give CPR to somebody who passed away from a heart attack. I might have started the hour thinking about discharging the child but now need to reprioritize to care for the cardiac patient.

Emergency nursing requires a good mixture of being organized and liking chaos. I know that sounds odd. If I have six patients and a really sick person is thrown into the mix, I have to figure out how to take care of everybody. In other words, you need to thrive on chaos while keeping organized.

3. What do you wish you had known going into this profession?

I was prepared because I had the advantage of working in a nursing home in high school. I do notice a lot of other nurses are surprised that this is a twenty-four-hour-a-day, 365-day-per-year job. New nurses graduate, hear they have to work Christmas Eve and Christmas, and say, "Wait, that's my family time." Well, no. Now you're a nurse, and that requires personal sacrifice.

4. Are there many job opportunities in your profession? In what specific areas?

Nursing, and especially emergency nursing, can't be taken over by automation. The population is growing. There will always be jobs in this field. Sometimes when you graduate as a nurse, you have to work in different areas and wait for an opening in the ED, which might be a few years down the road.

5. How do you see your profession changing in the next five years, how will technology impact that change, and what skills will be required?

One of the biggest changes nursing is experiencing is the rise of advanced practice. Nurse practitioner is a new educational level, and a lot of young nurses want to go right into it. That's going to be an issue for us. We may find advanced practice is more desirable than bedside nursing and have a re-engineering of our field on the horizon.

New technology is constantly being introduced, which means as a nurse you will constantly be on a learning curve. You are going to have to learn new skills and integrate the technology into your practice.

6. What do you enjoy most about your job? What do you enjoy least about your job?

I most like the camaraderie with my coworkers. Emergency nursing is a team sport. A bad trauma comes in, and we go in and do the impossible. It feels really good when a very difficult case comes through, and as a team you save a life and overcome a challenge.

The challenging aspects are the intense social needs emergency nurses are forced to see at work. I will care for celebrities and politicians, but I will also care for the homeless person, the person with a life sentence injured in prison, children beaten by parents, women beaten by husbands, or innocent people shot in a robbery attempt who then die in front of you. This is hard. A mentally ill patient comes in, and there's no hospital bed; what do I do with that person? It can wear on you.

7. Can you suggest a valuable "try this" for students considering a career in your profession?

Can I start with what they should not do? Do not base your decision to go into emergency nursing on TV dramas. That will give you a false sense of what we do. If you really, really want to see this work up close, the best way is to join a volunteer group. Every hospital has one, and many love to have high school students. You might work out front, you might work back in the ER passing out water.

This conversation was originally published in 2018.

MORE INFORMATION

For more information about registered nurses, including credentialing, visit

American Nurses Association
https: //www.nursingworld.org/

For more information about nursing education and being a registered nurse, visit

American Society of Registered Nurses
https: //www.asrn.org/

Johnson & Johnson, Nurses change lives
https: //nursing.jnj.com/home

National League for Nursing
http: //www.nln.org/

National Student Nurses' Association
https: //www.nsna.org/

For more information about undergraduate and graduate nursing education, nursing career options, and financial aid, vi

American Association of Colleges of Nursing
https: //www.aacnnursing.org/

For more information about the National Council Licensure Examination (NCLEX-RN) and a list of individual state boards of nursing, visit

National Council of State Boards of Nursing
https: //www.ncsbn.org/

For more information about clinical nurse specialists, including a list of accredited programs, visit

National Association of Clinical Nurse Specialists
https: //nacns.org/

O*NET
Acute Care Nurses
Advanced Practice Psychiatric Nurses
Clinical Nurse Specialists
Critical Care Nurses
Registered Nurses

Source

Bureau of Labor Statistics, U.S. Department of Labor, *Occupational Outlook Handbook*, Registered Nurses, on the Internet at https: //www.bls.gov/ooh/healthcare/registered-nurses.htm (visited January 20, 2019).

Rehabilitation Counselors

Snapshot

2017 Median Pay: $34,860 per year, $16.76 per hour

Typical Entry-Level Education: Master's degree

Work Experience in a Related Occupation: None

On-the-job Training: None

Number of Jobs, 2016: 119,300

Job Outlook, 2016-26: 13% (Faster than average)

Employment Change, 2016-26: 15,100

CAREER OVERVIEW

What Rehabilitation Counselors Do

Rehabilitation counselors help people with disabilities develop strategies to live with their disability and transition to employment.

Rehabilitation counselors help people with physical, mental, developmental, or emotional disabilities live independently.

They work with clients to overcome or manage the personal, social, or psychological effects of disabilities on employment or independent living.

Duties

- Rehabilitation counselors typically do the following:
- Provide individual and group counseling to help clients adjust to their disability
- Evaluate clients' abilities, interests, experiences, skills, health, and education
- Develop a treatment plan for clients, in consultation with other professionals, such as doctors, therapists, and psychologists
- Arrange for clients to obtain services, such as medical care or career training
- Help employers understand the needs and abilities of people with disabilities, as well as laws and resources that affect people with disabilities
- Help clients develop their strengths and adjust to their limitations
- Locate resources, such as wheelchairs or computer programs, that help clients live and work more independently
- Maintain client records and monitor clients' progress, adjusting the rehabilitation or treatment plan as necessary
- Advocate for the rights of people with disabilities to live in a community and work in the job of their choice

Rehabilitation counselors help people with disabilities at various stages in their lives. Some work with students, to develop strategies to live with their disability and transition from school to work. Others help veterans cope with the mental or physical effects of their military service. Still others help elderly people adapt to disabilities developed later in life from illness or injury. Some may provide expert testimony or assessments during personal-injury or workers' compensation cases.

Some rehabilitation counselors deal specifically with employment issues. These counselors, sometimes called ***vocational rehabilitation counselors***, typically work with older students and adults.

WORK ENVIRONMENT

Rehabilitation counselors work in a variety of settings, such as community rehabilitation centers, senior citizen centers, and youth guidance organizations.

Rehabilitation counselors held about 119,300 jobs in 2016. The largest employers of rehabilitation counselors were as follows:

Community and vocational rehabilitation services	30%
Individual and family services	19
State government, excluding education and hospitals	14
Nursing and residential care facilities	12
Self-employed workers	7

Rehabilitation counselors work in a variety of settings, such as community rehabilitation centers, senior citizen centers, and youth guidance organizations.

Work Schedules

Depending on where they work, some rehabilitation counselors may work evenings or weekends.

HOW TO BECOME A REHABILITATION COUNSELOR

Rehabilitation counselors typically need a master's degree in rehabilitation counseling or a related field. They may need to complete a period of supervised clinical experience as part of a master's degree. Some positions require certification or a license.

Education

Most employers require a master's degree in rehabilitation counseling or a related field. Master's degree programs teach students to evaluate clients' needs, formulate and implement job placement strategies, and understand the medical and psychological aspects of disabilities. These programs typically include a period of supervised clinical experience, such as an internship.

Although some employers hire workers with a bachelor's degree in rehabilitation and disability studies, these workers typically cannot offer the full range of services that a rehabilitation counselor with a master's degree can provide. Students in bachelor's degree programs learn about issues faced by people with disabilities and about the process of providing rehabilitation services. Some universities offer dual-degree programs in rehabilitation counseling, in which students can earn a bachelor's and master's degree in 5 years.

Licenses, Certifications, and Registrations

Licensing requirements for rehabilitation counselors differ by state and by type of services provided. Rehabilitation counselors who provide counseling services to clients and patients must attain a counselor license through their state licensing board. Rehabilitation counselors who provide other services, however, may be exempt from state licensing requirements. For example, rehabilitation counselors who provide only vocational rehabilitation services or job placement assistance may not need a license.

Licensure typically requires a master's degree and 2,000 to 4,000 hours of supervised clinical experience. In addition, counselors must pass a state-recognized exam. To maintain their license, counselors must complete annual continuing education credits.

Applicants should contact their state licensing board for information on which services or counseling positions require licensure. Contact information for these state licensing boards can be found through the Commission on Rehabilitation Counselor Certification.

Some employers prefer or require rehabilitation counselors to be certified. The Commission on Rehabilitation Counselor Certification offers the Certified Rehabilitation Counselor (CRC) certification.

Applicants must meet advanced education, work experience, and clinical supervision requirements and pass a test. Certification must be renewed every 5 years. Counselors must complete continuing education requirements or pass a reexamination to renew their certification.

ADVANCEMENT

Important Qualities

Communication skills. Rehabilitation counselors need to be able to communicate effectively with clients. They must express ideas and information in a way that is easy to understand.

Compassion. Rehabilitation counselors often work with people who are dealing with stressful and difficult situations. They must be compassionate and empathize with their clients.

Critical-thinking skills. Rehabilitation counselors must be able to develop a treatment plan to help clients reach their goals by considering each client's abilities and interests.

Interpersonal skills. Rehabilitation counselors must be able to work with different types of people. They spend most of their time working directly with clients, families, employers, or other professionals. They must be able to develop and maintain good working relationships.

Listening skills. Good listening skills are essential for rehabilitation counselors. They need to give their full attention in sessions in order to understand clients' problems, concerns, and values.

Patience. Rehabilitation counselors must have patience to help clients learn new skills and strategies to address their disabilities.

WAGES

Median annual wages, May 2017

Counselors, social workers, and other community and social service specialists: $43,860

Total, all occupations: $37,690

Rehabilitation counselors: $34,860

Note: All Occupations includes all occupations in the U.S. Economy. Source: U.S. Bureau of Labor Statistics, Occupational Employment Statistics

The median annual wage for rehabilitation counselors was $34,860 in May 2017. The lowest 10 percent earned less than $22,040, and the highest 10 percent earned more than $62,780.

In May 2017, the median annual wages for rehabilitation counselors in the top industries in which they worked were as follows:

State government, excluding education and hospitals	$48,380
Individual and family services	33,510
Nursing and residential care facilities	30,800
Community and vocational rehabilitation services	30,350

Depending on where they work, some rehabilitation counselors may work evenings or weekends.

JOB OUTLOOK

Percent change in employment, projected 2016-26

Counselors, social workers, and other community and social service specialists: 16%

Rehabilitation counselors: 13%

Total, all occupations: 7%

Note: All Occupations includes all occupations in the U.S. Economy. Source: U.S. Bureau of Labor Statistics, Employment Projections program

Employment of rehabilitation counselors is projected to grow 13 percent from 2016 to 2026, faster than the average for all occupations. Demand for rehabilitation counselors is expected to grow with the increase in the elderly population and with the continued rehabilitation needs of other groups, such as veterans and people with disabilities.

Older adults are more likely than other age groups to become disabled or injured. Rehabilitation counselors will be needed to help the elderly learn to adapt to any new limitations and learn strategies to live independently.

In addition, there will be a continued need for rehabilitation counselors to work with veterans who were disabled during their military service. They will also be needed to work with other groups, such as people who have learning disabilities, autism spectrum disorders, or substance abuse problems.

Job Prospects

Job prospects are expected to be good because of job growth and the need to replace workers.

**Employment projections data for
Rehabilitation counselors, 2016-26**

Occupational Title	SOC Code	Employment, 2016	Projected Employment, 2026	Change, 2016-26	
				Percent	Numeric
Rehabilitation counselors	21-1015	119,300	134,400	13	15,100

Source: Bureau of Labor Statistics, Employment Projections program

Famous First

About half of people with alcoholism will develop withdrawal symptoms upon reducing their alcohol consumption. Some develop delirium tremens (the DTs) or have seizures. The term delirium tremens appeared first in 1813, although the symptoms were well known since the 1700s. The word "delirium" is Latin for "going off the furrow," a plowing metaphor. It is also called shaking frenzy and Saunders-Sutton syndrome. Nicknames include the shakes, barrel-fever, blue horrors, bottleache, bats, drunken horrors, elephants, gallon distemper, quart mania, and pink spiders, among others.

Source: https://en.wikipedia.org/wiki/Delirium_tremens

SIMILAR OCCUPATIONS

This table shows a list of occupations with job duties that are similar to those of rehabilitation counselors.

OCCUPATION	JOB DUTIES	ENTRY-LEVEL EDUCATION	2017 MEDIAN PAY
Marriage and Family Therapists	Marriage and family therapists help people manage and overcome problems with family and other relationships.	Master's degree	$48,790
Occupational Therapists	Occupational therapists treat injured, ill, or disabled patients through the therapeutic use of everyday activities. They help these patients develop, recover, improve, as well as maintain the skills needed for daily living and working.	Master's degree	$83,200
Occupational Therapy Assistants and Aides	Occupational therapy assistants and aides help patients develop, recover, improve, as well as maintain the skills needed for daily living and working. Occupational therapy assistants are directly involved in providing therapy to patients; occupational therapy aides typically perform support activities. Both assistants and aides work under the direction of occupational therapists.	Associate's degree (assistants) High school diploma or equivalent (aides)	$56,690
Psychologists	Psychologists study cognitive, emotional, and social processes and behavior by observing, interpreting, and recording how individuals relate to one another and to their environments. They use their findings to help improve processes and behaviors.	PhD in psychology or a Doctor of Psychology (PsyD) degree	$77,030

OCCUPATION	JOB DUTIES	ENTRY-LEVEL EDUCATION	2017 MEDIAN PAY
School and Career Counselors	School counselors help students develop the academic and social skills needed to succeed in school. Career counselors help people choose careers and follow a path to employment.	Master's degree	$55,410
Social and Human Service Assistants	Social and human service assistants provide client services, including support for families, in a wide variety of fields, such as psychology, rehabilitation, and social work. They assist other workers, such as social workers, and they help clients find benefits or community services.	High school diploma or equivalent	$33,120
Special Education Teachers	Special education teachers work with students who have a wide range of learning, mental, emotional, and physical disabilities. They adapt general education lessons and teach various subjects, such as reading, writing, and math, to students with mild and moderate disabilities. They also teach basic skills, such as literacy and communication techniques, to students with severe disabilities.	Bachelor's degree	$58,980
Substance Abuse, Behavioral Disorder, and Mental Health Counselors	Substance abuse, behavioral disorder, and mental health counselors advise people who suffer from alcoholism, drug addiction, eating disorders, mental health issues, or other mental or behavioral problems. They provide treatment and support to help clients recover from addiction or modify problem behaviors.	Bachelor's degree	$43,300

OCCUPATION	JOB DUTIES	ENTRY-LEVEL EDUCATION	2017 MEDIAN PAY
Social Workers	Social workers help people solve and cope with problems in their everyday lives. Clinical social workers also diagnose and treat mental, behavioral, and emotional issues.	Bachelor's Bachelor's degree in social work (BSW) with supervised fieldwork or an internship for direct-service work Master's degree in social work (MSW) with supervised practicum or an internship, clinical work for clinical work	$47,980
Social and Community Service Managers	Social and community service managers coordinate and supervise social service programs and community organizations. They manage workers who provide social services to the public.	Bachelor's degree	$64,100

Fast Fact

One in five Americans has a disability, and the most common functional disability is difficulty walking or climbing stairs. That's according to a report from the Centers for Disease Control using data from 2013, as reported by the Voice of America.
Source: Brennan Center for Justice

Conversation With . . .
JOHN MOLLAHAN

Vocational Rehabilitation Counselor Oregon
Vocational Rehabilitation Services Portland,
OR Rehabilitation Counselor, 15 years

1. What was your individual career path in terms of education/training, entry-level job, or other significant opportunity?

Originally, I wanted to be a firefighter, so I did a lot of volunteer firefighting and earned an associate degree in fire science technology. The competition was pretty stiff, so I went back to school, got a bachelor's in sociology at Portland State University, and worked for 10 years as a residential life counselor at the Washington State School for the Blind.

While I was there, I returned to Portland State and earned a master's degree in counseling, education, and rehabilitation. I originally applied to become a community counselor, but a professor who was basically the father of vocational rehabilitation told me that with my background, I should think about rehab. I asked: "What's rehab?" We talked, I realized I had already been doing the work, and that's what prompted me to go into this field.

We assist people who have disabilities—sometimes acquired through a sports injury, although it could be anything—and help them get back to work. We break down the barriers to work, and seek accommodations. Every individual has unique needs. A good case in point is a client who came in with multiple concussions, all related to sports injuries. This guy was fairly well-educated. He was having memory problems and mental health issues such as depression. He was working in the sports industry, but couldn't continue because of the memory issues and fatigue. We tried to fully understand his condition, gathering medical records and determining his eligibility for services.

We sent him to get enhanced rehab at a specialized brain injury clinic to help him with organization, and maybe get adaptive equipment to help him remember things. He was also meeting other people adapting to their disabilities. A lot of rehab is grief over the loss of ability to perform at the level you're used to. This gentleman no doubt benefited from meeting others in a similar situation.

We're not therapists, although I do have a private practice for mental health therapy. We do counseling and guidance. We do a lot of referrals, including for physical capacity exams. We keep people employed, help them access employment, and advocate for them on the job. Maybe they need a special chair, or desk.

2. **What are the most important skills and/or qualities for someone in your profession?**

Interpersonal skills such as empathy—the ability to enter a person's world and walk with them. People in this position need a master's degree—usually a counseling background. It's also helpful if a vocational rehabilitation counselor has done a variety of jobs, whether it's working at Taco Bell or working as a laborer, so that you have a varied background to help a person enter a field.

3. **What do you wish you had known going into this profession?**

Rehab counselors do a lot of procurement of services. I wish I'd had more training on how to handle a budget. In my master's degree studies, we didn't talk a lot about allocating and spending money.

4. **Are there many job opportunities in your profession? In what specific areas?**

There are a number of jobs in the field. Vocational rehabilitation counseling is a relatively small field, but there are jobs in state and federal programs, including working with veterans, and jobs with insurance companies. Some insurance companies contract out their vocational rehab work to private counselors.

5. **How do you see your profession changing in the next five years as it relates to fitness and/or sports injuries? What role will technology play, and what skills will be required?**

We use case management software systems that are always being improved. What we struggle with is making sure our services are seamless, so we've moved toward online applications. Technology will continue to help people access our services, but you will always need some interpersonal interaction.

6. **What do you enjoy most about your job? What do you enjoy least about your job?**

I really enjoy helping people reach their job goals and overcome their disabilities. I least enjoy the bureaucracy involved in serving our clients.

7. **Can you suggest a valuable "try this" for students considering a career in your profession?**

Job shadow, do informational interviews, and volunteer to work for a social service agency. Become a camp counselor, work at the teen center, work at a Boys & Girls Club. See if working with people gives you pleasure.

This conversation was originally published in 2018.

MORE INFORMATION

For more information about counseling and information about counseling specialties, visit

American Counseling Association
https://www.counseling.org/

American Rehabilitation Counseling Association
http://www.arcaweb.org/

For more information about accredited degree programs in rehabilitation counseling, visit

Council for Accreditation of Counseling & Related Educational Programs
https://www.cacrep.org/

For more information about the Certified Rehabilitation Counselors certification and state licensing boards, visit

Commission on Rehabilitation Counselor Certification
https://www.crccertification.com/

Sources

Bureau of Labor Statistics, U.S. Department of Labor, *Occupational Outlook Handbook*, Probation Officers and Correctional Treatment Specialists.

Security Guards and Gaming Surveillance Officers

Snapshot

2017 Median Pay: $26,960 per year, $12.96 per hour

Typical Entry-Level Education: High school diploma or equivalent

Work Experience in a Related Occupation: Experience in surveillance or in casinos. Experience with video monitoring technology.

On-the-job Training: Short- to moderate-term on-the-job training; additional training for armed guards

Number of Jobs, 2016: 1,133,900

Job Outlook, 2016-26: 6% (As fast as average)

Employment Change, 2016-26: 71,000

CAREER OVERVIEW

What Security Guards and Gaming Surveillance Officers Do

Security guards control building access for employees and visitors.

Security guards and gaming surveillance officers patrol and protect property against theft, vandalism, and other illegal activity.

Duties

Security guards and gaming surveillance officers typically do the following:

- Enforce laws and protect an employer's property
- Monitor alarms and closed-circuit TV (CCTV) cameras
- Respond to emergencies
- Control building access for employees and visitors
- Conduct security checks over a specified area
- Write reports on what they observed while on duty
- Detain violators

Guards and officers must remain alert, looking out for anything unusual. In an emergency, they are required to call for assistance from police, fire, or ambulance services. Some security guards are armed.

A security guard's responsibilities vary from one employer to another. In retail stores, guards protect people, merchandise, money, and equipment. They may work with undercover store detectives to prevent theft by customers and employees, detain shoplifting suspects until the police arrive, and patrol parking lots.

In offices and factories, security guards protect workers and equipment and check the credentials of people and vehicles entering and leaving the premises.

Security guards work in many other environments, because they work wherever people and assets need to be protected.

Security guards, also called security officers, protect property, enforce rules on the property, and deter criminal activity. Some guards are assigned a stationary position from which they monitor alarms or surveillance cameras. Other guards are assigned a patrol area where they conduct security checks.

Gaming surveillance officers and gaming investigators act as security agents for casinos. Using audio and video equipment in an observation room, they watch casino operations for suspicious activities, such as cheating and theft, and monitor compliance with rules, regulations, and laws. They maintain and organize recordings from security cameras, which are sometimes used as evidence in police investigations.

WORK ENVIRONMENT

Some security guards monitor alarms or surveillance cameras from a desk.

Gaming surveillance officers and gaming investigators held about 10,700 jobs in 2016. The largest employers of gaming surveillance officers and gaming investigators were as follows:

Local government, excluding education and hospitals	47%
Gambling industries (except casino hotels)	25
Casino hotels	19
State government, excluding education and hospitals	4
Spectator sports	2

Security guards held about 1.1 million jobs in 2016. The largest employers of security guards were as follows:

Investigation, guard, and armored car services	58%
Educational services; state, local, and private	6
Accommodation and food services	6
Healthcare and social assistance	6
Government	4

Security guards work in a wide variety of places, including public spaces, stores, and office buildings. Gaming surveillance officers and investigators are employed only in locations where gambling is legal.

Most security guards spend considerable time on their feet, either at a single post or patrolling buildings and grounds. Some may sit for long periods behind a counter or in a guardhouse at the entrance to a gated facility or community.

Security guards who work during the day may have a great deal of contact with other employees and the public.

Most gaming surveillance officers sit behind a desk observing customers on video surveillance equipment.

Work Schedules

Security guards and gaming surveillance officers usually work in shifts of approximately 8 hours, with rotating schedules. Night shifts are common.

HOW TO BECOME A SECURITY GUARD OR GAMING SURVEILLANCE OFFICER

Most states require that guards be registered with the state in which they work.

Most security guard and gaming surveillance officer jobs require a high school diploma. Gaming surveillance officers sometimes need experience with security and video surveillance. Most states require security guards to be registered with the state, especially if they carry a firearm.

Education

Security guards generally need a high school diploma or equivalent, although some jobs may not have any education requirements. Gaming surveillance officers also need a high school diploma or equivalent and may need experience with video surveillance technology depending upon assignment.

Training

Although most employers provide instruction for newly hired security guards, the amount of training they receive varies. Most security guards, however, learn their job in a few weeks. During this time, the employer-provided training typically covers emergency procedures, detention of suspected criminals, and proper communication.

Many states recommend that security guards receive approximately 8 hours of pre-assignment training, 8–16 hours of on-the-job training, and 8 hours of annual training. This may include training in protection, public relations, report writing, deterring crises, first aid, and other specialized training related to the security guard's assignment.

Training is more rigorous for armed guards because they require weapons training. Armed guards may be tested periodically in the use of firearms.

Gaming surveillance officers and investigators receive training in topics such as the rules of casino games, gaming regulations, identifying cheating techniques, and the proper use of video and radio equipment.

Drug testing may be required both as a condition of employment and randomly during employment.

Work Experience in a Related Occupation

Gaming surveillance officers and investigators may need previous work experience in surveillance or in casinos. Experience with video monitoring technology is particularly helpful, and some workers gain this experience by working as a security guard.

Licenses, Certifications, and Registrations

Most states require that security guards be registered with the state in which they work. Although registration requirements vary by state, basic qualifications for candidates are as follows:

- Be at least 18 years old
- Pass a background check
- Complete training

Guards who carry weapons usually must be registered by the appropriate government authority. Armed guard positions have more stringent background checks and entry requirements than those of unarmed guards. Rigorous hiring and screening programs, including background, criminal record, and fingerprint checks, are required for armed guards in most states.

Some jobs may also require a driver's license.

ADVANCEMENT

Important Qualities

Communication skills. Security guards and officers must communicate effectively with others, even in stressful situations.

Good judgment. Security guards and officers must be able to quickly determine the best course of action when a dangerous situation arises.

Observation skills. Security guards and officers must be alert and aware of their surroundings, and be able to quickly recognize anything out of the ordinary.

Patience. Security guards and officers may need to spend long periods standing and observing their environment without distractions.

Famous First

Early gambling establishments in the United States were known as saloons. Four major cities were most particularly affected by the growth of saloons: New Orleans, St. Louis, Chicago and San Francisco. Travelers who patronized saloons could find people to talk to, drink with, and gamble with. Gambling was outlawed during the early 20th century in America, gambling became outlawed and banned by state legislation and social reformers of the time but, in 1931, gambling was legalized throughout the state of Nevada where America's first legalized casinos were set up. In 1976 New Jersey allowed gambling in Atlantic City, and it is now America's second largest gambling city.

Source: https://en.wikipedia.org/wiki/Casino

WAGES

Median annual wages, May 2017

Total, all occupations: $37,690

Gaming surveillance officers and gaming investigators: $33,260

Other protective service workers: $27,150

Security guards and gaming surveillance officers: $26,960

Security guards: $26,900

Note: All Occupations includes all occupations in the U.S. Economy. Source: U.S. Bureau of Labor Statistics, Occupational Employment Statistics

The median annual wage for gaming surveillance officers and gaming investigators was $33,260 in May 2017. The lowest 10 percent earned less than $23,010, and the highest 10 percent earned more than $54,480.

The median annual wage for security guards was $26,900 in May 2017. The lowest 10 percent earned less than $19,640, and the highest 10 percent earned more than $48,370.

In May 2017, the median annual wages for gaming surveillance officers and gaming investigators in the top industries in which they worked were as follows:

State government, excluding education and hospitals	$54,270
Casino hotels	36,600
Gambling industries (except casino hotels)	33,860
Spectator sports	32,170
Local government, excluding education and hospitals	30,610

In May 2017, the median annual wages for security guards in the top industries in which they worked were as follows:

Government	$33,170
Educational services; state, local, and private	32,010
Healthcare and social assistance	31,980
Accommodation and food services	27,850
Investigation, guard, and armored car services	25,170

Security guards and gaming surveillance officers usually work in shifts of approximately 8 hours, with rotating schedules. Night shifts are common.

JOB OUTLOOK

Percent change in employment, projected 2016-26

Total, all occupations: 7%

Other protective service workers: 7%

Security guards: 6%

Security guards and gaming surveillance officers: 6%

Gaming surveillance officers and gaming investigators: 4%

Note: All Occupations includes all occupations in the U.S. Economy. Source: U.S. Bureau of Labor Statistics, Employment Projections program

Overall employment of security guards and gaming surveillance officers is projected to grow 6 percent from 2016 to 2026, about as fast as the average for all occupations.

Employment of security guards is projected to grow 6 percent from 2016 to 2026, about as fast as the average for all occupations. Security guards will continue to be needed to protect both people and property because of concerns about crime and vandalism.

Employment of gaming surveillance officers and investigators is projected to grow 4 percent from 2016 to 2026, slower than the average for all occupations. Although states continue to legalize gambling and casinos continue to grow in number, advances in video surveillance and anti-cheating technology may limit the employment of gaming surveillance officers and investigators.

Job Prospects

Overall job opportunities are projected to be excellent, especially for security guards. The large size of the occupation and the number of workers who leave the occupation each year should result in many job openings. However, there will be more competition for higher paying positions that require more training and experience.

Candidates who have experience with video surveillance equipment should have the best job prospects in the gaming industry. Those with a background in law enforcement will also have an advantage.

**Employment projections data for
Security guards and gaming surveillance officers, 2016-26**

Occupational Title	SOC Code	Employment, 2016	Projected Employment, 2026	Change, 2016-26	
				Percent	Numeric
Security guards and gaming surveillance officers	33-9030	1,133,900	1,205,000	6	71,000
Gaming surveillance officers and gaming investigators	33-9031	10,700	11,100	4	400
Security guards	33-9032	1,123,300	1,193,900	6	70,600

Source: Bureau of Labor Statistics, Employment Projections program

Fast Fact

Because Native American casinos are located on tribal land, they are part of a free and sovereign nation. That means they have a right to their own police force.

Source: Cracked.

SIMILAR OCCUPATIONS

OCCUPATION	JOB DUTIES	ENTRY-LEVEL EDUCATION	2017 MEDIAN PAY
Correctional Officers and Bailiffs	Correctional officers are responsible for overseeing individuals who have been arrested and are awaiting trial or who have been sentenced to serve time in jail or prison. Bailiffs are law enforcement officers who maintain safety and order in courtrooms.	High school diploma or equivalent	$43,510
Gaming Services Workers	Gaming services workers serve customers in gambling establishments, such as casinos or racetracks. Some workers tend slot machines, deal cards, or oversee other gaming activities such as keno or bingo. Others take bets or pay out winnings. Still others supervise or manage gaming workers and operations.	High school diploma or equivalent	$22,300
Police and Detectives	Police officers protect lives and property. Detectives and criminal investigators, who are sometimes called agents or special agents, gather facts and collect evidence of possible crimes.	High school diploma or equivalent (police) Bachelor's degree (fish and game wardens) Bachelor's degree (federal agencies)	$62,960

OCCUPATION	JOB DUTIES	ENTRY-LEVEL EDUCATION	2017 MEDIAN PAY
Private Detectives and Investigators	Private detectives and investigators search for information about legal, financial, and personal matters. They offer many services, such as verifying people's backgrounds and statements, finding missing persons, and investigating computer crimes.	High school diploma or equivalent	$50,700
Firefighters	Firefighters control and put out fires and respond to emergencies where life, property, or the environment is at risk.	Postsecondary nondegree award	$49,080

Conversation With . . .
COLIN VICK

CPP

Security Officer, 14 years

1. What was your individual career path in terms of education/training, entry-level job, or other significant opportunity?

At one time I thought about becoming a law enforcement officer but police are often reactive. I wanted to be part of the solution that prevented incidents from occurring in the first place.

Initially I didn't have any formalized training and was hired on as a security officer, an entry-level position that allowed me to see the different types of security -- from mobile patrol service to providing security for retail stores, shopping malls, hotels, commercial buildings, and even some armed security jobs. That job really opened my eyes. I was in college so I left for awhile, but missed the operational aspects of security.

I started at Per Mar Security Services in November 2002, again as an entry-level security officer, and worked my way up. In that time, a greater emphasis has been placed on both security and emergency management due to a combination of heightened awareness since September 11, 2001 and the upgrades in technology we've seen. You almost need a background in electronics to know the inner workings of some of the technology. Many colleges and universities have added courses and offer degree programs in these fields since I started.

Different security organizations have certifications that enhance your credentials and your expertise. I took and passed a certification exam from ASIS International, a worldwide organization, to become a Certified Protection Professional in 2011. The certification is held in high esteem and, although the exam can be intimidating and exhausting, it is worth the effort.

2. What are the most important skills and/or qualities for someone in your profession?

I agree with the four values that guide our company: communication, so you have a solid foundation that is supported by a desire to communicate your expectations, your needs, your goals, or even simply what you witnessed; integrity, so your actions answer for what you do and say, and, finally, excellent service.

3. What do you wish you had known going into this profession?

I wish I'd had a better understanding of what it means to have an integrated protection program. In addition to a security guard, such a program includes access control (entry devices, card readers, computer and verification systems); display and assessment (CCTV, workstations, fixed security posts and patrols); barriers (fences, gates, lighting, locking devices or clear zones), communications (radios, telephone equipment, intercoms, and data networks), identification (photos, fingerprints, signatures, ID cards, and vehicle decals), intrusion detection (exterior sensors, interior sensors, and duress sensors), and operations procedures, such as standards, training, policies, and crisis management.

4. What do you wish you had known going into this profession?

Many, including supervisory and management positions. I work for a contract security company. We are hired to provide companies with contracted security officers. Some companies have their own proprietary security program and hire their own officers. The breakdown throughout the United States is close to 50% contract and 50% proprietary.

5. How do you see your profession changing in the next five years? What role will technology play in those changes, and what skills will be required?

Technology will play a huge role. The automation and biometrics fields have grown by leaps and bounds and this trend will continue. Leveraging greater security technological needs with security officers who can successfully navigate these systems will become a greater need. Many companies will have dedicated security operations centers -- a nerve center -- and security officers will need to know how to run access control systems, closed circuit television systems, building automation systems, central alarm monitoring, and communication systems, all from one console.

6. What do you enjoy most about your job? What do you enjoy least?

I enjoy doing physical security surveys for clients, which is an overview of vulnerability at a given facility or site. It allows me to take an objective look at an overall security program. This is often a puzzle that combines a mix of science and art to give the facility an upgraded security program that fits both their needs and their budget.

The thing I like least is dealing with people who don't take security seriously. While I believe this is rare, sometimes people work within this industry and just see it as a job.

7. Can you suggest a valuable "try this" for students considering a career in your profession?

Contact a security company and see if you can interview one of the managers about their day-to-day responsibilities. If that looks like something you might be interested in doing, perhaps an internship or a part-time job with the company might be an option. Also, many security organizations or magazines offer or sponsor free online webinars about various topics that are relevant within the security realm.

MORE INFORMATION

Sources

Bureau of Labor Statistics, U.S. Department of Labor, *Occupational Outlook Handbook*, Security Guards and Gaming Surveillance Officers.

Social and Community Service Managers

Snapshot

2017 Median Pay: $64,100 per year, $30.82 per hour

Typical Entry-Level Education: Bachelor's degree

Work Experience in a Related Occupation: Less than 5 years

On-the-job Training: None

Number of Jobs, 2016: 147,300

Job Outlook, 2016-26: 18% (Much faster than average)

Employment Change, 2016-26: 26,500

CAREER OVERVIEW

What Social and Community Service Managers Do

Social and community service managers meet with community members and funding providers to discuss their programs.

Social and community service managers coordinate and supervise social service programs

and community organizations. They manage workers who provide social services to the public.

Duties

Social and community service managers typically do the following:

- Work with community members and other stakeholders to identify necessary programs and services
- Oversee administrative aspects of programs to meet the objectives of the stakeholders
- Analyze data to determine the effectiveness of programs
- Suggest and implement improvements to programs and services
- Plan and manage outreach activities to advocate for increased awareness of programs
- Write proposals for social services funding

Social and community service managers work for a variety of social and human service organizations. Some of these organizations focus on working with a particular demographic, such as children, people who are homeless, older adults, or veterans. Others focus on helping people with particular challenges, such as substance abuse, mental health needs, chronic hunger, and long-term unemployment.

Social and community service managers are often expected to show that their programs and services are effective. They collect statistics and other information to evaluate the impact their programs have on the community or their target audience. They are usually required to report this information to administrators or funders. They may also use evaluations to identify opportunities to improve their programs, such as providing mentorship and assessments for their staff.

Although the specific job duties of social and community service managers may vary with the size of the organization, most managers must recruit, hire, and train new staff members. They also supervise staff, such as social workers, who provide services directly to clients. Additionally, they may perform some of the services of the workers they oversee.

In large agencies, social and community service managers tend to have specialized duties. They may be responsible for running only one program in an organization and reporting to the agency's upper management. They usually do not design programs but instead supervise and implement programs set up by administrators, elected officials, or other stakeholders.

In small organizations, social and community managers often have many roles. They represent their organization through public speaking engagements or in communitywide committees; they oversee programs and execute their implementations; they spend time on administrative tasks, such as managing budgets; and they also help with raising funds and meeting with potential donors.

WORK ENVIRONMENT

Social and community service managers held about 147,300 jobs in 2016. The largest employers of social and community service managers were as follows:

Individual and family services	27%
Religious, grantmaking, civic, professional, and similar organizations	12
Local government, excluding education and hospitals	11
Nursing and residential care facilities	11
Community and vocational rehabilitation services	10

Social and community service managers work for nonprofit organizations, private for-profit social service companies, and government agencies. They also work in a variety of settings, including offices, clinics, hospitals, and shelters.

Work Schedules

The majority of social and community service managers work full time. They may work extended hours to meet deadlines or when preparing new programs; about 1 in 4 worked more than 40 hours per week in 2016.

HOW TO BECOME A SOCIAL AND COMMUNITY SERVICE MANAGER

Social and community service managers typically need at least a bachelor's degree and Work Experience in a Related Occupation.

Social and community service managers typically need at least a bachelor's degree and work experience. However, some positions also require a master's degree.

Education

Most social and community service manager jobs require a bachelor's degree in social work, public or business administration, public health, or a related field. However, some positions also require a master's degree.

Work Experience

Workers usually need experience in order to become a social and community service manager, and it is essential for those with a bachelor's degree. Lower-level management positions may require only a few years of experience, although social and community service directors typically have much more experience. Candidates can get this experience by working as a social worker, substance abuse counselor, or in a similar occupation.

ADVANCEMENT

Important Qualities

Analytical skills. Social and community service managers need to understand and evaluate data in order to provide strategic guidance to their organization. They must be able to monitor and evaluate current programs as well as determine new initiatives.

Communication skills. Social and community service managers must be able to speak and write clearly so that others can understand them. Public speaking experience is also helpful because social and community service managers often participate in community outreach.

Managerial skills. Social and community service managers spend much of their time administering budgets and responding to a wide variety of issues.

Problem-solving skills. Social and community service managers must be able to address client, staff, and agency-related issues as they occur.

Time-management skills. Social and community service managers must prioritize and handle numerous tasks for multiple customers, often in a short timeframe.

WAGES

Median annual wages, May 2017

Other management occupations: $88,720

Social and community service managers: $64,100

Total, all occupations: $37,690

Note: All Occupations includes all occupations in the U.S. Economy. Source: U.S. Bureau of Labor Statistics, Occupational Employment Statistics

The median annual wage for social and community service managers was $64,100 in May 2017. The lowest 10 percent earned less than $39,730, and the highest 10 percent earned more than $109,990.

In May 2017, the median annual wages for social and community service managers in the top industries in which they worked were as follows:

Local government, excluding education and hospitals	$82,100
Religious, grantmaking, civic, professional, and similar organizations	67,580
Nursing and residential care facilities	60,970
Community and vocational rehabilitation services	59,450
Individual and family services	57,990

The majority of social and community service managers work full time. They may work extended hours to meet deadlines or when preparing new programs; about 1 in 4 worked more than 40 hours per week in 2016.

JOB OUTLOOK

Percent change in employment, projected 2016-26

Social and community service managers: 18%

Other management occupations: 8%

Total, all occupations: 7%

Note: All Occupations includes all occupations in the U.S. Economy. Source: U.S. Bureau of Labor Statistics, Employment Projections program

Employment of social and community service managers is projected to grow 18 percent from 2016 to 2026, much faster than the average for all occupations.

Much of the job growth in this occupation is the result of an aging population. An increase in the number of older adults will result in a need for more social services, such as adult daycare and meal delivery, creating demand for social and community service managers. Employment of social and community service managers is expected to increase the most in industries serving the elderly, such as services for the elderly and persons with disabilities.

In addition, employment growth is projected as people continue to seek treatment for their addictions, and as illegal drug offenders are increasingly sent to treatment programs rather than to jail. As a result, managers who direct treatment programs will be needed.

Job Prospects

Job prospects are expected to be good because of the continued expected demand for individual and family social services.

Employment projections data for
Social and community service managers 2016-26

Occupational Title	SOC Code	Employment, 2016	Projected Employment, 2026	Change, 2016-26	
				Percent	Numeric
Social and community service managers	11-9151	147,300	173,800	18	26,500

Source: Bureau of Labor Statistics, Employment Projections program

Fast Fact

Mental disorders increase the risk of getting other diseases such as cardiovascular disease, diabetes, and HIV -- and having one of those diseases increases the likelihood of a person developing a mental illness.
Source: World Health Organization

SIMILAR OCCUPATIONS

This table shows a list of occupations with job duties that are similar to those of social and community service managers.

OCCUPATION	JOB DUTIES	ENTRY-LEVEL EDUCATION	2017 MEDIAN PAY
Health Educators and Community Health Workers	Health educators teach people about behaviors that promote wellness. They develop and implement strategies to improve the health of individuals and communities. Community health workers collect data and discuss health concerns with members of specific populations or communities.	Bachelor's degree (health educators) High school diploma or equivalent (community health workers)	$45,360
Marriage and Family Therapists	Marriage and family therapists help people manage and overcome problems with family and other relationships.	Master's degree	$48,790
Probation Officers and Correctional Treatment Specialists	Probation officers and correctional treatment specialists provide social services to assist in rehabilitation of law offenders in custody or on probation or parole.	Bachelor's degree	$51,410

OCCUPATION	JOB DUTIES	ENTRY-LEVEL EDUCATION	2017 MEDIAN PAY
Rehabilitation Counselors	Rehabilitation counselors help people with physical, mental, developmental, or emotional disabilities live independently. They work with clients to overcome or manage the personal, social, or psychological effects of disabilities on employment or independent living.	Master's degree	$34,860
School and Career Counselors	School counselors help students develop the academic and social skills needed to succeed in school. Career counselors help people choose careers and follow a path to employment.	Master's degree	$55,410
Social and Human Service Assistants	Social and human service assistants provide client services, including support for families, in a wide variety of fields, such as psychology, rehabilitation, and social work. They assist other workers, such as social workers, and they help clients find benefits or community services.	High school diploma or equivalent	$33,120
Social Workers	Social workers help people solve and cope with problems in their everyday lives. Clinical social workers also diagnose and treat mental, behavioral, and emotional issues.	Bachelor's degree in social work (BSW) with supervised fieldwork or an internship for direct-service work Master's degree in social work (MSW) with supervised practicum or an internship, clinical work for clinical work	$47,980

OCCUPATION	JOB DUTIES	ENTRY-LEVEL EDUCATION	2017 MEDIAN PAY
Substance Abuse, Behavioral Disorder, and Mental Health Counselors	Substance abuse, behavioral disorder, and mental health counselors advise people who suffer from alcoholism, drug addiction, eating disorders, mental health issues, or other mental or behavioral problems. They provide treatment and support to help clients recover from addiction or modify problem behaviors.	Bachelor's degree	$43,300
Medical and Health Services Managers	Medical and health services managers, also called healthcare executives or healthcare administrators, plan, direct, and coordinate medical and health services. They might manage an entire facility, a specific clinical area or department, or a medical practice for a group of physicians. Medical and health services managers must direct changes that conform to changes in healthcare laws, regulations, and technology.	Bachelor's degree	$98,350

MORE INFORMATION

For more information about social and community service managers, visit

The Network for Social Work Management
https://socialworkmanager.org/

National Association of Social Workers
https://www.socialworkers.org/

Council on Social Work Education
https://www.cswe.org/

Source

Bureau of Labor Statistics, U.S. Department of Labor, *Occupational Outlook Handbook*,Social and Community Service Managers.

Social Workers

Snapshot

2017 Median Pay: $47,980 per year, $23.07 per hour

Typical Entry-Level Education: Bachelor's degree in social work (BSW) with supervised fieldwork or an internship for direct-service work, Master's degree in social work (MSW) with supervised practicum or an internship, clinical work for clinical work

Work Experience in a Related Occupation: None

On-the-job Training: Two years of supervised training and experience after obtaining an MA degree for clinical social workers.

Number of Jobs, 2016: 682,100

Job Outlook, 2016-26: 16% (Much faster than average)

Employment Change, 2016-26: 109,700

CAREER OVERVIEW

What Social Workers Do

Social workers help people solve and cope with problems in their everyday lives. Clinical social workers also diagnose and treat mental, behavioral, and emotional issues.

Duties

Social workers typically do the following:
- Identify people and communities in need of help
- Assess clients' needs, situations, strengths, and support networks to determine their goals
- Help clients adjust to changes and challenges in their lives, such as illness, divorce, or unemployment
- Research, refer, and advocate for community resources, such as food stamps, childcare, and healthcare to assist and improve a client's well-being
- Respond to crisis situations such as child abuse and mental health emergencies
- Follow up with clients to ensure that their situations have improved
- Maintain case files and records
- Develop and evaluate programs and services to ensure that basic client needs are met
- Provide psychotherapy services

Social workers help people cope with challenges in their lives. They help with a wide range of situations, such as adopting a child or being diagnosed with a terminal illness.

Advocacy is an important aspect of social work. Social workers advocate or raise awareness with and on behalf of their clients and the social work profession on local, state, and national levels.

Some social workers—referred to as *bachelor's social workers* (BSW)—work with groups, community organizations, and policymakers to develop or improve programs, services, policies, and social conditions. This focus of work is referred to as macro social work.

Social workers who are licensed to diagnose and treat mental, behavioral, and emotional disorders are called *clinical social workers* (CSW) or *licensed clinical social workers* (LCSW). They provide individual, group, family, and couples therapy; they work with clients to develop strategies to change behavior or cope with difficult situations; and they refer clients to other resources or services, such as support groups or other mental health professionals. Clinical social workers can develop treatment plans with the client, doctors, and other healthcare professionals and may adjust the treatment plan if necessary based on their client's progress. They may work in a variety of specialties. Clinical social workers who have not completed two years of supervised work are often called *master's social workers* (MSW).

The following are examples of types of social workers:

Child and family social workers protect vulnerable children and help families in need of assistance. They help families find housing or services, such as childcare, or apply for benefits, such as food stamps. They intervene when children are in danger of neglect or abuse. Some help arrange adoptions, locate foster families, or work to reunite families.

School social workers work with teachers, parents, and school administrators to develop plans and strategies to improve students' academic performance and social development. Students and their families are often referred to social workers to deal with problems such as aggressive behavior, bullying, or frequent absences from school.

Healthcare social workers help patients understand their diagnosis and make the necessary adjustments to their lifestyle, housing, or healthcare. For example, they may help people make the transition from the hospital back to their homes and communities. In addition, they may provide information on services, such as home healthcare or support groups, to help patients manage their illness or disease. Social workers help doctors and other healthcare professionals understand the effects that diseases and illnesses have on patients' mental and emotional health. Some healthcare social workers specialize in geriatric social work, hospice and palliative care, or medical social work.

Mental health and substance abuse social workers help clients with mental illnesses or addictions. They provide information on services, such as support groups and 12-step programs, to help clients cope with their illness. Many clinical social workers function in these roles as well.

WORK ENVIRONMENT

Social workers held about 682,100 jobs in 2016. Employment in the detailed occupations that make up social workers was distributed as follows:

Child, family, and school social workers	317,600
Healthcare social workers	176,500
Mental health and substance abuse social workers	123,900
Social workers, all other	64,000

The largest employers of social workers were as follows:

Individual and family services	18%
State government, excluding education and hospitals	14
Ambulatory healthcare services	13
Local government, excluding education and hospitals	13
Hospitals; state, local, and private	12

Although most social workers work in an office, they may spend time visiting clients. School social workers may be assigned to multiple schools and travel around the school district to see students. Understaffing and large caseloads may cause the work to be stressful.

Social workers may work remotely through distance counseling, using videoconferencing or mobile technology to meet with clients and organize support and advocacy groups.

Injuries and Illnesses

"Social workers, all other" have one of the highest rates of injuries and illnesses of all occupations. ("All other" titles represent occupations with a wide range of characteristics that do not fit into any of the other detailed occupations.)

Work Schedules

The majority of social workers worked full time in 2016. They sometimes work evenings, weekends, and holidays to see clients or attend meetings, and they may be on call.

HOW TO BECOME A SOCIAL WORKER

Although some social workers only need a bachelor's degree in social work, clinical social workers must have a master's degree and 2 years of experience in a supervised clinical setting after they've completed their degree. Clinical social workers must also be licensed by their state to provide mental health or counseling services.

Education and Training

There are multiple educational pathways to becoming a social worker, depending on the specialty.

A bachelor's degree in social work (BSW) is the most common requirement for entry-level administrative positions. However, some employers may hire workers who have a bachelor's degree in a related field, such as psychology or sociology.

A BSW prepares students for direct-service positions such as caseworker or mental health assistant. These programs teach students about diverse populations, human behavior, social welfare policy, and ethics in social work. All programs require students to complete supervised fieldwork or an internship.

Clinical positions require a master's degree in social work (MSW), which generally takes 2 years to complete. MSW programs prepare students for work in their chosen specialty by developing clinical assessment and management skills. All programs require students to complete a supervised practicum or an internship.

A bachelor's degree in social work is not required in order to enter a master's degree program in social work. Although a bachelor's degree in almost any major is acceptable, courses in psychology, sociology, economics, and political science are recommended. Some programs allow graduates with a bachelor's degree in social work to earn their master's degree in 1 year.

In 2017, there were more than 500 bachelor's degree programs and more than 200 master's degree programs accredited by the Council on Social Work Education.

Two years of supervised training and experience after obtaining an MA degree is typically required for clinical social workers.

Licenses, Certifications, and Registrations

All states require clinical social workers to be licensed, and most states require licensure or certification for nonclinical social workers. Becoming a licensed clinical social worker requires a master's degree in social work and a minimum of 2 years of supervised clinical experience after graduation. After completing their supervised experience, clinical social workers must pass a clinical exam to be licensed.

Because licensing requirements vary by state, those interested should contact their state licensure board. For more information about regulatory licensure boards by state, visit the Association of Social Work Boards.

Important Qualities

Communication skills. Clients talk to social workers about challenges in their lives. To provide effective help, social workers must be able to listen to and understand their clients' needs.

Emotional skills. Social workers often work with people who are in stressful and difficult situations. To develop strong relationships, they must have patience, compassion, and empathy for their clients.

Interpersonal skills. Social workers need to be able to work with different groups of people. They need strong interpersonal skills to foster healthy and productive relationships with their clients and colleagues.

Organizational skills. Social workers must help and manage multiple clients, often assisting with their paperwork or documenting their treatment.

Problem-solving skills. Social workers need to develop practical and innovative solutions to their clients' problems.

WAGES

Median annual wages, May 2017

Social workers: $47,980

Counselors, social workers, and other community and social service specialists: $43,860

Total, all occupations: $37,690

Note: All Occupations includes all occupations in the U.S. Economy. Source: U.S. Bureau of Labor Statistics, Occupational Employment Statistics

The median annual wage for social workers was $47,980 in May 2017. The lowest 10 percent earned less than $29,560, and the highest 10 percent earned more than $79,740.

Median annual wages for social workers in May 2017 were as follows:

Social workers, all other	$61,980
Healthcare social workers	54,870
Child, family, and school social workers	44,380
Mental health and substance abuse social workers	43,250

In May 2017, the median annual wages for social workers in the top industries in which they worked were as follows:

Hospitals; state, local, and private	$58,490
Local government, excluding education and hospitals	52,900
Ambulatory healthcare services	48,340
State government, excluding education and hospitals	46,120
Individual and family services	40,800

The majority of social workers worked full time in 2016. They sometimes work evenings, weekends, and holidays to see clients or attend meetings, and they may be on call.

Overall employment of social workers is projected to grow 16 percent from 2016 to 2026, much faster average for all occupations. Increased demand for healthcare and social services will drive demand for social workers, but growth will vary by specialization.

JOB OUTLOOK

Percent change in employment, projected 2016-26

Social workers: 16%

Counselors, social workers, and other community and social service specialists: 16%

Total, all occupations: 7%

Note: All Occupations includes all occupations in the U.S. Economy. Source: U.S. Bureau of Labor Statistics, Employment Projections program

Employment of child, family, and school social workers is projected to grow 14 percent from 2016 to 2026, faster than the average for all occupations. Child and family social workers will be needed to work with families to strengthen parenting skills, prevent child abuse, and identify alternative homes for children who are unable to live with their biological families. In schools, more social workers will be needed as student enrollments rise. However, employment growth of child, family, and school social workers may be limited by federal, state, and local budget constraints.

Employment of healthcare social workers is projected to grow 20 percent from 2016 to 2026, much faster than the average for all occupations. Healthcare social workers will continue to be needed to help aging populations and their families adjust to new treatments, medications, and lifestyles.

Employment of mental health and substance abuse social workers is projected to grow 19 percent from 2016 to 2026, much faster than the average for all occupations. Employment will grow as more people seek treatment for mental illness and substance abuse. In addition, drug offenders are increasingly being sent to treatment programs, which are staffed by these social workers, rather than being sent to jail.

Job Prospects

Overall, job prospects should be very good, particularly for clinical social workers. The continuing growth of healthcare spending and treatment increases the opportunities for clinical social workers as compared to social workers who do not offer treatment services. This table shows a list of occupations with job duties that are similar to those of social workers.

Employment projections data for Social workers, 2016-26

Occupational Title	SOC Code	Employment, 2016	Projected Employment, 2026	Change, 2016-26	
				Percent	Numeric
Social workers	21-1020	682,100	791,800	16	109,700
Child, family, and school social workers	21-1021	317,600	362,600	14	45,000
Healthcare social workers	21-1022	176,500	212,000	20	35,400
Mental health and substance abuse social workers	21-1023	123,900	147,900	19	23,900
Social workers, all other	21-1029	64,000	69,300	8	5,300

Source: Bureau of Labor Statistics, Employment Projections program

SIMILAR OCCUPATIONS

OCCUPATION	JOB DUTIES	ENTRY-LEVEL EDUCATION	2017 MEDIAN PAY
Health Educators and Community Health Workers	Health educators teach people about behaviors that promote wellness. They develop and implement strategies to improve the health of individuals and communities. Community health workers collect data and discuss health concerns with members of specific populations or communities.	Bachelor's degree (health educators) High school diploma or equivalent (community health workers)	$45,360
Marriage and Family Therapists	Marriage and family therapists help people manage and overcome problems with family and other relationships.	Master's degree	$48,790
Probation Officers and Correctional Treatment Specialists	Probation officers and correctional treatment specialists provide social services to assist in rehabilitation of law offenders in custody or on probation or parole.	Bachelor's degree	$51,410
Psychologists	Psychologists study cognitive, emotional, and social processes and behavior by observing, interpreting, and recording how individuals relate to one another and to their environments. They use their findings to help improve processes and behaviors.	PhD in psychology or a Doctor of Psychology (PsyD) degree	$77,030

OCCUPATION	JOB DUTIES	ENTRY-LEVEL EDUCATION	2017 MEDIAN PAY
Rehabilitation Counselors	Rehabilitation counselors help people with physical, mental, developmental, or emotional disabilities live independently. They work with clients to overcome or manage the personal, social, or psychological effects of disabilities on employment or independent living.	Master's degree	$34,860
School and Career Counselors	School counselors help students develop the academic and social skills needed to succeed in school. Career counselors help people choose careers and follow a path to employment.	Master's degree	$55,410
Social and Community Service Managers	Social and community service managers coordinate and supervise social service programs and community organizations. They manage workers who provide social services to the public.	Bachelor's degree	$64,100
Social and Human Service Assistants	Social and human service assistants provide client services, including support for families, in a wide variety of fields, such as psychology, rehabilitation, and social work. They assist other workers, such as social workers, and they help clients find benefits or community services.	High school diploma or equivalent	$33,120
Substance Abuse, Behavioral Disorder, and Mental Health Counselors	Substance abuse, behavioral disorder, and mental health counselors advise people who suffer from alcoholism, drug addiction, eating disorders, mental health issues, or other mental or behavioral problems. They provide treatment and support to help clients recover from addiction or modify problem behaviors.	Bachelor's degree	$43,300

Conversation With . . .
NICKI J. HOMLES

Adult protective services field, 11 years

Nicki J. Holmes is the Adult Protective Services Manager for the Oregon Department of Human Services (DHS) in Klamath Falls, Oregon.

1. **What was your individual career path in terms of education/training, entry-level job, or other significant opportunity?**

Working with older people came naturally to me. When I was young and my mom went looking for me in the neighborhood, she would find me at older peoples' homes.

I earned my associate degree in criminal justice at Portland Community College and my bachelor's in business management at Northwest Christian University. I then spent eight years in parole and probation. I dealt with people who are not the easiest to work with because they had criminal histories and criminal thinking. You learn to ask good questions to find truths. Realizing people make poor choices and bad mistakes made me learn to meet people where they are in their lives.

I got laid off and started at DHS as an adult foster home licenser. When you are a regulator, you deal with allegations of abuse and neglect and work hand in hand with adult protective services investigators. Given my past, investigation was right up my alley. I spent five years as an investigator and handled hundreds of cases, then I took a supervisor position in the same unit that I have held for five years. I help coach investigators through my experience, things that work and do not work.

For instance, there was a lady, retired from NASA, our office had been aware of. She had a substantial amount of money and was raising a grandson. As he got older, he got emotionally and verbally abusive and eventually conditioned her to hand over whatever finances he needed. She even gave him a house she had bought as a rental property for a penny on the deed. When we first investigated the case, she had good mental capacity wanted help, and we were able to help her change her bank account so he could not get to it.

Two years later, the grandson and his wife were having domestic issues and she kicked him out of the house where the grandmother lived with them. He called us that time, telling us the wife was abusing the grandmother, whose mental capacity had diminished.

We were ultimately able to get her into a nice adult foster home. She had had a stroke and needed someone to take care of her. One day I was sitting with her on the sofa as she ran her hand over her ring finger and said, "I wish I had my wedding ring back." She had given it to her grandson and his wife because they said they needed money. They pawned it for $500 and promised to get it back. It had been about a year and a half, but ours is a fairly small town so I took a gamble. I also took law enforcement with me. We found the ring. The pawnshop knew it was worth about $16,000. We were able to get it back through legal channels. The detective came when we gave it back and was able to see the look on her face. She was shocked we found it but smiled and cried and held my hand. Those wins do not happen very often.

The end of the story is that the grandson was prosecuted for minor charges, but he deeded the house back as restitution. She sold it and went to live with her son in the Midwest.

2. What are the most important skills and/or qualities for someone in your profession?

You have to be caring and compassionate, tenacious, curious, and able to think outside the box. You need skin that is a little thick, and the ability to listen so you take in good observations. You also need good writing skills because if you cannot put everything on paper, you cannot articulate the work you did.

3. What do you wish you had known going into this profession?

You cannot ever place judgment on why people do things.

I also wish I'd known more about vicarious trauma, which we learn skills to deal with. It is really hard not to take victims' situations home with you and leave work at work.

4. Are there many job opportunities in your profession? In what specific areas?

I can speak best to Oregon, where there are protective services jobs in a variety of capacities. In our adult protective services world, we have investigators, screeners, and support staff. You can go up to management and be a field expert or a policy analyst. A lot of people don't stay in this for their entire career; burnout is pretty significant if people don't take care of themselves.

5. How do you see your profession changing in the next five years? How will technology impact that change, and what skills will be required?

The skillset will not change a lot. You're dealing with human behavior and people. I think the sheer number of people turning 65 over the next ten years as baby boomers age is going to change the work substantially. The number of jobs that will potentially open will be substantial. That growth is also going to change the way we do business. Oregon just rolled out a database, the Central Abuse Management System, so, for example, we will be able to track perpetrators. Since baby boomers have more money than other generations, we anticipate more financial exploitation. A lot of work is being done with banks to make them savvier about what to look for. New laws are rolling out to allow more exchange of information.

6. What do you enjoy most about your job? What do you enjoy least about your job?

The older generation has amazing stories to tell. I have learned a tremendous amount of history by talking to a Holocaust victim, for example. I knew an elderly guy who lived through nine plane crashes. I also love putting an investigation's intricate puzzle pieces together, and part of me likes to watch the bad guys get punished, so there is justice for a victim. Now, as a supervisor, it brings me a lot of pride to see my team carry on this work.

It is hard to keep yourself in check and not lose faith in humanity. When all you see is bad, the bad can take over your mindset. You also have to walk away from somebody who doesn't want help sometimes because they do have rights. And, finally, people can have unrealistic expectations of what we can do.

7. Can you suggest a valuable "try this" for students considering a career in your profession?

Volunteer at a hospital or any place where you're working with a geriatric population. Also, investigative work lets you test those skills, such as a police department program that allows high school students to be a junior cop. This work is a mesh between social work and law enforcement.

Conversation With . . .
LENNY FONTES

Child protective services,
forensic interviewer, 18 years

*Lenny Fontes is the Associate Director for Children's Cove in Hyannis,
Massachusetts.*

**1. What was your individual career path in terms of education/training,
entry-level job, or other significant opportunity?**

I got into the field of children's advocacy after a short career in juvenile probation.
I got a degree in physical education with a minor in recreation at Bridgewater
State University, with the goal of becoming a gym teacher and football coach in my
hometown.

But, my first job out of college was at a residential facility in Plymouth, MA for boys
from 10 to 14 years old. They were victims of neglect, physical abuse and sexual
abuse—significant childhood trauma. It was a difficult population, but I found I loved
working with the kids and teaching them sportsmanship and social skills.

I moved to Texas for a few years and got a job as a juvenile probation officer in a
rural community south of Dallas, where I was promoted to a supervisory position at a
short-term detention facility.

When I returned to Massachusetts, I was again hired as a juvenile probation officer
in Brockton. I enjoyed working with high-risk youth. I felt there was a lack of services
and individuals willing to work with this population—oftentimes they were the kids
that were difficult to engage and required a lot of patience. I could see that job
coming to an end because of state budget problems and applied for an advertised
position at Children's Cove.

The Cove is a county agency known as a child advocacy center that provides
services to victims of child sexual abuse and severe physical abuse. At first, I ran a
recreation program for children and non-offending parents. I planned everything from
beach barbecues to holiday parties. After a couple of years, Children's Cove sent me
to Huntsville, Alabama, to become trained as a forensic interviewer.

As an interviewer, I meet with the child in a room with a two-way mirror. On the
other side, there are representatives of law enforcement and the state department of
children and families, medical and mental health experts, and others who make up

a multidisciplinary team. The goal is to minimize trauma to children by limiting how many times they have to tell their story.

Forensic interviewers are trained not to ask leading questions but to get as many details as possible about a possible crime scene—everything from the color of the walls to the number of windows in a room—as well as details regarding what has happened to them.

I was promoted to Sexual Abuse Intervention Network (SAIN) coordinator before being named associate director. After eighteen years with Children's Cove, I still do forensic interviews.

2. What are the most important skills and/or qualities for someone in your profession?

You have to like kids. The things that happened to them—it is not their fault. This is not a job where you can show up to work grumpy or out of sorts. You have to make a connection with every family that walks through the door. Kids can read through the lines. They will not engage if you are just going through the motions. But, you have to be able to turn it off at the end of the day and not take it home with you. This work can be taxing, and self-care is important. My family, faith, and hobbies have pulled me through.

3. What do you wish you had known going into this profession?

I wish I had known early on that the main goal of the job is not always criminal prosecution. The healthiest outcome for the child is what is most important.

Our agency gives children a chance to talk about their trauma and provides follow-up care to make sure they are okay in school or the community, enrolled in activities and seeing a trauma-informed therapist if necessary.

4. Are there many job opportunities in your profession? In what specific areas?

Every one of the nation's child advocacy centers has at least one forensic interviewer. Centers in cities have more.

There are lots of related jobs in child protective services, such as response workers for state departments of children and families. Other jobs that help children at risk include juvenile probation officers and school resource officers.

5. How do you see your profession changing in the next five years? How will technology impact that change, and what skills will be required?

Technological advances will play a role in this field over the next few years, especially regarding data collection, case tracking, and the ability to capture recordings of the forensic interviews.

As we learn more about the impact of trauma, there is going to be a need for more clinicians with a specialty in evidence-based practices and trauma focused modalities.

We also need more male forensic interviewers. I'm the only male interviewer at a Massachusetts child advocacy center.

The job is personality, not gender, driven. You need a good rapport with the kids.

6. What do you enjoy most about your job? What do you enjoy least about your job?

There is nothing better than connecting with a child who has gone through some form of trauma and helping them understand they have done nothing wrong. That is the best part of the job—seeing kids rebound from the trauma and going on to live healthy lives.

It is gratifying to see people taking child abuse seriously. We used to see kids who had been abused multiple times. Now they tell me about it happening once and maybe twice and then they report it. Parents know what to do with the information. They can call Children's Cove or an agency like it. There are twelve of us across the state and 750 nationwide.

I enjoy supervising staff and making sure they keep a healthy outlook. Sometimes it is difficult when employees face burnout dealing with hard cases. In management, you have to address vicarious trauma when you see it.

7. Can you suggest a valuable "try this" for students considering a career in your profession?

Visit the closest child advocacy center and have the staff show you around. Ask your school to arrange an internship.

Famous First

Social work as a practice and profession has a relatively modern origin. It was developed out of individual casework, social administration and social action. The Charity Organization Society, founded in the mid-19th century, was the pioneering organization of the social theory that led to the emergence of social work as a professional occupation, based on individual casework. Social administration, which included poverty had its roots in the English Poor Laws of the 17th century. Social action put the emphasis on political action and working through the community to improve social conditions and thereby alleviate poverty; this approach was developed originally by the Settlement House Movement.

Source: https://en.wikipedia.org/wiki/Social_work#History

Fast Fact

Social workers provide the majority of mental health services in the United States; are often the only providers in rural, remote communities; and outnumber psychologists, psychiatrists, and psychiatric nurses combined

Source: https://www.kvc.org/blog/10-things-about-social-workers/

MORE INFORMATION

For more information about social workers and clinical social workers, visit

American Board of Examiners in Clinical Social Work
https://abecsw.org/

National Association of Social Workers
https://www.socialworkers.org/

Association for Community Organization and Social Administration
http://www.acosa.org/joomla/

For more information about accredited social work degree programs, visit

Council on Social Work Education
https://www.cswe.org/

Online MSW Programs
https://www.onlinemswprograms.com/

MSW Guide
https://www.mswguide.org/

For more information about licensure requirements, visit

Association of Social Work Boards
https://www.aswb.org/

Sources

Bureau of Labor Statistics, U.S. Department of Labor, *Occupational Outlook Handbook*, Social Workers.

Substance Abuse, Behavioral Disorder, and Mental Health Counselors

Snapshot

2017 Median Pay: $43,300 per year, $20.82 per hour

Typical Entry-Level Education: Bachelor's degree

Work Experience in a Related Occupation: None

On-the-job Training: Substance abuse and behavioral disorder counselors in private practice must be licensed. Mental health counselors must complete a period of postdegree supervised clinical work under the supervision of a licensed counselor and must be licensed,

Number of Jobs, 2016: 260,200

Job Outlook, 2016-26: 23% (Much faster than average)

Employment Change, 2016-26: 60,300

CAREER OVERVIEW

What Substance Abuse, Behavioral Disorder, and Mental Health Counselors Do

Substance abuse, behavioral disorder, and mental health counselors advise people who suffer from alcoholism, drug addiction, eating

disorders, mental health
issues, or other mental
or behavioral problems.
They provide treatment
and support to help clients
recover from addiction or
modify problem behaviors.

Duties

Substance abuse, behavioral disorder, and mental health counselors
typically do the following:

- Evaluate clients' mental and physical health, addiction, or
  problematic behavior and assess their readiness for treatment
- Develop, recommend, and review treatment goals and plans with
  clients and their families
- Assist clients in developing skills and behaviors necessary to
  recover from their addiction or modify their behavior
- Work with clients to identify behaviors or situations that interfere
  with their recovery
- Teach clients' family members about addiction or behavior
  disorders and help them develop strategies to cope with those
  problems
- Refer clients to other resources and services, such as job placement
  services and support groups
- Conduct outreach programs to help people identify the signs of
  addiction and other destructive behavior, as well as steps to take to
  avoid such behavior

Substance abuse counselors and ***behavioral disorder counselors***,
also called addiction counselors, work with clients individually and in
group sessions. Many incorporate the principles of 12-step programs,
such as Alcoholics Anonymous (AA), to guide their practice. They
teach clients how to cope with stress and life's problems in ways that
help them recover. Furthermore, they help clients rebuild professional
relationships and, if necessary, reestablish their career. They also help
clients improve their personal relationships and find ways to discuss
their addiction or other problems with family and friends.

Some addiction counselors work in facilities that employ many types of healthcare and mental health professionals. Addiction counselors may work with psychologists, psychiatrists, social workers, physicians, and registered nurses to develop treatment plans and coordinate care for patients.

Some counselors work with clients who have been ordered by a judge to receive treatment for addiction. Others work with specific populations, such as teenagers, veterans, or people with disabilities. Some specialize in crisis intervention; these counselors step in when someone is endangering his or her own life or the lives of others. Other counselors specialize in noncrisis interventions, which encourage a person with addictions or other issues, such as difficulty managing anger, to get help. Noncrisis interventions often are performed at the request of friends and family.

Mental health counselors provide treatment to individuals, families, couples, and groups. Some work with specific populations, such as the elderly, college students, or children. Mental health counselors treat clients with a variety of conditions, including anxiety, depression, grief, low self-esteem, stress, and suicidal impulses. They also help with mental and emotional health issues and relationship problems.

WORK ENVIRONMENT

Substance abuse, behavioral disorder, and mental health counselors held about 260,200 jobs in 2016. The largest employers of substance abuse, behavioral disorder, and mental health counselors were as follows:

Outpatient mental health and substance abuse centers	19%
Individual and family services	17
Residential mental health and substance abuse facilities	11
Hospitals; state, local, and private	11
Government	9

Substance abuse, behavioral disorder, and mental health counselors work in a wide variety of settings, including mental health centers, prisons, probation or parole agencies, and juvenile detention facilities. They also work in halfway houses, detox centers, or in employee assistance programs (EAPs). EAPs are mental health programs provided by some employers to help employees deal with personal problems.

Some addiction counselors work in residential treatment centers, where clients live in the facility for a fixed period of time. Others work with clients in outpatient treatment centers. Some counselors work in private practice, where they may work alone or with a group of counselors or other professionals.

Although rewarding, the work of substance abuse, behavioral disorder, and mental health counselors is often stressful. Many counselors have to deal with large workloads. They do not always have enough resources to meet the demand for their services. Also, they may have to intervene in crisis situations or work with agitated clients, which can be difficult.

Work Schedules

Most substance abuse, behavioral disorder, and mental health counselors work full time. In some settings, such as inpatient facilities, they may need to work evenings, nights, or weekends.

HOW TO BECOME SUBSTANCE ABUSE, BEHAVIORAL DISORDER, OR MENTAL HEALTH COUNSELOR

Substance abuse, behavioral disorder, and mental health counselors need a license in private practice.

Most positions require at least a bachelor's degree. Although educational requirements can vary from a high school diploma and certification to a master's degree for substance abuse and behavioral disorder counselors, a master's degree and an internship is typically required to become a mental health counselor. Substance abuse, behavioral disorder, and mental health counselors need a license in private practice.

Education

Most substance abuse, behavioral disorder, and mental health counselor positions require at least a bachelor's degree. However, depending on the state and employer, educational requirements for substance abuse, behavioral disorder, and mental health counselors can vary from a high school diploma and certification to a master's degree. Workers with psychology, clinical social work, mental health counseling, and similar master's degrees can provide more services to their clients, such as private one-on-one counseling sessions, and they require less supervision than those with less education. Those interested should research their state's educational requirements.

Licenses, Certifications, and Registrations

Substance abuse and behavioral disorder counselors in private practice must be licensed. Licensing requirements vary by state, but all states require these counselors to have a master's degree and 2,000 to 4,000 hours of supervised clinical experience. In addition, counselors must pass a state-issued exam and complete continuing education every year. Contact information for your state's regulating board can be found through the National Board for Certified Counselors.

The licensure criteria for substance abuse and behavioral disorder counselors outside of private practice vary from state to state. For example, not all states require applicants to have a specific degree, but many require them to pass an exam. Contact information for individual states' licensing boards can be found through the Addiction Technology Transfer Center Network.

All states require mental health counselors to be licensed, after completing a period of postdegree supervised clinical work under the supervision of a licensed counselor.

Other Experience

There is a long tradition of people who have overcome their own addictions to be involved in counseling others to overcome their addictions. Counselors with personal experience overcoming alcohol or drug addictions are sometimes viewed as especially helpful and insightful to those seeking treatment.

ADVANCEMENT

Important Qualities

Compassion. Substance abuse, behavioral disorder, and mental health counselors often work with people who are dealing with stressful and difficult situations, so they must be compassionate and empathize with their clients.

Interpersonal skills. Substance abuse, behavioral disorder, and mental health counselors must be able to work with different types of people. They spend most of their time working directly with clients or other professionals and must be able to develop and nurture good relationships.

Listening skills. Substance abuse, behavioral disorder, and mental health counselors need good listening skills. They must give their full attention to a client to be able to understand that client's problems and values.

Patience. Substance abuse, behavioral disorder, and mental health counselors must be able to remain calm when working with all types of clients, including those who may be distressed or angry.

Speaking skills. Substance abuse, behavioral disorder, and mental health counselors need to be able to effectively communicate with clients. They must express ideas and information in a way that their clients easily understand.

WAGES

Median annual wages, May 2017

Counselors, social workers, and other community and social service specialists: $43,860

Substance abuse, behavioral disorder, and mental health counselors: $43,300

Total, all occupations: $37,690

Note: All Occupations includes all occupations in the U.S. Economy. Source: U.S. Bureau of Labor Statistics, Occupational Employment Statistics

The median annual wage for substance abuse, behavioral disorder, and mental health counselors was $43,300 in May 2017. The lowest 10 percent earned less than $27,310, and the highest 10 percent earned more than $70,840.

In May 2017, the median annual wages for substance abuse, behavioral disorder, and mental health counselors in the top industries in which they worked were as follows:

Government	$50,600
Hospitals; state, local, and private	47,000
Individual and family services	42,190
Outpatient mental health and substance abuse centers	42,140
Residential mental health and substance abuse facilities	37,210

Most substance abuse, behavioral disorder, and mental health counselors work full time. In some settings, such as inpatient facilities, they may need to work evenings, nights, or weekends.

Famous First

Physicians like Philippe Pinel at the Bicêtre Hospital in France and William Tuke at the York Retreat in England believed that mental illness was a disorder that required compassionate treatment in order to effect rehabilitation of the patient. The advent of institutions devoted to those afflicted "madness" got its start in the nineteenth century with first public mental asylums in Britain; the County Asylums Act 1808 empowered magistrates to build asylums in every county to house what were referred to as "pauper lunatics." The Act required asylums to have written regulations and to have a resident physician. The first public asylum opened in 1812 in Nottinghamshire. By 1828, the Commissioners in Lunacy licensed and supervised private asylums.

Source: https://en.wikipedia.org/wiki/Psychiatric_hospital

JOB OUTLOOK

Percent change in employment, projected 2016-26

Substance abuse and behavioral disorder counselors: 23%

Mental health counselors: 23%

Substance abuse, behavioral disorder and mental health counselors: 23%

Counselors, social workers, and other community and social service specialists: 16%

Total, all occupations: 7%

Note: All Occupations includes all occupations in the U.S. Economy. Source: U.S. Bureau of Labor Statistics, Employment Projections program

Employment of substance abuse, behavioral disorder, and mental health counselors is projected to grow 23 percent from 2016 to 2026, much faster than the average for all occupations. Employment growth is expected as people continue to seek addiction and mental health counseling services.

Demand for substance abuse, behavioral disorder, and mental health counselors is also expected to increase as states seek treatment and counseling services for drug offenders rather than jail time. In recent years, the criminal justice system has recognized that drug and other substance abuse addicts are less likely to offend again if they get treatment for their addiction. As a result, sentences often require drug offenders to attend treatment and counseling programs. In addition, some research suggests that these programs are more cost effective than incarceration and states may use them as a method to reduce recidivism rates.

In addition, there will be a continued need for counselors to work with military veterans to provide them the appropriate mental health or substance abuse counseling care.

Job Prospects

Job prospects are expected to be very good for substance abuse and behavioral disorder counselors, particularly for those with a bachelor's or master's degree. In addition, many workers leave the field after a few years and need to be replaced. As a result, those interested in entering this field should find favorable prospects.

Job prospects are also expected to be very good for mental health counselors, particularly in rural areas or other communities that are underserved by mental health practitioners.

Employment projections data for
Substance abuse, behavioral disorder, and mental health
counselors, 2016-26

Occupational Title	SOC Code	Employment, 2016	Projected Employment, 2026	Change, 2016-26	
				Percent	Numeric
Substance abuse, behavioral disorder, and mental health counselors	—	260,200	320,400	23	60,300
Substance abuse and behavioral disorder counselors	21-1011	102,400	126,200	23	23,800
Mental health counselors	21-1014	157,700	194,200	23	36,500

Source: Bureau of Labor Statistics, Employment Projections program

Fast Fact

Opioid overdoses kill more than 130 people every day in the United States
Source: National Institute on Drug Abuse.

SIMILAR OCCUPATIONS

This table shows a list of occupations with job duties that are similar to those of substance abuse, behavioral disorder, and mental health counselors.

OCCUPATION	JOB DUTIES	ENTRY-LEVEL EDUCATION	2017 MEDIAN PAY
Marriage and Family Therapists	Marriage and family therapists help people manage and overcome problems with family and other relationships.	Master's degree	$48,790
Physicians and Surgeons	Physicians and surgeons diagnose and treat injuries or illnesses. Physicians examine patients; take medical histories; prescribe medications; and order, perform, and interpret diagnostic tests. They counsel patients on diet, hygiene, and preventive healthcare. Surgeons operate on patients to treat injuries, such as broken bones; diseases, such as cancerous tumors; and deformities, such as cleft palates.	Doctoral or professional degree	This wage is equal to or greater than $208,000 per year.
Psychologists	Psychologists study cognitive, emotional, and social processes and behavior by observing, interpreting, and recording how individuals relate to one another and to their environments. They use their findings to help improve processes and behaviors.	PhD in psychology or a Doctor of Psychology (PsyD) degree	$77,030
Registered Nurses	Registered nurses (RNs) provide and coordinate patient care, educate patients and the public about various health conditions, and provide advice and emotional support to patients and their family members.	Bachelor's degree	$70,000

Rehabilitation Counselors	Rehabilitation counselors help people with physical, mental, developmental, or emotional disabilities live independently. They work with clients to overcome or manage the personal, social, or psychological effects of disabilities on employment or independent living.	Master's degree	$34,860
School and Career Counselors	School counselors help students develop the academic and social skills needed to succeed in school. Career counselors help people choose careers and follow a path to employment.	Master's degree	$55,410
Social and Community Service Managers	Social and community service managers coordinate and supervise social service programs and community organizations. They manage workers who provide social services to the public.	Bachelor's degree	$64,100
Social and Human Service Assistants	Social and human service assistants provide client services, including support for families, in a wide variety of fields, such as psychology, rehabilitation, and social work. They assist other workers, such as social workers, and they help clients find benefits or community services.	High school diploma or equivalent	$33,120

Social Workers	Social workers help people solve and cope with problems in their everyday lives. Clinical social workers also diagnose and treat mental, behavioral, and emotional issues.	Bachelor's degree in social work (BSW) with supervised fieldwork or an internship for direct-service work Master's degree in social work (MSW) with supervised practicum or an internship, clinical work for clinical work	$47,980
Health Educators and Community Health Workers	Health educators teach people about behaviors that promote wellness. They develop and implement strategies to improve the health of individuals and communities. Community health workers collect data and discuss health concerns with members of specific populations or communities.	Bachelor's degree (health educators) High school diploma or equivalent (community health workers)	$45,360
Probation Officers and Correctional Treatment Specialists	Probation officers and correctional treatment specialists provide social services to assist in rehabilitation of law offenders in custody or on probation or parole.	Bachelor's degree	$51,410

MORE INFORMATION

For more information about addiction counselors, visit

Addiction Technology   **NAADAC, The Association for**
Transfer Center Network   **Addiction Professionals**
https://attcnetwork.org/   https://www.naadac.org/

For more information about counseling and counseling specialties, visit

American Counseling
Association
https://www.counseling.org/

For contact information for state regulating boards, visit

National Board for Certified
Counselors
https://www.nbcc.org/

Sources

Bureau of Labor Statistics, U.S. Department of Labor, *Occupational Outlook Handbook*, Substance Abuse, Behavioral Disorder, and Mental Health Counselors.

What Are Your Career Interests?

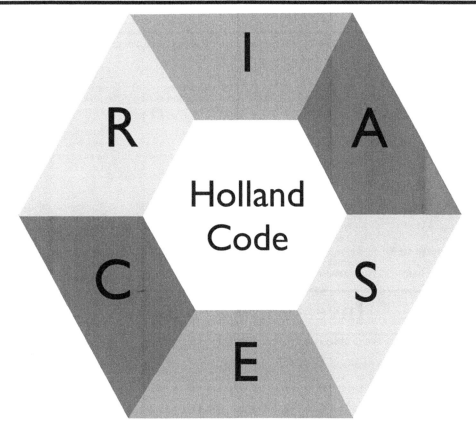

Holland Code

This is based on Dr. John Holland's theory that people and work environments can be loosely classified into six different groups. Each of the letters above corresponds to one of the six groups described in the following pages.

Different people's personalities may find different environments more to their liking. While you may have some interests in and similarities to several of the six groups, you may be attracted primarily to two or three of the areas. These two or three letters are your "Holland Code." For example, with a code of "RES" you would most resemble the Realistic type, somewhat less resemble the Enterprising type, and resemble the Social type even less. The types that are not in your code are the types you resemble least of all.

Most people, and most jobs, are best represented by some combination of two or three of the Holland interest areas. In addition, most people are most satisfied if there is some degree of fit between their personality and their work environment.

The rest of the pages in this booklet further explain each type and provide some examples of career possibilities, areas of study at MU, and co-curricular activities for each code. To take a more in-depth look at your Holland Code, take a self-assessment such as the SDS, Discover, or a card sort at the MU Career Center with a Career Specialist.

<u>R</u>ealistic *(Doers)*

People who have athletic ability, prefer to work with objects, machines, tools, plants or animals, or to be outdoors.

Are you?
practical
straightforward/frank
mechanically inclined
stable
concrete
reserved
self-controlled

independent
ambitious
systematic

<u>Can you?</u>
fix electrical things
solve electrical problems
pitch a tent
play a sport
read a blueprint
plant a garden
operate tools and machine

<u>Like to?</u>
tinker with machines/vehicles
work outdoors
be physically active
use your hands
build things
tend/train animals
work on electronic equipment

Career Possibilities
(Holland Code):

Air Traffic Controller (SER)
Archaeologist (IRE)
Athletic Trainer (SRE)
Cartographer (IRE)
Commercial Airline Pilot (RIE)
Commercial Drafter (IRE)
Corrections Officer (SER)

Dental Technician (REI)
Farm Manager (ESR)
Fish and Game Warden (RES)
Floral Designer (RAE)
Forester (RIS)
Geodetic Surveyor (IRE)
Industrial Arts Teacher (IER)

Laboratory Technician (RIE)
Landscape Architect (AIR)
Mechanical Engineer (RIS)
Optician (REI)
Petroleum Geologist (RIE)
Police Officer (SER)
Practical Nurse (SER)

Property Manager (ESR)
Recreation Manager (SER)
Service Manager (ERS)
Software Technician (RCI)
Ultrasound Technologist (RSI)
Vocational Rehabilitation
   Consultant (ESR)

<u>I</u>nvestigative *(Thinkers)*

People who like to observe, learn, investigate, analyze, evaluate, or solve problems.

Are you?
inquisitive
analytical
scientific
observant/precise
scholarly
cautious

intellectually self-confident
Independent
logical
complex
Curious

Can you?
think abstractly
solve math problems
understand scientific theories
do complex calculations
use a microscope or computer
interpret formulas

Like to?
explore a variety of ideas
work independently
perform lab experiments
deal with abstractions
do research
be challenged

Career Possibilities
(Holland Code):

Actuary (ISE)
Agronomist (IRS)
Anesthesiologist (IRS)
Anthropologist (IRE)
Archaeologist (IRE)
Biochemist (IRS)
Biologist (ISR)

Chemical Engineer (IRE)
Chemist (IRE)
Computer Systems Analyst (IER)
Dentist (ISR)
Ecologist (IRE)
Economist (IAS)
Electrical Engineer (IRE)

Geologist (IRE)
Horticulturist (IRS)
Mathematician (IER)
Medical Technologist (ISA)
Meteorologist (IRS)
Nurse Practitioner (ISA)
Pharmacist (IES)

Physician, General Practice (ISE)
Psychologist (IES)
Research Analyst (IRC)
Statistician (IRE)
Surgeon (IRA)
Technical Writer (IRS)
Veterinarian (IRS)

Artistic *(Creators)*

People who have artistic, innovating, or intuitional abilities and like to work in unstructured situations using their imagination and creativity.

Are you?
creative
imaginative
innovative
unconventional
emotional
independent
Expressive

original
introspective
impulsive
sensitive
courageous
complicated
idealistic
nonconforming

Can you?
sketch, draw, paint
play a musical instrument
write stories, poetry, music
sing, act, dance
design fashions or interiors

Like to?
attend concerts, theatre, art
  exhibits
read fiction, plays, and poetry
work on crafts
take photography
express yourself creatively
deal with ambiguous ideas

Career Possibilities (Holland Code):

Actor (AES)
Advertising Art Director (AES)
Advertising Manager (ASE)
Architect (AIR)
Art Teacher (ASE)
Artist (ASI)

Copy Writer (ASI)
Dance Instructor (AER)
Drama Coach (ASE)
English Teacher (ASE)
Entertainer/Performer (AES)
Fashion Illustrator (ASR)

Interior Designer (AES)
Intelligence Research Specialist
  (AEI)
Journalist/Reporter (ASE)
Landscape Architect (AIR)
Librarian (SAI)

Medical Illustrator (AIE)
Museum Curator (AES)
Music Teacher (ASI)
Photographer (AES)
Writer (ASI)
Graphic Designer (AES)

Social *(Helpers)*

People who like to work with people to enlighten, inform, help, train, or cure them, or are skilled with words.

Are you?
friendly
helpful
idealistic
insightful
outgoing
understanding

cooperative
generous
responsible
forgiving
patient
kind

Can you?
teach/train others
express yourself clearly
lead a group discussion
mediate disputes
plan and supervise an activity
cooperate well with others

Like to?
work in groups
help people with problems
do volunteer work
work with young people
serve others

Career Possibilities (Holland Code):

City Manager (SEC)
Clinical Dietitian (SIE)
College/University Faculty (SEI)
Community Org. Director
  (SEA)
Consumer Affairs Director
  (SER)Counselor/Therapist
  (SAE)

Historian (SEI)
Hospital Administrator (SER)
Psychologist (SEI)
Insurance Claims Examiner
  (SIE)
Librarian (SAI)
Medical Assistant (SCR)
Minister/Priest/Rabbi (SAI)
Paralegal (SCE)

Park Naturalist (SEI)
Physical Therapist (SIE)
Police Officer (SER)
Probation and Parole Officer
  (SEC)
Real Estate Appraiser (SCE)
Recreation Director (SER)
Registered Nurse (SIA)

Teacher (SAE)
Social Worker (SEA)
Speech Pathologist (SAI)
Vocational-Rehab. Counselor
  (SEC)
Volunteer Services Director
  (SEC)

Enterprising (*Persuaders*)

People who like to work with people, influencing, persuading, leading or managing for organizational goals or economic gain.

Are you?
self-confident
assertive
persuasive
energetic
adventurous
popular

ambitious
agreeable
talkative
extroverted
spontaneous
optimistic

Can you?
initiate projects
convince people to do things
  your way
sell things
give talks or speeches
organize activities
lead a group
persuade others

Like to?
make decisions
be elected to office
start your own business
campaign politically
meet important people
have power or status

Career Possibilities
(Holland Code):

Advertising Executive (ESA)
Advertising Sales Rep (ESR)
Banker/Financial Planner (ESR)
Branch Manager (ESA)
Business Manager (ESC)
Buyer (ESA)
Chamber of Commerce Exec
  (ESA)

Credit Analyst (EAS)
Customer Service Manager
  (ESA)
Education & Training Manager
  (EIS)
Emergency Medical Technician
  (ESI)
Entrepreneur (ESA)

Foreign Service Officer (ESA)
Funeral Director (ESR)
Insurance Manager (ESC)
Interpreter (ESA)
Lawyer/Attorney (ESA)
Lobbyist (ESA)
Office Manager (ESR)
Personnel Recruiter (ESR)

Politician (ESA)
Public Relations Rep (EAS)
Retail Store Manager (ESR)
Sales Manager (ESA)
Sales Representative (ERS)
Social Service Director (ESA)
Stockbroker (ESI)
Tax Accountant (ECS)

Conventional (*Organizers*)

People who like to work with data, have clerical or numerical ability, carry out tasks in detail, or follow through on others' instructions.

Are you?
well-organized
accurate
numerically inclined
methodical
conscientious
efficient
conforming

practical
thrifty
systematic
structured
polite
ambitious
obedient
persistent

Can you?
work well within a system
do a lot of paper work in a short
  time
keep accurate records
use a computer terminal
write effective business letters

Like to?
follow clearly defined
  procedures
use data processing equipment
work with numbers
type or take shorthand
be responsible for details
collect or organize things

Career Possibilities
(Holland Code):

Abstractor (CSI)
Accountant (CSE)
Administrative Assistant (ESC)
Budget Analyst (CER)
Business Manager (ESC)
Business Programmer (CRI)
Business Teacher (CSE)
Catalog Librarian (CSE)

Claims Adjuster (SEC)
Computer Operator (CSR)
Congressional-District Aide (CES)
Cost Accountant (CES)
Court Reporter (CSE)
Credit Manager (ESC)
Customs Inspector (CEI)
Editorial Assistant (CSI)

Elementary School Teacher
  (SEC)
Financial Analyst (CSI)
Insurance Manager (ESC)
Insurance Underwriter (CSE)
Internal Auditor (ICR)
Kindergarten Teacher (ESC)

Medical Records Technician
  (CSE)
Museum Registrar (CSE)
Paralegal (SCE)
Safety Inspector (RCS)
Tax Accountant (ECS)
Tax Consultant (CES)
Travel Agent (ECS)

GENERAL BIBLIOGRAPHY

Cybersecurity

Kim, Peter. *The Hacker Playbook: [2]*. CreateSpace Independent Publishing, 2015. Print.

Wong, Caroline. *Secure Metrics: A Beginners Guide*. Berkeley, Calif: Osborne/McGraw-Hill, 2011. Print.

Wright, Joshua, and Johnny Cache. *Hacking Exposed Wireless: Wireless Security Secrets and Solutions*. McGraw-Hill Education, 2015. Print.

Firefighting

Clayton, Bill, David Day, and Jim McFadden. *Wildland Firefighting*. North Highlands, CA: State of California Office of Procurement, 1987. Print.

Firefighting. St. John's, Newfoundland: the Institute, 1985. Print.

Lepore, Paul S. *The Aspiring Firefighter's 2 Year Plan: The Complete Road Map to Becoming a Firefighter*. Freespool Publications, 2012. Print.

Wasser, Al, and Donna Kimble. *Mastering the CPAT: A Comprehensive Guide*. Clifton Park, NY: Thomson/Delmar Learning, 2007. Print.

Nursing, EMTs, Paramedics and Ambulance Drivers

Careers in Emergency Medical Services: Emt—Paramedic, Care, Rescue and Transportation: Helping People in Their Worst Hour of Need. Chicago, Ill.: Institute for Career Research, 2007. Internet resource.

Dick, Thom, Steve Berry, Jeff Forster, and Mike Smith. *People Care: Career-friendly Practices for Professional Caregivers*. Van Nuys, CA: Cygnus Business Media, 2005. Print

Frazier, Margaret S, Christine Malone, and Connie Morgan. *Medical Assisting: Foundations and Practices*. Upper Saddle River, N.J: Pearson, 2010. Print.

Patrick, William B. *The Call of Nursing: Stories from the Front Lines of Health Care*. Hudson Whitman/Excelsior College Press, 2013. Print.

Police, Detectives, and Investigators

Blum, Lawrence N. *Force Under Pressure: Why Cops Live and Why They Die*. New York: Lantern Books, 2000. Print.

Brown, Steven K. *The Complete Idiot's Guide to Private Investigating.* New York: Penguin, 2013. Print.

Glennon, Jim. *Arresting Communication: Essential Interaction Skills for Law Enforcement.* San Francisco: Calibre Press, 2010. Print.

Koletar, Joseph W. *The Fbi Career Guide: Inside Information on Getting Chosen for and Succeeding in One of the Toughest, Most Prestigious Jobs in the World.* New York: AMACOM, 2006. Print.

Wynn, Michael. *Rising Through the Ranks: Leadership Tools and Techniques for Law Enforcement.* New York: Kaplan Pub, 2008. Print.

Social Work

Gawande, Atul. *Being Mortal.* Anchor, Canada, 2017. Print.

Grobman, Linda M. *More Days in the Lives of Social Workers: 35 "real-Life" Stories of Advocacy, Outreach, and Other Intriguing Roles in Social Work Practice.* Harrisburg, Pa: White Hat Communications, 2005. Print

Klein, Jessie. *The Bully Society: School Shootings and the Crisis of Bullying in America's Schools.* New York: New York University Press, 2013. Print.

ORGANIZATIONS & WEB RESOURCES

ABET
https://www.abet.org/

Addiction Technology Transfer Center Network
https://attcnetwork.org/

American Academy of Forensic Sciences
https://www.aafs.org/

American Association of Colleges of Nursing
https: //www.aacnnursing.org/

American Board of Criminalistics
http://www.criminalistics.com/

American Board of Examiners in Clinical Social Work
https://abecsw.org/

American Board of Industrial Hygiene
http://www.abih.org/

American Board of Medicolegal Death Investigators
https://abmdi.org/

American College of Epidemiology
https://www.acepidemiology.org/

American Counseling Association
https://www.counseling.org/

American Epidemiological Society
https://www.americanepidemiologicalsociety.org/

American Geosciences Institute
https://www.americangeosciences.org/

American Industrial Hygiene Association
https://www.aiha.org//Pages/default.aspx

American Nurses Association
https://www.nursingworld.org/

American Probation and Parole Association
http://www.appa-net.org/eweb/

American Public Health Association
https://www.apha.org/

American Registry of Professional Animal Scientists
https://www.arpas.org/

American Rehabilitation Counseling Association
http://www.arcaweb.org/

American Society for Engineering Education
http://www.asee.org/

American Society of Agronomy
https://www.agronomy.org/

American Society of Animal Science
https://www.asas.org/

American Society of Home Inspectors
https://www.homeinspector.org/

American Society of Registered Nurses
https://www.asrn.org/

American Society of Safety Engineers
https://www.assp.org/

American Society of Safety Engineers
https://www.assp.org/education/certificate-programs

ASIS International
https://www.asisonline.org/

Association for Community Organization and Social Administration
http://www.acosa.org/joomla/

Association for Computing Machinery
https://www.acm.org/

Association of Construction Inspectors
http://www.aci-assoc.org/

Association of Firearm and Tool Mark Examiners
https://afte.org/

Association of Public-Safety Communications Officials
https://www.apcointl.org/

Association of Social Work Boards
https://www.aswb.org/

Association of State and Territorial Health Officials
http://www.astho.org/

Board of Certified Safety Professionals
https://www.bcsp.org/

Bureau of Alcohol, Tobacco, Firearms and Explosives
https://www.atf.gov/

Centers for Disease Control and Prevention, National Institute for Occupational
Safety and Health (NIOSH)
https://www.cdc.gov/niosh/

Centers for Disease Control and Prevention
https://jobs.cdc.gov/

Commission on Accreditation of Allied Health Education Programs
https://www.caahep.org/

Commission on Rehabilitation Counselor Certification
https://www.crccertification.com/

Computing Research Association
https://cra.org/

Council for Accreditation of Counseling & Related Educational Programs
https://www.cacrep.org/

Council of State and Territorial Epidemiologists
https://www.cste.org/default.aspx

Council on Social Work Education
https://www.cswe.org/

Disaster Recovery Institute International
https://drii.org/

Discover Corrections
http://www.discovercorrections.com/

Drug Enforcement Administration
https://www.dea.gov/

Ecological Society of America
https://www.esa.org/esa/

Federal Bureau of Investigation
https://www.fbi.gov/

Federal Bureau of Prisons
https://www.bop.gov/

Forest Stewards Guild
http://www.forestguild.org/

Future Farmers of America
https://www.ffa.org/

IEEE Computer Society
https://www.computer.org/

Institute of Food Technologists
https://www.ift.org/

Institute of Hazardous Materials Management
https://www.ihmm.org/certificants/chmm

International Academies of Emergency Dispatch
https://www.emergencydispatch.org/

International Association of Arson Investigators
https://www.firearson.com/

International Association of Certified Home Inspectors (InterNACHI)
https://www.homeinspector.org/

International Association of Directors of Law Enforcement Standards and Training
https://www.iadlest.org/

International Association of Electrical Inspectors
https://www.iaei.org//

International Association of Emergency Managers
https://www.iaem.org/

International Association of Fire Fighters
https://client.prod.iaff.org/

International Association of Plumbing and Mechanical Officials
http://www.iapmo.org/

International Association of Women in Fire & Emergency Services
https://www.i-women.org/

International Code Council
https://www.iccsafe.org/

International Council on Systems Engineering
https://www.incose.org/

International Crime Scene Investigators Association
https://www.icsia.org/

International Municipal Signal Association
http://www.imsasafety.org/

Johnson & Johnson, Nurses change lives
https://nursing.jnj.com/home

MSW Guide
https://www.mswguide.org/

NAADAC, The Association for Addiction Professionals
https://www.naadac.org/

NACE International
http://www.nace.org/home

National Academy for State Health Policy
https://nashp.org/

National Association of Clinical Nurse Specialists
https://nacns.org/

National Association of Elevator Safety Authorities International
https://www.naesai.org/

National Association of Emergency Medical Technicians
http://www.naemt.org/

National Association of Fire Investigators
https://www.nafi.org/

National Association of Legal Investigators
https://www.nalionline.org/

National Association of Social Workers
https://www.socialworkers.org/

National Association of State EMS Officials
https://nasemso.org/

National Board for Certified Counselors
https://www.nbcc.org/

National Center for Women & Information Technology
https://www.ncwit.org/

National Commission for Health Education Credentialing, Inc.
https://www.nchec.org/

National Council of Examiners for Engineering and Surveying
https://ncees.org/

National Council of State Boards of Nursing
https://www.ncsbn.org/

National Emergency Management Association
https://www.nemaweb.org/

National Emergency Number Association
https://www.nena.org/default.aspx

National Environmental Health Association
https://www.neha.org/

National Fire Academy, U.S. Fire Administration
https://www.nfpa.org/

National Fire Academy
https://www.usfa.fema.gov/training/nfa/index.html

National Fire Protection Association
https://www.nfpa.org/

National Highway Traffic Safety Administration, Office of Emergency Medical
Services
https://www.ems.gov/

National Institutes of Health
https://www.nih.gov/

National League for Nursing
http://www.nln.org/

National Maritime Center, U.S. Coast Guard Headquarters
https://www.dco.uscg.mil/national_maritime_center/

National Registry of Emergency Medical Technicians
https://www.nremt.org/rwd/public

National Registry of Emergency Medical Technicians
https://www.nremt.org/rwd/public/

National Society of Professional Engineers
https://www.nspe.org/

National Student Nurses' Association
https://www.nsna.org/

Online MSW Programs
https://www.onlinemswprograms.com/

Public Health Foundation
http://www.phf.org/Pages/default.aspx

Smithsonian Institution
https://www.si.edu/

Society for Public Health Education
https://www.sophe.org/

Society for Range Management
http://rangelands.org/

Society of American Foresters
https://www.eforester.org/

Soil Science Society of America
https://www.soils.org/

Technology Student Association
https://tsaweb.org/

The Network for Social Work Management
https://socialworkmanager.org/

The Society for Healthcare Epidemiology of America
http://www.shea-online.org/

U.S. Customs and Border Protection
https://www.cbp.gov/

U.S. Department of Agriculture
https://www.usda.gov/

U.S. Department of Homeland Security
https://www.dhs.gov/

U.S. Department of Labor, Occupational Safety and Health Administration (OSHA)
https://www.osha.gov/

U.S. Fire Administration
https://www.usfa.fema.gov/

U.S. Fish & Wildlife Service
https://www.fws.gov/

U.S. Food and Drug Administration
https://www.fda.gov/

U.S. Forest Service
https://www.fs.fed.us/

U.S. Marshals Service
https://www.usmarshals.gov/

U.S. Office of Personnel Management
https://www.opm.gov/

U.S. Secret Service
https://www.secretservice.gov/

UCAR (University Corporation for Atmospheric Research)
https://www.ucar.edu/

USAJOBS
https://www.usajobs.gov/

Where to Hunt
https://www.nssf.org/hunting/where-to-hunt/

INDEX